CW01271322

The Story
of Us

First published in 2024
An Eyewear Publishing book, The Black Spring Press Group
Maida Vale, London W9,
United Kingdom

Cover and jacket design by **Matt Broughton**
Typeset by **Edwin Smet**
Cover photo by **Serena Yang**
Author photo by **Jenny Magee**
Copyediting by **Jo Tuscano**
Proofreading by **Evie Rowan**

Printed and bound in Great Britain by Clays Ltd, Elcograf S.p.A.

All rights reserved
© 2024 Caitlin Robson
The right of Caitlin Robson to be identified as author of this work has been asserted in accordance with section 77 of the Copyright, Designs and Patents Act 1988

ISBN 978-1915406798

blackspringpressgroup.com

TAYLOR SWIFT

The Story of Us

A Swiftie's Journey Through The Eras

Caitlin Robson

xx *Caitlin*

THE **BLACK SPRING**
PRESS GROUP

to Lachlan
You are the biggest inspiration to me; I want to be you
when I grow up. I love you every minute I am alive.

to Brett and Bronwyn
Thank you for championing your loud daughter and raising
me to know that I am enough just the way I am.

to Bec and my fellow Swifties
You are RED, golden, and every screaming colour,
thank you for dancing with me.

and to Taylor
My goodness my dear, thank you for every song on every album,
and for our hug back in 2012.
Here's to the boys who break our hearts because,
you are the longest and best relationship I've ever had.

it starts and ends with singing Taylor in my bedroom... — 8

1. Introducing...*Taylor Swift*. — 14
2. Being *fearless*, believing in love stories. — 36
3. The 2009 MTV Video Music Awards and Kanyegate. — 57
4. Having the courage to *speak now*. — 74
5. What colour is love? — 98
6. "I was born in the year, *1989*!" — 128
7. "There will be no explanation, there will just be *reputation*." — 154
8. "If something says in parentheses (Taylor's Version) that means I own it." — 184
9. Heralding a return to romance. — 212
10. The wistful storytelling of *folklore* and *evermore*. — 244
11. How do you spend your *midnights*? The sleepless lyricism of failed romances and The Eras Tour. — 272
12. Aren't we all just tortured poets? — 304
13. The Taylor Swift Effect. — 325

Taylor Swift (Caitlin's Version) — 362
album secret messages — 364
acknowledgements — 367
Works Cited (Caitlin's Version) — 372

August 23, 2019. 2:29 pm, Sydney, Australia.

It's my birthday and Taylor's album is out. Now.

And I'm listening to it in a bathroom. And it's beautiful.
And I know she's happy.

11:48 pm

So, I'm lying in bed and it's nearly not my birthday anymore.

I'm tired. Today was full. Of sunshine. Of happiness. Of ramen. Of little golden daffodils and new things. Of music and lyrics that I will grow to love and listen to.

But most all, friends. Those people who mean the most to me. They all sat at the same table and I try not to tear up when they say nice things or smile at me, which is nearly the same as 'I love you.'

I am forever grateful for the people who let me in and let me be me.

And it's hard and overwhelming sometimes but l am never alone. You dance with me and you hug me and say this is who you are and I love it.

I woke up next to my childhood best friend and spent nearly the whole day with my father. He is something else and every part of him is good and tomorrow I get to see my mum.

AND TAYLOR. Thank you my dear. You are the reason for most of my singing and laughing and I'm glad that my friends like you.

To release an album on my birthday is pretty unbelievable. To think that sixteen-year-old girl who hugged you on the 9th of March 2012, all those years later would know how it is to be loved.

Because of the way you write.

In 2010 I sang your songs loud and I wanted your curls. I didn't know back then about the kind of romantic love you sang about.

It is 2019 and I have known that love and I have lost it. And because of your songs I know I will find it again. Thank you for sharing your heart with the world. It must be so hard at times but you know it is worth the while. Thank you for standing up and fighting for women.

I want to tell stories like you. And it is okay that mine is only just getting started.

Because I write about other people and I watch, and I want.

But ultimately, I will wait, and you know as well as I do that is more than okay.

Forever and always,

Caitlin x

It starts and ends with singing Taylor in my bedroom...

August 5, 2024. 5:01 pm, London, England.

I find it intriguing that I spent a lot of the time writing this book sitting on my bed, because this has also been the place where I have listened to songs written by Taylor Swift since I was thirteen years old. If I can't sleep and my mind is racing, I will put my phone under my pillow on a low volume, and lay my head down again, knowing the lyrics I know by heart will lull me into unconsciousness. On bad days, the same practice will eventually stop uncontrollable sobbing, because I concentrate on each word Taylor sings, calming myself down enough to hear. When I was in high school, I would often play her songs getting ready for school dancing my way into a good mood for the day. Over a decade later, I still do the same thing.

When I tell someone that I have followed the path of her career for sixteen years, I do get some weird looks. "That's a long time," they will say. It sure is. The 10,000-hour rule was explained by Malcolm Gladwell, in his book *Outliers: The Story of Success*. It takes 10,000 hours of practice until you are an expert at something. His example is The Beatles and their schedule of performing live over 1,200 times as a group in Hamburg at the beginning of their career, between 1960-1964. When you do the quick maths, 8,760 hours is equivalent to one year, and thus 140,160 hours is sixteen years. By Gladwell's calculation I have achieved this tenfold, and along the way I have learnt about myself at the same time as memorising things about her. She has made me unapologetic for being a loud woman, for sharing wisdom that comes through heartbreak, and for giving me the lyrical tools to find lost things. She teaches me every day that it's okay to want to live in a world that doesn't hurt you and every time someone starts a conversation with, "Did you see Taylor do this?" and I'm listening in, I can't help but smile.

In an interview with *BBC Radio 1*'s Live Lounge in September

2019, Taylor spoke about negativity. "The worst kind of person is someone who makes someone feel bad, dumb, or stupid for being excited about something." I like to repeat this when I need a reminder of the joy she brings to my life. A few of my family members constantly belittle me for being a fangirl, some make fun of me in front of other people and say her name in a mocking tone, or tell me I've wasted my money when I buy merchandise or tickets, because they won't listen to me to understand why she means a lot. They all have families, and I have had two relationships, at the same age that my parents already had two children.

If you're a fan, chances are you don't need to be retold a lot of history but I know you will read anyway. We're already friends or would get along more than fine. If you're *not* a fan, chances are you've heard her name and either rolled your eyes, or nodded in acknowledgement. Either way you know who she is. Ideally this book will add to the Taylor Swift fandom community a few more (casual is fine) listening ears. For this reason, it has been my pleasure to lay out her story in a timeline of nearly 19 years, and 11 albums. This book is a joyous nostalgic trip through eras filled with cowboy boots and curls, sparkles and ball gowns, red lipstick, 22nd birthday parties and immaculate bangs (fringes for non-North American readers). There are call-backs to eighties synth dance tracks, seagulls and big city dreams, snakes and black leather combat boots, angst and sparkly revenge, pastel pinks and blues and wedding bands and romance returned, lockdown melancholy mixed with fairytales, midnights spent wondering about lost loves and poetry written in the depths of self-love and self-loathing. This is the discography of Taylor so far, filled with secret messages, easter eggs and colour, waiting for you to choose your favourites and stay for a while. You are about to read her story, interwoven with fragments of mine.

I have seen her perform live eight times, and there are other Swifties I know who have seen her eight times in a year, but I feel very lucky to even have those times to count. If you know me well enough, it won't shock you that I'm writing about Taylor. In the beginning, my best friend Rebecca Vickery and I listened to *Fearless* in the back row of our high school English class on her purple iPod Nano. The teacher knew we had one earphone in each ear; she couldn't really do much about it. I can remember those early listening days like they happened last week.

There were other times where I used to hide in the library when other "friends" decided not to talk to me that day, and when my mum picked me up from school and "You Belong With Me" came on the radio, it was an instant distraction because I would sing about a boy who I wouldn't meet for eight years.

Recently, I made that old boyfriend (who was once antagonistic towards my listening habits) a Spotify playlist of her underrated tracks from each album. He listened to them. "Maybe I'm getting older, but I'm actually liking her songs more and more. 21-year-old me would be deeply ashamed." My response? "I'll make you a playlist." This is exactly the kind of redemption story arc I aim for, where you're allowed to be ambivalent, but you're not allowed to hate for no reason. My best friend Annalise, who isn't a Swiftie once surprised me by joining in with me singing the chorus to "All Too Well" in the passenger seat of my car and I burst into tears. It is exhausting trying to justify how much I love her to the people who like to criticise the joy she brings me. Will I get taken seriously by them now that her name and mine share a front cover? Probably not. But do I care? Also, nope. Like her or not, you cannot deny the phenomenon that is Taylor Swift.

The struggles of being a woman are intertwined with Taylor's lasting cultural impact. Not being taken seriously because you were "too much" or louder than the other girls is one. I am, and always will be, the token loud friend, and I feel extremely validated that Taylor and I share this trait; we're not afraid to be heard. We can operate at any volume we want to. Constantly fighting a battle of comparison and being pitted against other women also frequently rears its ugly face. Regardless of how many Grammys you have to your name. To all of the women in my life, thank you for being supportive of each other, and killing the tradition of witch-burning.

    Every little girl has had the same dream, where she stands in the front of a crowd and somehow becomes a rockstar. Much to my piano teacher's horror, instead of focusing on Mozart, Chopin, and Tchaikovsky, I wanted to learn Taylor's songs. I am a half-decent dancer, so the stage was not a foreign concept for me. Often, I would wake up from pretending I was brave enough to be in a talent show, standing in front of a piano with a microphone, and then afterwards my friends would tell me I was cool. For a lot of little girls like Billie Eilish, Camila Cabello, Ice Spice, Doja Cat, Megan Thee Stallion, Phoebe Bridgers, Olivia Rodrigo, Sabrina Carpenter, Halsey, Ariana Grande, Maggie Rogers, Kelsea Ballerini, Lorde, Maisie Peters, Cate, Griff and Gretta Ray, those dreams really did come true. They have grown up not in Taylor's shadow, but guided by her glittering light through an industry that regularly enjoys objectifying us as much as it does catapulting females to stardom.

    I have always wanted to be a music journalist and write for *Rolling Stone*, entertaining this idea of exploring the inside workings of music and stories told to me by the artists themselves. Fuelled by this *Almost Famous* fantasy, I have poured my heart and soul into writing down everything I know and love about Taylor. In my creative writing degree, I fell in love with the idea of non-academic personal essay writing which is what this book is filled with. If you're someone who reads and listens to music at the same time, there is chapter that matches each album. Taylor and I are obsessed with telling stories and writing down our feelings. Now you get to read my longest love letter yet. To everyone who picks up this book, I hope you find out some things about Taylor you don't already know, and maybe you'll pick an album after the last page, go and sit on your bed like I do, and press play.

                                            Are you ready for it?

Debut era
2004 – 2008.

Introducing... *Taylor Swift.*

In 2024, it is "cool" to like Taylor Swift again. This resurgence is because The Eras Tour has brought fans, old friends, and new listeners to packed-out stadiums for the highest-grossing tour of all time, beginning in 2023. In February, Taylor played to 96,000 fans in Melbourne, the biggest crowd of her career. That kind of astronomical success is rarely the beginning of any story. Jump in a DeLorean car and strap yourself in. Come back in time to the middle of the 2000s, when not only was it not cool to listen to Taylor Swift, but it wasn't actually cool *to be* Taylor Swift.

Taylor Alison Swift was born on December 13, 1989, in West Reading, Pennsylvania, USA, to parents Scott and Andrea. She was named after country and blues icon James Taylor. Her mother believed that when her daughter was older, it was better to have a gender-neutral name to succeed in business. Heart-melting archival home video footage of tiny Taylor can be found by watching the music videos for "The Best Day" (2009) and "Christmas Tree Farm" (2022). In "Christmas Tree Farm," footage shows her receiving what could be her first guitar in 1997, age eight, but she wouldn't learn to play properly until a few years later. In the *Miss Americana* documentary, we see an extended clip where she exclaims, "GUITAARRR. I...AM...HAPPY..." She has a decorative bow on top of her head.

Scott worked as a stockbroker for Merrill Lynch. Before she had children, Andrea was a mutual fund marketing executive while also running the Christmas tree farm where Taylor and her younger brother, Austin, grew up. She attended a Montessori kindergarten, went on summer holidays to New Jersey, and, at age nine, showed a keen interest and talent for musical theatre. There are various clips on Reddit and early performances on YouTube and Instagram show her in lead roles for the Berks Youth Theatre Academy in Pennsylvania. She was Sandy in *Grease*, Kim McAfee in *Bye Bye Birdie* and Maria in *The Sound of Music*. In fourth grade, when she was ten, she won a national poetry competition with her submission titled "A Monster in My Closet," and in 2002, at age eleven, she sang the national anthem at a Philadelphia 76ers NBA basketball game.

My name is Caitlin Louise Robson, and I was born on August 23, 1995, in Sydney, New South Wales, Australia. My parents, Brett and Bronwyn, named me after Welsh poet Dylan Thomas' wife and my parent's closest friend. Brett has been in the banking sector for 40 years, and Bronwyn has been a health professional for the same amount of time. Neither mine nor Taylor's parents had careers in the creative industries, but both sets of parents did not stop their daughters from pursuing their dreams in place of what some parents might see as more stable and sensible options rather than a degree or career in the creative arts. I didn't grow up on a Christmas tree farm. I grew up on the beaches, explored the rock tidepools down the road from my house and swam with dolphins and seals. I was late for school because my mum wanted to show us the whales migrating. My parents have quite the archive of home videos (as all parents from the 90s would) from holidays up north and opening presents on birthdays and big events. I had far too many hobbies; I loved sports and did ballet for nearly nine years alongside other dance styles throughout my teenage years. I could read before I started school at age five, and at nine, I started piano lessons that continued for a decade.

I loved English, Art and Music at school, and from a very early age, I loved movies, often reciting entire scenes to my family until they told me to choose something else to do. Taylor and I both only have one sibling, a younger brother. My brother, Lachlan, was born two months after I turned two. I did the maths; we are 795 days apart. Taylor and her brother Austin are 819 days apart, which is a difference of 24 days, but taking into account time zones, we can take off a day and turn it to 23 and 23 is my favourite number.

In 2002, I was in my second year at school, and the biggest moment for me was probably seeing *Harry Potter and the Chamber of*

Secrets in the cinemas. For Taylor Swift, perhaps the one particular day in 2002 that would change the course of her life was when a computer repairman named Ronnie brought a guitar to her house. He taught her three chords, left it with her to borrow that week, and she wrote her first song, "Lucky You" that night.

For most music artists in the beginning stage of their careers, there is often a singular moment or seminal event that propels them into the limelight, bringing about an instant change from being a "regular" human who can do their groceries or eat at restaurants without being disturbed into a non-regular human who is chased, harassed, stalked or stopped while walking down the street. Taylor didn't have that instant *snap* into fame that perhaps Justin Bieber did with his viral YouTube videos picked up by Usher or One Direction's iconic *X-Factor* run. There were a few years of fighting to be noticed, but eventually, it would be her turn. She visited Nashville for the first time on her spring break, driving around with her mum, as she recounts, "I had this demo CD of me singing karaoke music [of the Chicks, Dolly Parton and LeAnne Rimes], and marched up and down Music Row into every major record label and was like, 'Hey I'm Taylor, I'm 11, I want a record deal, if you could give me a call that'd be awesome.'"

Those demo CDs held a substantial number of unreleased songs that have surfaced on sites like Tumblr and Reddit. "Dark Blue Tennessee," "Smokey Black Nights," "American Boy," and some of my personal favourites, "I Heart?" and "Lucky You" are some of them. Whole lists exist online: the demos also had songs that fans will recognise from her EP of Christmas songs, "Christmas Must Be Something More," and others that would make the cut onto her first album, like "The Outside," "Picture to Burn," "Teardrops on My Guitar" and "The Outside." A select few of the unreleased songs can be found on unofficial YouTube channels. It was apparent even back then that this was a girl on a mission to be heard.

In 2003, Taylor started working with a New York-based talent manager Dan Dymtrow. Through Dymtrow, she modelled for the clothing brand Abercrombie and Fitch in a 'Rising Stars' national campaign. An early song of hers, "The Outside," would later become Track 6 on her debut album and was featured on a compilation CD, *Maybelline New York Presents Chicks With Attitude* in 2004. Other early musical influences are easy to spot; the early 2000s in country music were filled with women pushing their way through the glass ceiling of country music; artists like Shania Twain, Kellie Pickler, The Chicks, Miranda Lambert, Carrie Underwood and LeAnne Rimes. These were women Taylor saw as doing what she wanted to do, but with so many swimming in the talent pool, it was clear she had to make herself stand out. "I need to be different; they see that sort of thing every single day," she said in an early interview. "She [LeAnn Rimes] was one of the reasons I got involved in country music and became in love with it because I got her album, *Blue* when I was six, and just absolutely fell in love with the way she sang and the kind of music she sang...she is definitely a catalyst for a lot of this." In the 27 years since her awards, LeAnn Rimes still holds the title as the youngest individual artist to win a Grammy, at 14 years old, with two awards in 1997 for Best New Artist and Best Female Country Vocal Performance.

When she was 14, Taylor wrote a non-autobiographical novel titled *A Girl Named Girl*, about "a mother who wants a son but instead has a girl." This is a critical dramatic moment in Swift-lore because this sentence is all we know of the book's plot. It remains unpublished, with the sole draft remaining in the hands of her parents. There was a trademark filed for the title in 2015, and the trademark was renewed in 2023. It could be published at any time, or it could be the planned title for a future biography. Nobody knows. In 2005, her family moved to Nashville to further Taylor's performing career. She was the youngest artist signed to Sony/ATV Music with a publishing deal, and she worked with great Music Row songwriters such as Brett James, Mac McAnally, the Warren

Brothers, Troy Verges and Brett Beavers. It was here she formed a lasting writing relationship with Liz Rose. If you are remotely close to Nashville, fans will tell you that a significant place of pilgrimage is the Bluebird Café. I've yet to visit, but – one day.

Navigating fame at an early age was a natural thing for Taylor. She was determined and hard-working and knew exactly what she wanted and how to get it. This drive, however, was paired with the vulnerability of being a teenager, unafraid to share details about the boys in her songs with her young audience in order to be relatable. Her personality is her superpower, but it also can be her downfall. I am not an expert on the Zodiac, but I know this: Taylor and I are both fire signs: Leo and Sagittarius. We're loud and confident, we know what we want and how to get it, we're kind and genuine towards our friends (and strangers) and unafraid of speaking our minds. A lot of people enjoy how much energy we have, but there are always people who don't.

In various interviews, Taylor has said, "Back then, I used to try to change everything about myself that was different. I hated my curly hair, I straightened it every day, I lived in fear if the local newspaper would write something about my music because I knew the next day I was going to have to be absolutely tortured at [middle] school. But when we moved to Hendersonville, Tennessee, everything just clicked." In a radio interview, she told SiriusXM, "I wasn't cool in school or anything, I didn't have that many friends, well I did for a while, and then they didn't want to be friends with me anymore." She tells another story about the time "Mum and I went to the mall, and I had asked all of my friends to go with me that day, 'So I want to go to the mall, do you guys want to go,' [and the responses were], 'no I'm busy...no, my mum says I can't go.' And so we get there, and we run into all of the friends that I had called to go to the mall, and they were all there without me." In an interview, Taylor's mother, Andrea, said that Taylor struggled with friendships, "because all the other little girls were going to sleepovers, and playing soccer and Taylor wanted to sing on a stage and that was a little bit different...my worst time of the day was when I went to go pick up Taylor at school and I would know that things hadn't been so great that day...and that was tough to hear about the ostracising and the shunning, where she would sit down at a table with her lunch tray, and everyone would move."

I used to cry in the car on the way home from school because girls weren't interested in spending lunchtimes at high school with me. Even now, moving through another decade of countless friendship breakdowns and sadness over situations that I can't seem to fix, it's difficult to reconcile with the people who chose to hurt me because I was different. I come from a small coastal region close to a big city, and I had dreams of being a writer. A friend I had at high school has the same birthday as Taylor, and she hated it whenever I mentioned it. There was no space in our friendship for me loving a musician so much that it was all I could seem to talk about, and she got bored pretty quickly. When I moved to Sydney, I lost more friends because the short distance from my coastal town to Sydney apparently wasn't manageable for keeping in contact, and we didn't see each other as often. And moving to London meant more people weren't really interested in staying in touch. What being bullied taught me was this: people are afraid of those of us who attract attention because of our personalities. We stand out. To this day, sadly, I still possess the ability to push people away, but I have come to understand that if I am "too much" for you, then go and find less, and alongside my parent's constant support and encouragement, it was Taylor who taught me that.

A TV segment on YouTube shows a local Nashville station, WSMV4, putting a spotlight on Taylor a few months away from the release of her debut. It's 2005, and the cameras follow her through the day in a normal setting: high school. Hendersonville High School was where Taylor spent her days for just shy of two years and where she completed her studies and graduated a year earlier than her classmates. One boy in the segment says, "My dad says that he's really impressed with your music, and he wanted me to tell you." "Really!!" "He said you sound like you're like twenty-five..." Perhaps this is an odd compliment, and it's unclear whether the boy could be referring to the sound of her voice or her emotional maturity, but I think it's the latter. Taylor sings about quintessential youth experiences that other teenagers couldn't translate into songwriting.

And soon, it was time for an album. On June 19, 2006, the first of five singles from her upcoming debut album was released, including the song "Tim McGraw." Tim McGraw is a country music singer and actor (he played Sandra Bullock's husband in The Blind Side) who rose through the charts in the 1990s and is also married to fellow country queen and dynamo Faith Hill. Taylor was astute enough to make these associations early. In an interview with Anne Hudson on Hill Country, daytime American country music television in 2006, Taylor says, "I never even thought anything of this song after I wrote it, I came up with the idea for "Tim McGraw" when I was sitting in math class, my freshman year and I just starting singing...after school I went in and wrote the song in 15 minutes on piano." In the years to come, Taylor would become ambivalent about her muses and inspiration for songs, but in the early years, there was a youthful honesty present in her music. She shared everyday adolescent experiences, and they became chart-toppers. Why? Because it brought a new sub-audience to the genre. Teenage girls were starting to listen to country music. Taylor was singing stories they could relate to.

Starting a song and an album with a simple conversation between a boy and a girl is a brilliant way to introduce us to the romance that will follow. The first line has a boy comparing a girl's eyes to the stars. The girl, rather than accepting the flattery, tells the boy he is lying. So begins Track 1, "Tim McGraw." Sam Lansky, writing for TIME, said, "Even for country music, these lyrics are literary – conjuring a romantic fantasy, then deflating it a line later." Eyes and the beauty of them (love in its simplest form) are often something that hold power and attention when you begin a relationship, but the magic gets lost as the years go by. To return to first loves is what Taylor is asking of us with this first song. She sings about remembering happiness and the clothes she wore at that time and of her head on the chest of the boy she loved. When speaking on Hill Country, she said,

> I applied it to the situation I was in which I was dating a guy who was going off to college, and you know I knew we were going to break up, and just thinking about all the things that I knew, that would remind him of me, and I never played it for anybody for about three months and I didn't demo it, I didn't do anything with this song until on an off-chance I played it for the president of my record label, and he looked at me and was like 'well, that's your first single.'

Everyone's experience of love is different, but we all share in knowing what those beginning-of-a-relationship shiny new feelings are and perhaps feeling a pure form of love. It is no different for Taylor. Many teenagers have a box of their most precious objects in their bedrooms amongst their schoolbooks and shelves filled with old and new toys. These are our memories in their tangible form that are associated with times we won't forget, gifts that we can't bring ourselves to give away. It's the same for the pieces of lost love that we keep. Memories exist in driving on highways and seeing the same cars that your once-was person used to drive, or looking at the shoes or clothes they used to wear that now you see on strangers. Memories are in the music they listened to and the songs you sang with them. They are in letters that never will be read, and the beautiful space you occupied together at an exact moment in time. Regardless of the relationship's duration, the memories stay. Whether you're like my parents and are still with the same person after many years, or whether a twist of fate or tragic accident pulled the one you love away from you, or like me, you made decisions that changed everything, you still have memories. Taylor knows that *every* love story is worth singing about. This is the core of her songwriting that has carried her through her career of 11 albums. "Tim McGraw" was her first ever single to chart.

Taylor told Katie Cook on CMT *Insider Special Edition* promoting *Fearless* in 2008,

> When I was making the rounds first trying to get a record deal, the thing that I heard the most was country music does not have a young demographic. So, you being a teenager, are not going to fit into country music because the only people that listen to country music on country radio are 35-year-old females. I just kept thinking, that can't be accurate, because I listen to country music, and I know there have to be other girls everywhere who listen to country music and want some music that is maybe directed more towards them.

At an industry showcase in 2005, Taylor performed and standing in the room was Scott Borchetta, preparing to start an independent record label, Big Machine Records. Taylor would become one of the first signings for the new label, and her father purchased a three per cent stake for an estimated $120,000 USD. Critics disapproved of Borchetta's signing of a baby-faced 16-year-old, but similar to the 11 publishers that turned down *Harry Potter and the Philosopher's Stone* before Bloomsbury took its chance, they learnt not to underestimate the power of a younger demographic.

Taylor sang the national anthem again on September 24, 2006, for a Pittsburgh Steelers NFL game, and as part of the promotions for her new album, spent much of 2006 and 2007 opening the national tours for other country artists: Brad Paisley, George Strait, Rascall Flatts (October 19 to November 3, 2006), Tim McGraw and Faith Hill.

Another country music star, Kenny Chesney, met Taylor when she was unsigned, and she was initially slated to be an opening act for Chesney on his world tour in 2007-2008. Because of a legality, she was unable to because "there was some sort of legal, contractual thing where people weren't comfortable with having an alcohol-sponsored show and having a 17- or 18-year-old on the show." Chesney said, "I had to call Taylor and tell her that she couldn't do that tour. And I gave her, as an 'I'm sorry' present, I gave her a lot of money." She told TIME in 2023 she was "devastated" when she couldn't open for Chesney's tour. However, his generous gift "was for more money than I'd ever seen in my life...I was able to pay my band bonuses. I was able to pay for my tour buses. I was able to fuel my dreams."

If Swifties were to listen to Chesney's 2002 song "Big Star," they would find some uncanny resemblances to Taylor in the lyrics (though it was written when she was still in middle school) when he sings about a girl who took to the stage, despite being unsure of herself, and brought the house down. In Chesney's lyrics he mentions a 20,000 plus crowd full of young girls with the same dreams, and when I saw Taylor perform for the first time, it was to 27,900 people in Sydney's Allphones/QUDOS Bank Arena.

On the recorded version featuring Taylor, Chesney introduces it as, "This song is about a girl... who had a dream and followed it, and I know from living in this town for so many years that there's a lot of girls out there with a lot of dreams in their heads and this song goes out to you." The two have performed the song together live twice (both in Nashville), once on Taylor's Speak Now World Tour in 2011 and on Chesney's The Big Revival Tour in 2015.

On October 24, 2006, Taylor Swift's self-titled debut was released, and she debuted it on *Good Morning America* and *The Megan Mullally Show* in New York City that same day. The album cover of *Taylor Swift* is whimsical. She stares back at you with her piercing blue eyes and untamed curly blond hair, set against a backdrop of blue and green patterns and butterflies, with what looks like a lake and the forest imprinted behind. The album was largely promoted by Swift through Myspace, engaging directly with fans and on country music stations in the United States. She was 16, almost 17 years old. Despite selling a modest 40,000 in its first week, the year after its release, sales would skyrocket to over 1,000,000 copies in November 2007. Compared to the week of release, the album reached its highest sales week on the Billboard 200 on January 5, 2008, when it sold 187,000 copies and was #8 on the charts. *Taylor Swift* spent 157 weeks on the US Billboard 200 and peaked at #5. With this release, Taylor became the first female country music artist to write or co-write every track on a US platinum-certified debut album. This was the longest stay on the chart of any release in the US in the 2000s. In 2020, *Rolling Stone* put "Tim McGraw" at #11 on their 'The 100 Greatest Debut Singles of All Time' list, writing, "With her first song, Swift immediately showed her Nashville peers she could beat any of them at their own game, acing the classic genre trope of nostalgic country song about how country music is nostalgic." I recently discovered that this first album was released everywhere else apart from North America almost 17 months later.

February 13, 2007, was her first appearance on *The Tonight Show* with Jay Leno, and that week, on February 19, "Teardrops on My Guitar" would be released as her third single. A tale of unrequited love, setting the table for "You Belong With Me" to arrive next, critics have a range of opinions on the genre classification of the song. NPR categorised it as pop, Ed Masley, writing for the *Arizona Republic*, called it "A soft-rock ballad with plenty of banjo and steel-guitar touches," and Grady Smith from *Rolling Stone* deemed it one of Swift's "countriest" songs. I think it could be all three at once. A blog from February 28, 2007, from *Great American Country*, called, 'Ask the Artist,' Taylor answered questions sent in by fans. They ranged from musical influences and being a role model to more complex issues like writing songs about self-confidence and even trickier to navigate questions to do with eating disorders. "What do you do to balance being a popular recording artist and just being a teenager?" asks one listener.

Taylor: I was in regular high school up until last year. I went to two proms, had the coolest friends in the world and had a great time, but there were some things that I didn't really like to do that other teenagers my age like to do. I have never really been a partier. I'm kind of a big dork. I was always afraid to go to parties because I was afraid people would be drinking, and maybe the cops would show up and I couldn't risk it, I just couldn't. Part of who I am, and trying to be a role model is having responsibility. I like to hang out with my friends. I love going to the mall. I love doing all that stuff, but part of me is afraid of being a regular teenager [and] making those mistakes because for me there are bigger consequences. If I get in trouble, I get written up in newspapers. I have to constantly be afraid of that. Being a regular teenager to me is just having friends and coming back home every once in a while. I just love being on tour, I really do. It's like me being a soccer player, volleyball player. I am just gone a lot more and I am homeschooled.

Another questioner asks, "Taylor, you are my role model, and you always will be. What do you have to say to us girls who look up to you?"

Taylor: Being a role model is one of the coolest things. I really do love it. When people come up to me and tell me that a song has really moved them or helped them in some way, I love that because I *was* that girl. I had role models that I looked up to and I know how beneficial it can be to your life – if you find a song that can say what you are thinking in a way that you thought you couldn't say. What I have to say to those girls is, thank you! That is the coolest thing that I have become a role model to people. I really just love it! It is so cool. I know how tough it is to become a role model to people. It is pretty tough criteria. I've been a 16-year-old girl, I've been a 17-year-old girl, you know, and you're really tough with your music choices. I mean, you don't just listen to anything. It's gotta be good. You've gotta believe it, because people see through stuff and you can tell when something is honest and when it's not. All I have to say is, thank you from the bottom of my heart. Please, please always be there for me because I'll always be here for you.

To be considered a role model at such an early age is quite a huge amount of responsibility; one slip of the finger and it could all be over. Taylor was already acutely aware of that, and her request for loyalty at the end is simple and effective because she shows us that it's a friendship, not just a fandom. There is also mention of Track 7, "Tied Together With A Smile," a song she wrote about a school friend suffering from an eating disorder. "I always thought that one of the biggest overlooked problems American girls face is insecurity. Whether insecurity spurs anorexia or whether it spurs some other eating disorder or not liking yourself, suicide, or hurting other people. It is all based on insecurity and not being OK with yourself."

This is the first song, before "The Best Day" on *Fearless*, that I direct people to when they say to me, "Oh, but Taylor Swift only writes about break-ups." No, she does not.

Taylor's first time playing on the main stage at the CMA Music Festival was June 9, 2007. She introduced herself by saying, "This whole thing started for me last year [June 11, 2006] at the CMA Music Festival out on the 'Riverfront' stages where nobody knew about a song called "Tim McGraw," and this morning they told me that my album is platinum and tonight I'm standing on this stage, and I can't believe it y'all! Thank you so much!" She starts to sing the song she just referenced, wearing a white flowy dress, blue cowboy boots and the same guitar in the photograph on this front cover, which she now uses to play surprise songs on The Eras Tour. Justin Beckner, writing for *Guitar.com*, says this,

> If there's one guitar that we think might be Taylor's most sentimental instrument, it's this one – this stunning guitar has a flamed koa body with a distinctive matching soundhole cover and a 'Taylor Swift' in [what is called] a 'Byzantine inlay' on the fingerboard... a custom-build, based on Taylor's super-high-end Presentation Serie PS-24ce Grand Auditorium model, but with a very unconventional 'Florentine' cutaway, which has a sharp point, unlike a regular GA model. The guitar also has an ebony peghead and bridge, Gotoh tuners and ivoroid binding.

Her red-carpet debut was the 2006 *Country Music Television Music Awards* on April 10, and it would be the next year (April 16, 2007) that she would win the CMT Award for Breakthrough Video of the Year for "Tim McGraw," and then the year after that, (April 14, 2008) she would win Video of the Year and also Female Video of the Year for "Our Song." Taylor's songwriting style convinces fans to listen to the same songs over and over and over again. Take it from me, we do not tire of it.

Track 11, the last song on her debut album, and her second single released on September 4, 2007, "Our Song," has a sole writing credit of just Taylor. Interviewed on 'Story Behind the Song' on *theboot.com*, Taylor said,

> I wrote this song in my freshman year of high school, for my ninth-grade talent show. So, I was sitting there thinking, I've gotta write a song that's gonna relate to everyone in the talent show, and it's gotta be upbeat...And at that time, I was dating a guy, and we didn't have a song. So I went ahead and wrote us one, and I played it at the talent show at the end of the year...months later, people would come up to me, and they're like, 'I loved that song that you played – "Our Song."' And then they'd start singing lines of it back to me. And they'd only heard it once, so I thought, 'There must be something here!'

This song has a more upbeat tempo than "Tim McGraw." Again, there is a story of romance and good times, unlike the melancholia of "Cold As You," the loneliness of "The Outside," or the angst of "Picture to Burn." She is covering the full spectrum of emotions with her debut, which is undeniably a characteristic of being a teenager. I find myself infectiously happy when listening to this ballad. "Our Song" is the final track on the album and there is a very clever message in the lyrics where Taylor asks God if he can play it (the date night) again. Not only does Taylor wish for a repeat of her time with a new romantic interest, but she is telling listeners with embedded messaging to "Go on, restart the whole album, I dare you." I did indeed play it again because this song was one of the first of Taylor's I tried to learn on the piano. Nearly 16 years later, I play it or listen to it on iTunes, and I still love every minute of its beautiful innocence and unbridled joy.

The exact sparkle-rhinestone guitar (Taylor Guitars GS6), which made its first appearance in "Our Song," only her third ever and released on a September 24 music video, was retired in 2013 and replaced with an almost identical Gibson J-180. It's important to note here that the guitar brand, not affiliated with the artist herself, is also called Taylor. It pays homage to the original model in the *Fearless* set of The Eras Tour that started last year, where she brings out a different version of the iconic guitar on a white finish instead of a black one and sings the songs that catapulted her to stardom. Beckner, for *Guitar.com*, says, "The new guitar featured around 5,400 Swarovski Lead Crystals attached with silicone epoxy by Taylor and her family just days before the tour...one notable difference between the new guitar and the original – the addition of a '13' rhinestone pattern just behind the bridge."

I could write a coffee table book about this guitar and its many appearances. Taylor said in an interview, "I think it came about because we had ordered a black guitar, and it was damaged, and so you know the number one way to fix stuff is glue sparkly stuff on it, so that's what we did. I've taken it on tour..." I've come to see this sparkly guitar as a metaphor. If country music were an instrument, it would be the acoustic guitar (or the banjo; she's played both). Jazz has the trumpet; Rock has the electric guitar and drums, and she wouldn't pick that one up just yet. Early reviews and criticism of Taylor's music lay in her age and demographic, so what did she do in response to that challenge? Picked up an instrument that defined a genre of songs about broken hearts sung mainly by men and added feminine diamantes and rhinestones. It started as an accident and has evolved into something almost as iconic as her blonde corkscrew curls. A version of the guitar has been on tour with her ever since.

On November 7, 2007, Taylor performed "Our Song" (on a certain aforementioned sparkly guitar) at the CMA Awards in Nashville, where she also won the Horizon Award. Upon presenting the award, Carrie Underwood, the previous year's winner, said, "This is an award that means you have truly arrived in country music." Some may criticise Taylor for her reactions to awards show wins, but I find them endearing, especially this first big one. She thanked her producers and her family, "and the fans...you have changed my life, I can't even believe this, this is definitely the highlight of my senior year." Taylor graduated from high school a year early in order to focus on her music. Nurturing the popularity of young people and what they pay attention to has led to historic musical discoveries. Many iconic stars were discovered in their teenage years, and have subsequently changed the music world; groups like the Beatles, the Rolling Stones, Destiny's Child, and artists like Madonna, Britney Spears and Lorde.

The Taylor Swift Holiday Collection was her first EP released as a Target exclusive on October 14, 2007, by Big Machine Records and released to other retailers on December 2, 2008. It has six tracks in total: two original songs, "Christmases When You Were Mine" "Christmas Must Be Something More," and four covers, the best of which, a cover of Wham's "Last Christmas" reached #28 on Billboard's Hot Country Songs. The following year, all EP songs charted again for the holiday season. It is currently certified platinum and has sold over 1,000,000 copies in the US. In February 2008, Taylor lost the Best New Artist Grammy to Amy Winehouse, who won five awards that evening. She was nominated alongside Feist, Ledisi and a band also from Tennessee called Paramore, who, in 2024, was her opener for the European leg of The Eras Tour. In April 2008, she appeared again on *Good Morning America*, singing "Our Song" and "Picture to Burn" with her sparkly guitar.

Debut's final single, "Should've Said No," was released on May 19, 2008, and is one of my favourites. It has lyrical parallels with the fourth single, "Picture to Burn," the two existing as angry twins on the album, whereas "Teardrops on My Guitar" is more melancholy. Taylor is, again, the sole songwriter on this, along with "Our Song" and "The Outside". I can already hear hints of pop in the opening guitar riff even here, and since day one, Taylor Swift has laid out a clear set of instructions, a 'how to' if you will, on the right way to court her. There is a very clever subtle hint to "Tim McGraw" in the opening line and we know that we are about to get a very different song from almost the opposite perspective, as the lyrics refer to a future where the songs, the smiles and the flowers and are now gone. In "Should've Said No" the lyrics address a cheating lover and the reasons why the relationship cannot continue. Here, Taylor uses the literary device of anaphora where the same words or phrase is repeated for dramatic affect; to show her anger and why it is justified. Folks, there will be no more singing about Tim McGraw. She's been wronged.

William Congreve, in his tragic play, *The Mourning Bridge*, performed in 1697, wrote, "Heaven has no rage like love to hatred turned, nor hell a fury like a woman scorned," and so the more popular idiom, "Hell hath no fury like a woman scorned," emerged. As women, we are *allowed* to get angry; we are reacting to being hurt; this often is misinterpreted as the sexist stereotype of an "over-reaction." The recurring theme of being wronged in relationships will quickly become Taylor's brand, threading an invisible string from this album all the way to her most recent, *The Tortured Poets Department*, released on April 19, 2024.

Track 6, "The Outside," wasn't a single, but it was one that I sang many times over. It comes from a place of insecurity and self-consciousness. Though many people feel normal levels of insecurity if you don't talk about it with close friends and family members, and it goes unchecked for too long, it hurts no one but yourself. The secret album message left in this song in all caps in the album booklet was 'You are not alone' (all of the album's secret messages are in the back of this book). Taylor wrote "The Outside" alone when she was 12 years old. In this song Taylor explains to her listeners how hurtful it is to be isolated and to long for acceptance. She is young, allowing us to see her vulnerability and inviting us to imagine what life is like for those who don't belong. She alludes to the poet Robert Frost in this song, of his road less travelled because she understands what it's like to follow a path that most don't take. It's astounding that she can write those lyrics at the age she did. Most recently, she performed it on piano as a surprise song on February 9, 2024, of The Eras Tour in Tokyo.

On July 15, 2008, Taylor's second EP release was *Beautiful Eyes*. On Myspace she wrote, "I'm only letting my record company make a small amount of these – the last thing I want any of you to think is that we are putting out too many releases. I'm not going to be doing a bunch of promotion for it, because I don't want there to be confusion about whether it's the second album or not." It was sold exclusively to Walmart stores in the US and online through Big Machine Records with a limited physical release. I downloaded the two unreleased tracks, "Beautiful Eyes" and "I Heart?" early in the 2000s, and they have been on my iTunes ever since, along with a few other unreleased songs. The other four songs on the EP are alternate/acoustic and radio edit versions of tracks from her debut; "Should've Said No," "Teardrops on My Guitar," "Picture to Burn," and the debut deluxe edition's "I'm Only Me When I'm with You."

We know it's a business of course, but Taylor has for a long time understood where revenue comes from. It isn't multi-national sponsorship deals; it is predominantly us, the ones who buy the albums, vinyls, merchandise and the tickets. As a teenager, she took the time to greet hundreds of fans who went to early shows, and once she developed a fanbase, there was no limit to what Taylor was capable of. When it comes to her capacity for graciousness, there is no one like her. The biggest star in the world takes time to give back to her primary source of income: us, her fans. In an interview with Andrea, she said about her daughter, "If she could thank every fan that's been to one of her shows, she would. She's tried." There are quite a few of us now, and many more than in 2006 with the release of her first album.

I didn't know much about Taylor Swift in her debut era. When you discover a new television series in its second season, you don't go onto the third until you retrace your steps and start from the beginning. I fell in love with *Fearless* and then went backwards and became obsessed with her debut, which marked the start of my listening journey. *Taylor Swift (Taylor's Version)* is yet to have a release date, and with it comes the much-anticipated hidden catalogue of vault tracks from her unreleased music.

I would fall to pieces if songs like "Lucky You," the first one she ever wrote, "I'd Lie," "Your Face," "Permanent Marker," and "Dark Blue Tennessee" finally got their time in the limelight on the vault tracks for the re-release of her debut. It is predicted that this album will be the last of the re-recorded releases, and there is a certain symmetry with ending exactly where she started. It is inevitable that she is going to sound a lot different in her debut re-record than in a few of the newer albums where it is difficult to distinguish between her original vocals and the updated tracks. If I were to make a prediction, since she has done two re-records every two years (*Fearless* and *Red*, 2021) (*Speak Now* and *1989*, 2023), it could be close to the end of The Eras Tour that she announces *reputation (Taylor's Version)* and we could anticipate *Taylor Swift (Taylor's Version)* the debut re-recordings, maybe in the middle of 2025. I know she has a habit of promoting chaos and keeping us guessing. She has yet to finish The Eras Tour and who knows what tricks she is busy conceptualising as I am writing. Taylor loves doing what the fans want her to, so only time will tell. A recent TikTok video I saw said, "We're Swifties, we're gonna be delusional about when Taylor Swift is gonna release her next album." It will be a great day for the fandom when the masters of her entire discography, including her debut, are once again all hers.

Fearless era
2008 – 2010.

Believing fearlessly in love stories.

I began writing this book somewhere close to March 2009, at the start of my second year of high school. There was a song on the radio I heard every time I was in the back seat or passenger seat of my parent's cars. I learnt the words, and I started to believe them even more quickly. The song was "Love Story." The lyrics are for hopeless romantics, alluding to princes and princesses, and the magic word: yes. If you're a hopeless romantic like me, then *Fearless* is your album. In the pandemic, when I started conceptualising and then self-published my first poetry collection, *Underwater Musings*, about the ocean, a thought bubble surfaced: if I'm writing about the things I love, surely one day I could write about Taylor Alison Swift.

Fearless was the first album I heard in full, and I found out recently that even though it was released 11 November, 2008, in North America, everywhere else in the world, it was released on March 9, 2009. Seven out of 13 tracks had Taylor as a solo writing credit on this album. I started listening in January because my friend Bec had downloaded it off the internet. We listened to it by hiding her purple iPod under the table in our English class. "Love Story" wouldn't debut on Australian radio until March 23, 2009 (it would become her first number one in the country), but we heard it almost three months before that. On the *Billboard* 200, it debuted at #1, selling 592,000 copies in its first week and spending 11 non-consecutive weeks at #1, it was the longest run of any album in the 2000s decade.

By the time the four follow-up singles were released in the US ("White Horse" – December 8, 2008, "You Belong With Me" – April 20, 2009, "Fifteen" – August 31, 2009, and "Fearless" – January 4, 2010) the rest of the world was finally starting to take notice. Whenever I play the beginning chords of *Fearless* (both the song and album), I instantly move into a parallel universe where I'm standing in the kitchen of my childhood home, taking my lunch box off the counter, putting it in my school bag and walking out the door to start my second year of high school. I was 13, and I don't think I knew what fearless meant back then. So, I let Taylor define it for me. In the album booklet (that Taylor designed herself, photos and all) is a paragraph that is repetitive and clear. I typed it out and stuck it on the covers of my schoolbooks so I could read it every day in lessons.

> This album is called FEARLESS, and I guess I'd like to clarify why we chose that as the title. To me, "FEARLESS" is not the absence of fear. It's not being completely unafraid. To me, FEARLESS is having fears. FEARLESS is having doubts. Lots of them. To me, FEARLESS is living in spite of those things that scare you to death. FEARLESS is falling madly in love again, even though you've been hurt before. FEARLESS is walking into your freshman year of high school at fifteen. FEARLESS is getting back up and fighting for what you want over and over again...even though every time you've tried before, you've lost. It's FEARLESS to have faith that someday things will change. FEARLESS is having the courage to say goodbye to someone who only hurts you, even if you can't breathe without them. I think it's FEARLESS to fall for your best friend, even though he's in love with someone else. And when someone apologises to you enough times for things they'll never stop doing, I think it's FEARLESS to stop believing them. It's FEARLESS to say "you're NOT sorry", and walk away. I think loving someone despite what people think is FEARLESS. I think allowing yourself to cry on the bathroom floor is FEARLESS. Letting go is FEARLESS. Then, moving on and being alright...That's FEARLESS too. But no matter what love throws at you, you have to believe in it. You have to believe in love stories and prince charmings and happily ever after. That's why I write these songs. Because I think love is FEARLESS.

Most of the time, I'm not easily scared by things. I'm an adrenaline-seeker with a little too much bravery, like my mother. "Not a lot shakes us," she told me in my early twenties. Being fearless is an experience that Taylor talks about and most of all, she wants us to know that at the core of life's melting pot of emotions and disappointments is love. Love conquers all. This is somewhat ironic because I think one of the only real fears I have right now, in 2024, is that I won't get the chance to spend my life with someone. Everyone's timeline is different, not everyone gets married at twenty-two (some of us are busy forcing our boyfriends to host Taylor Swift-themed treasure hunts), not everyone has one or two babies at twenty-eight, and some people find love and lose a loved one way too early than is fair. Some people have four, five or six goes at the "catch and release" game of dating before finding "the one." Some people find it on their first try. Some of my best friends were married before thirty and had babies. That was all that I ever wanted. I believe in the love stories that Taylor writes about because I've seen them in the people I love and their partners. It's not a question of the existence of love; it's more down to the timing and perfect circumstances and a matter of happenstance and chemical reactions.

At this moment in time, I am also afraid of being with someone who pretends to reciprocate feelings. There are four fixes for that kind of hurt, three of which I can afford. 1. A hug from my dad 2. A reassuring conversation with my mum 3. A very good psychologist and 4. Taylor Swift lyrics. Heartache, heartbreak, heart-bruising didn't exist when I listened to *Fearless* for the first time. So, it makes me laugh, re-reading her words from 2008 with the beautiful sparkle of foreshadowing. Her last dedication, after acknowledging the people that helped her with her sophomore album, rings true for the albums that followed: "To the boys who inspired this album, you had fair warning." (Her debut ended with a similar message, "to all the boys who thought they would be cool and break my heart, guess what? Here are 11 songs written about you. HA.")

I miss Taylor's Myspace diary-entry writing style that existed for a long time from around 2005 until 2010. It was a pure stream-of-consciousness trail that could be seen as either infuriating or very, very entertaining. Today, with Myspace a shell of its former self and media criticisms rife waiting for Taylor to misstep, this writing style is rare, but it is truly an example of Taylor's relatability, and here she was still just a teenager (18 when *Fearless* was released, turning 19 a month later). On August 30, 2008, Taylor wrote,

> So now is the time for planning. In 73 days, 11 November will be here, and so will the release date of my new album. And so right now I'm in the middle of writing my 'thank you' section and thinking about track listing order (wondering 'What song should go first…? Or last? How do you get the perfect flow of an album? What IS the "flow" of an album? Hmmm…'). And I'm also thinking about the secret codes to put into the lyrics. […] This next record is on my mind 24/7, all the time. It never stops. I'm always either listening to a new mix of a song or scanning through pictures to make sure we've chosen the right ones, or wondering which songs you guys are going to like the best. I'm just so obsessed with it right now, all the planning. And sometimes I just have to sit back and remind myself that 73 days is not going to be here any sooner if I obsess. It's still going to be 73 days away.

For those who have tendencies towards long-running medical dramas and pets of the feline nature (her Scottish Fold cat she has had since 2011 is called Meredith Grey), be enthused by the fact you and Taylor would get along well. On September 25, in another Myspace entry, we see Taylor writing in a very normal way as a fangirl would, oversharing about her favourite TV show.

> Let me tell you a story: Once upon a time, there was a girl. She was born in 1989 and was bald until she was like two.

Then she got a blonde afro. As a kid, she liked doing school projects and didn't have that many friends. She hung out with her mom a lot. And her cat. Then she started writing songs about all those awesome rejected feelings and blah blah blah..one thing led to another, and she went on tour. Then a show came out called Grey's Anatomy. It came out the same time her world was starting to change. Every time she would feel alone or stressed out, she would watch Grey's Anatomy.

Soon she just started to refer to it as "her show" and got all the seasons on DVD as soon as they came out and played them on repeat in the bus and downloaded every song that was EVER on Grey's Anatomy episodes, and decided that one day she was inevitably going to name one of her future daughters Izzie.

When Denny died in season 3, she couldn't stop crying for days and it was borderline embarrassing. Anyway, this show became her favorite thing ever and she watched it obsessively for years and years. And then one day, she got a call – and she found out that one of HER songs that SHE wrote............ was going to be played on THE SEASON PREMIERE of her FAVORITE SHOW (possibly the BEST show EVER CREATED)...Grey's Anatomy. And she started jumping up and down and started hugging people she didn't know in the hotel lobby and sobbing hysterically – again, borderline embarrassing. And it was the best day ever. And then she blogged about it and hopes that you don't think she's weird for obsessing over a TV show so much. The End.

Guys, I can't BELIEVE this! The song you'll hear on Grey's tomorrow night (TOMORROW NIGHT!!) is called "White

> Horse" and it's one of my favorites on the new album. It's a two hour premiere and I can't wait to see it. The coolest thing is, I would've been counting down to tomorrow anyway, because that's my show. I need to watch it, or the world ends. But now I'm counting down the seconds. I'm playing a show tomorrow night in Tulsa, Oklahoma, so I hope the times line up to where I can catch it when I get offstage. I've been in LA for the past few days, and it's been a blast. And I recorded a new song the other day for Fearless. I think it's fun to put yourself under crazy pressure to finish a song by a certain deadline. That's what I did with this last song. And that makes 13 songs on the new album. 13..... I think that's a good number of songs to end up with.... <3
>
> Grey's Anatomy rules. Lovelovelove -T-

One line I love is where she hopes her concert will be done in time to go and watch the TV. Celebrities really are just like us, right? The song she's referring to as just finished is Track 11, "Forever and Always." There is something cathartic about reading these Myspace entries because, once upon a time, all early 2000s teenagers wrote like that on the internet. In the early days of my Facebook usage, I professed my love for Zac Efron being in Sydney, blue digital cameras, yellow Volkswagen Beetles, *The Hunger Games*, *Doctor Who* and whenever I was lucky enough, my unhinged usage of capital letters appeared.

> October 17, 2014 at 11:50 am.
> TAYLOR SWIFT IS IN MY COUNTRY. NOT COPING RIGHT NOW.

Taylor played her first show out of the United States in London on September 3, 2008 at the King's College Student Union. There were only a few hundred people there when she sang three songs from

Fearless and three from her debut with a cover of Amy Winehouse's "Rehab." On October 5, for the third game of the World Series, Taylor sang the national anthem for the Philadelphia Phillies and Tampa Bay Rays. Even though she moved to Nashville as a teenager, she still knows how to honour her home. Writing for *The New York Times* in November 2008, Jon Caramanica refers to the constant use of early social media, mainly Myspace, to engage with fans and cement her legacy as caring and open towards the hundreds of people who operated online. Hundreds turned into thousands of people in real life who bought and interacted with her music. This would come full circle almost ten years later with the creation of the secret sessions. Caramanica writes,

> Right before the show in Chattanooga, as she does before every performance, Ms Swift loaded her wrists with bracelets that she would later toss out to fans, allowing them to take home a small piece of her. And after she finished singing "Should've Said No," about a boy who cheated on her, she dropped to her knees and bent forward, holding her head still as fans in the front rows patted it concernedly. It was a scarily intimate moment but essential to her self-presentation that there is no barrier between her and her songs, and their listeners, the consumers. That insistence informs every aspect of her work...It has also led to the decimation of her privacy. 'Every single one of the guys that I've written songs about has been tracked down on Myspace by my fans,' she said, a little giddy. 'I had the opportunity to be more general on this record, but I chose not to. I like to have the last word.'...She has aggressively used online social networks to stay connected with her young audience in a way that is proving to be revolutionary in country music...helping country reach a new audience.

Caramanica also commented on the genre-blending that Taylor mastered with the second album and refers to the early criticism of long-established demographics for country music. "She has placed the concerns of young women at the centre of her songs, subject matter that generally has been anathema in the more mature world of country singers. Most importantly, though, she very much sees country music as part of the larger pop panorama." There is a youthfulness in *Fearless* that is truly Taylor. The original album cover is more stripped back than the debut, with a colour scheme of creams, white, and soft gold. Her trademark curls aren't framing her face in a wild mane of natural beauty this time; they are mid-flight, and her head is turned with her profile in dead centre. It's a mid-shoulder framed shot, not allowing for too much detail, saving that for the words within. The updated cover of *Fearless (Taylor's Version)* is tinted golden-brown with a low shot looking up at Taylor. Her head is turning the opposite way, perhaps a metaphor for looking forward, not back. Her hair is still defying gravity, naturally styled, flying in the wind.

Taylor and Miley Cyrus joined forces to sing "Fifteen" at the Grammys in February 2009. Miley has also lasted through the decades, emerging from my early teenage poster girl eras, proving to the world that she is also an incredible woman with a long career creating great pop music. In April, my world's collided when Taylor had two songs released on the *Hannah Montana: The Movie* soundtrack. My parents will tell you I was obsessed with it for at least two years, and it would have been difficult to be around me in the early days of my Taylor fandom. These additions to the soundtrack were the closest that Taylor came to being classified as part of the Disney machine, and although she attended a lot of premieres with her friends, she never starred in a Disney Channel show and was in no other Disney-affiliated films aside from appearing as herself in the February 2009 concert film, *Jonas Brothers: The 3D Concert Experience* singing "Should've Said No," and making an uncredited cameo in *Hannah Montana: The Movie* when she sang "Crazier" in a barn dance scene. Accompanied by Rascall Flatts, she was still very firmly placing herself in the genre as a country artist, and this was her first in a long line of soundtrack singles. "Crazier" is an interesting song that could have suited either her debut or *Fearless*, so for it to exist in the in-between space of her two albums shows that maybe it was one that didn't make the cut for either and found a home somewhere else. The finale song, "You'll Always Find Your Way Back Home" which Miley/Hannah sings, was penned by Taylor. I would give anything to hear her sing that live, and I have unwavering optimism that it will happen one day. Lucas Till, who played the male romantic lead role in *Hannah Montana: The Movie*, is arguably the same character in the "You Belong With Me" music video, which premiered on May 4, 2009. This wasn't an accident; they met on the movie set, and Taylor would have seen his potential to carry the character into a different format and imagined a different existence with romance at the core. With over 1 billion views, it is the most-viewed country music video on YouTube.

If you were to ask me my favourite Taylor song, I would not be able to give you a straight one-sentence answer, but I would come very close to telling you about "You Belong With Me." Amidst the fairytales in *Fearless*, I learned the definition of the word 'unrequited' because of this song. Now, in 2024, having reached an expert level of experience on that kind of love, I sing it as loudly now as I did when I was 13. Desperation floods this song, easily summarised as, CHOOSE ME NOT HER. The girl in the song can see that the boy she likes is in a toxic relationship, but he just can't see it. It plays with the popular tropes of high school love triangles; the quiet pining girl, the popular football captain and the head cheerleader. These aren't defined or created by Taylor, but she understands her teenage audience's viewing habits very well. For every generation there is always defining American high school film, from James Dean's *Rebel Without a Cause* to *Grease, Say Anything, The Breakfast Club, Clueless, Mean Girls, Bring it On!, High School Musical* and recent films like *Love, Simon* and *The Kissing Booth*. Every character in those films has that moment captured in "You Belong With Me" where she sings about the day when the person she loves finally wakes up and sees that what he has been looking for is right in front of him.

Her lyrics immerse listeners in the American high school cafeteria environment. I didn't know what words like 'bleachers' were, and yet I still sang them into my hairbrush in my bedroom. One of Taylor's early television appearances was on *The Tonight Show* with Jay Leno promoting *Fearless* on April 2, 2009. This interview is fascinating because it presents her Myspace blog-writing persona to a live audience. I know some people are infuriated by the way she presents herself in interviews, but I find her to be quite a comedian. Taylor has a lot of fixations; cats and sparkly things are well-documented, but fans know the obsession she has with the number 13 is next level. During the *Fearless* and *Speak Now* era, she had her mum Andrea write the number on her hand with permanent marker and blue glitter. This practice has become a trend for her fans to copy to this day. In the Leno interview, she is quoted as saying,

> I was born on the 13th, I turned 13 on Friday the 13th, my first album went gold in 13 weeks, also my first song that ever went number one; it had a 13 second intro. I didn't even do that on purpose. And every time I've ever won an award at an awards show I've either been seated in the 13th row, row M, which is the 13th letter, and when I won the Horizon Award at the CMA awards, the producer came up to me when we were sound-checking and said, alright we're gonna go in 13 seconds. So many numbers!

Jay Leno responds by wiggling his fingers as if casting a spell, making a "WOoOooOOo" noise to visibly encourage the 'spookiness' of all of her coincidences with the number. There might be a tendency for a television personality like Leno to attribute this perceived childish way of speaking and naivety to her age, and Leno references this,

"How old are you – you're *only* 20?" but ultimately, here we get an unfiltered and honest monologue that speaks to her genuineness. She is unafraid of the quirkiness that comes with sharing her unique fixations on national television. Years later, in her *Rolling Stone* interview in October 2020 with Paul McCartney, she is perhaps more adult in the way that she reflects on this continued fixation. "It's lucky for me. It's my birthday. It's all these weird coincidences of good things that have happened. Now, when I see it places, I look at it as a sign that things are going the way they're supposed to. They may not be good now, they could be painful now, but things are on track. I don't know, I love the numerology." Paul responds with, "It's spooky, Taylor. It's very spooky… but…I like that, where certain things you attach yourself to, and you get a good feeling off them. I think that's great."

On May 6 2009, Taylor performed her second UK show at London's Shepherd's Bush Empire. Gillian Orr, writing for *The Independent*, called her "country's squeaky clean new queen." And for a very long while Taylor tried hard to adhere to that. This interview shows just how far "the brand of high-school heartache" has come with young women. Nowadays, women like Olivia Rodrigo, Sabrina Carpenter, Maisie Peters and Billie Eilish dominate the charts and tell their romantic stories in unique ways. Orr writes,

> It will be interesting to see if Swift can maintain her country fanbase now that she's found mainstream pop success. There's the odd nod to country, but with all the electric guitars and drums going on, the sound is much more pop-rock lite. It's a terribly bland style of music, but it's done extremely well. Like a Häagen-Dazs French Vanilla ice cream as opposed to Tesco own brand. But it's all still vanilla…The show is unashamedly girly (at one point, she even uses a guitar covered in pink crystals) and its defiantly PG. You won't find Swift doing raunchy routines (although

she's not averse to a bit of awkward dancing), and even her sparkly black dress comes down to her knees...There's no denying that Swift is a polished performer, can write a great little pop song and seems like a thoroughly nice girl. In an age of Paris, Lindsay et al, perhaps such a wholesome role model for younger girls shouldn't be sniffed at. But isn't it just a bit disappointing to see so many blinkered teenagers, so thoroughly into this when musically, really, there's so much more out there?

I love reading this review with hindsight, knowing that I was a blinkered teenager back then as much as I still like to think I am now. Since 2008, Taylor's fanbase has been cracked open to make way for people of all ages sharing together in her love stories and songs. I have friends who have come up to me over the years and said, "We miss country-Taylor" and that's strange to me because I don't think that version of her every fully left, she just took a hiatus through 1989, *reputation* and *Lover* to escape into quarantine and write a beautiful country-folk album in *folklore*. A mention of my favourite sparkly guitar is there, which Gillian Orr recognises as a symbol for girliness; however, I see it as an infiltration into a male-dominated genre. As for maintaining that country fanbase, in 2024, there is still space for reinvention and return; she re-entered the country charts with the rerecordings of *Fearless* and *Red*, and we have not yet seen the release of *Taylor Swift (Taylor's Version)*, which will no doubt chart in the country genre and with each new album heralding an experiment in sound production there is room for people to choose which Taylor they want to hear. Her fans began in a particular demographic, "girls brought up on a cultural diet of High School Musical and Hannah Montana," but there is substantial proof the fanbase has transcended. We now see grandparents taking their grandchildren and dads chaperoning their daughters to The Eras Tour.

I desperately wanted to fall in love when I was a teenager. Teenage love is an overused trope in American-centric high school romance movies. They tell us that when you're young, falling in love is full of fanfare, life, colour, and, of course, drama. I wanted to feel like the girl in the "You Belong With Me" music video. The pyjamas she wore were my outfit for my Eras Tour show at Wembley, night six on August 17, 2024. I wanted someone to notice me, but it would take a few years. Swift was the surname of the boy who was my first kiss. If nothing more than a beautiful coincidence, it was just another novel fact added to my personal history books. We have mutual friends, and he made me laugh a lot (and probably still could), but then it all came crashing down. He hurt me pretty badly, and I haven't seen him in a few years, but I've done a lot of healing. I'm sure our paths will cross again one day, and I can't tell if I liked him because he had the same name as her or if he was genuinely charming. I didn't love him like the songs said, but I let my guard down and got burned so the walls went back up. As far as first kisses go, it was mortifying, but when are they not? Only in Taylor Swift songs and Nancy Meyers films are first kisses flawless.

When *Fearless* was released, for the week that ended November 29, 2008, Track 2, "Fifteen" debuted at number 79 on the Billboard Hot 100. Along with six other songs, this meant that Taylor set a record to tie her with Hannah Montana (Miley Cyrus) for a solo female, having the most songs charting at once in the same week. In 2020, with *folklore*'s release, she beat her own record with 16 songs charting simultaneously. "Fifteen" re-entered the chart at number 94 on the week ending October 3, 2009, after its release as a single. Taylor sings about a girl named Abigail who becomes her instant best friend in her freshman (first) year of high school. Unlike the who-could-it-be mysteries laced through her lyrics, this one is easily solved. Taylor and Abigail Anderson met in freshman year when they attended Hendersonville High School, sitting next to each other in class. They are still friends to this day. Every Taylor friend I know has their own version of Abigail: that girl you met in your formative adolescence who has been with you through thick and thin, held your hand as you cried and held your hair as you sat next to a toilet bowl, kept you sane throughout school and celebrated all of your wins. There is a line from "Fifteen," where Taylor sings about wanting to leave school as soon as possible, laughing the girls who think they are "so cool." It is an important lyric for me because, at that age, I did want high school to fly by, because I hadn't yet found my place in the world. Taylor implores us to enjoy our young lives before we turn fifteen because we start to navigate the world as a teenager.

My cousin has twin daughters, Olive and Amelia, who are very special to me and at this moment, are 15 years old. I remember them when I write about this song. When I tell them, "I remember being 15," I feel like a wizened dinosaur, but I have had the absolute privilege of knowing them since the day they were born. Family is something I hold close and being over a whole decade older than them wields a lot of responsibility. The three of us at the *reputation* Stadium Tour was one of the best nights of my life. "Fifteen" would immortalise a certain birthday, like its older sister "22." Taylor is always ready for a fun, age-defining celebration. If you have a 15-year-old, play this song on for them, and you can sing it together for a whole year.

Everyone knows that one person (hopefully more) who is a ball of sunshine, the life of the party, lives at the speed of light, dancing at every live music event and chasing sunsets across the world. For me, that's my friend Bec. She radiates kindness, and her hugs are medicine. We met when we were eight years old and started and finished high school together. She showed me *Fearless* before it was released in Australia, and we still talk endlessly about Taylor's antics. Back then, our schoolbooks were covered in magazine cut-outs, and growing up with her by my side was a dream. Now we see each other whenever we're in the same country, which is not often. If Bec was the reason for me listening to Taylor, I wanted to find out how she began her journey.

"One day, my childhood friend Ellen showed me "Love Story." Her mum was driving us around somewhere, and she said, 'Look at this new song I found', and then that day, we proceeded to play it 50 times, Apple Music [back then it was iTunes] had a counter, and we played Monopoly while listening to it on repeat all day, and I thought, 'Who is this girl?' and then I realised she was dating Joe Jonas, and I thought again, 'How do I not know about this girl?' and then I got my dad to download Fearless and he put in on my little iPod Nano and the rest is history. That is my favourite album of ALL TIME, and I've been hooked ever since, loved every album, and the Fearless tour was my first ever concert I went to in March 2010. I've been to every tour since. Crazy times."

When I hear this song, I think of Bec, and I know it isn't too much of a long shot that one day, we could be listening to this song on opposite sides of the world at the same time. With everyone I interviewed for this book, I asked them about their 'holy trinity' of albums, their top three of the 11 released. It is a gauge of how listening tastes are matching or polarising. It doesn't come as a surprise to me at all that hers and mine are almost identical: Fearless, 1989 and Lover for me and the same first two, and folklore for Bec.

"With each album, Taylor shows her ability to make a hard turn on genre. Not necessarily on Fearless, but it is the one I found her in, and then 1989 was the huge turn to pop, another favourite and then folklore, a huge turn from everything else she's done, so that's kind of a weird coincidence. Actually, strangely, they were also the three that won Album of the Year too [before Midnights]."

Continuing the obsession Taylor and I have with sentimentality, Track 12 is "The Best Day." There is always a certain song on each album with a particular person in mind, and this one is about her mum, Andrea. The music video was released on May 1, 2009 as a part of a Big Machine Records Mother's Day promotion, and it is a rare glimpse into Taylor's unseen childhood through home video footage. In a 2015 video interview for Vogue's '73 Questions' Taylor answers, "What's the most difficult song to perform on stage and why?" with this song. "It's just hard to sing because it makes me really emotional." I have rarely listened to this song at the time of writing this book because my family lives on the other side of the world. The opening chords make me tear up, my loved ones are not a car ride away or in the next room. That's been really difficult, but I know they wanted me to go and chase my writing dreams.

In "The Best Day," Taylor describes her early painful school bullying experiences and how she found comfort driving around with her mum. I sang this song in the car with my mum next to me hundreds of times. The next song to come on was a song called "Change," and optimistic little me really believed that things could because I had this insanely strong and incredibly kind mother always beside me.

As we've seen with any new celebrity's rise to fame: 1) you have to start somewhere, and 2) any publicity is obviously important and for actors and even recording artists, scheduled television appearances play a very important role. While promoting the album, Taylor scored her first credited acting job, a guest role on a season nine episode of the long-running US crime serial *CSI: Crime Scene Investigation*, which aired on March 5, 2009. Track 9, "You're Not Sorry," received a CSI-remix, and featured in the credits of the episode. I love her dearly, but Taylor's strength lies in her songwriting, not her acting skills. I've watched this episode; it's melodramatic. Perhaps that's her acting modus operandi, in that case, she nails the brief, and it certainly supports the complexities of the teenage character she presents in her lyrics.

Taylor also made her first two appearances on the comedy sketch show *Saturday Night Live* (SNL) in 2009, debuting in January as a musical guest and performing "Love Story" and "Forever and Always" while also starring in a skit titled 'Save Broadway' where she played orphan Annie. In early November, she returned as host, performing her "Monologue Song," especially written for the show. One of the head writers at the time, successful comedian and talk show host Seth Meyers, called it "not only a beautiful song, but a 'perfect' SNL monologue, fully formed" in a radio interview with Howard Stern in 2023. There was careful attention paid to the joke-making from Taylor's side. The VMAs moment was very much a seminal moment in pop culture at the time because of the overwhelming press it received, she was a month off, turning 20, still very young to have so much spotlight on her.

The monologue song was clever, acerbic and a perfect way to strike back at the people who had hurt her, boyfriends included, and those who constantly speculate about her romantic life, and at others who had treated her badly. The lyrics were stinging, but were sung in a cute, girly voice with a smile. There are lines about what happened at the VMA Awards with Kanye West, delivered with obvious sarcasm but with a happy face, a big smile and a playful attitude. It was clear she was having fun. There are two very public mentions of past relationships in this monologue, which is a rarity for her, but at the same time important in showing that she knows exactly how to play her promotional cards right. Middle member of the Jonas Brothers, Joe Jonas, and *Twilight* actor Taylor Lautner were two very early relationships that caught the attention of the public as she was beginning her career. They are documented in paparazzi photos, but more importantly, Taylor chooses to leave the details out of interviews and put references into the lyrics of her songs to tell us more of a story.

There are very few times where she is clear and specific about song inspirations, with "Forever and Always" being an example. Talking on *Ellen*, on album release day in November 2008, she was shown a photograph of Joe Jonas and responded with, "That guy's not in my life anymore unfortunately…that's an ouch." When pressed further about whether there were any songs about Joe on the album, Taylor said, "There's one…My label let me record that song, right before the album had to be done." Ellen continued her line of questioning (read, interrogation) "What's the name of the song that's about that?" "It's called Forever and Always." "Is it sarcasm, forever and always?" "Definitely" Taylor replies, and "When I find that person that is right for me and he'll be wonderful and when I look at that person, I'm not even gonna be able to remember the boy who broke up with me over the phone in twenty-five seconds when I was 18." A decade later, she responded to the question, "What was the most rebellious thing you did as a teenager?" in Ellen's Burning Questions segment with, "Probably when I put Joe Jonas on blast on your show, that was too much, I was 18, we laugh about it now, that was some mouthy teenage stuff." In a song on *folklore*, she would bring this full circle in "invisible string," singing about the decisions made and relationships gone through on the journey to finding the one you're supposed to stay with. Here, she sings of her feelings towards the men who have broken her heart; the harsh imagery is created by words like 'cold,' 'axe' 'steel' 'broke' and give the listener a taste of her hurt. Detective Swifties know this is Joe Jonas because he has had two children with his now ex-wife Sophie Turner, and Sophie and Taylor have remained close friends.

Of all Taylor's past relationships, Taylor Lautner has definitely been the most supportive of her post-break-up. They briefly dated after meeting on the set of the film *Valentine's Day*, and he is the only one of Taylor's ex-boyfriends to have confirmed to media that he is the inspiration behind a particular song, "Back to December," without badmouthing her or claiming that its existence ruined his career. He appeared on stage to premiere *Speak Now (Taylor's Version)* while also starring in the music video for "I Can See You."

On November 11, 2009, Taylor won four awards at the CMA Awards; Entertainer, Album, Female Vocalist and Music Video ("Love Story"). This was a huge sweep, as on that night, Taylor, at 19, became the youngest person in CMA history to be nominated for and win Entertainer of the Year. Her curls that normally cascaded down her back were elegantly gathered up and her glittery gold tulle dress still influences prom gown choices everywhere.

    Fearless (Taylor's Version) was released April 9, 2021, and was the first of the original six albums to be re-recorded due to the masters dispute with her previous label, Big Machine Records. With the opportunity to release the album again came the phenomenon of the 'vault track.' Songs that had been shelved for various reasons and left off the original album were now given the opportunity to be heard for the first time. This was truly a gift to her fans, but she didn't make it easy. Taylor likes to tease, so the vault tracks were released with the letters jumbled together on a video posted to social media, and sure enough, the internet sleuths wasted no time cracking the lyrical codes. The six tracks from the *Fearless* vault are "You All Over Me (feat. Maren Morris)," "Mr. Perfectly Fine," "We Were Happy," "That's When (feat. Keith Urban)," "Don't You" and "Bye Bye Baby." Having featured artists is important, showing that Taylor realigned herself with country sounds. She is saying to her fans, "Please remember that I will never forget the genre that raised me, and I can and will come back to it whenever I see an opportunity."

    As the *Fearless* era ends in this book (but not in real life because I can just play the album again and again), I will forever be grateful for the people who showed me her music, for the songs that are time machines taking me back to being 15, the songs that always will remind me of my family, and the early days of being a fan. The first time I saw Taylor was when the *Fearless* Tour made it to Sydney on February 6, 2010. The crowd was 27,900. My mum and high school friend Jess danced with me close to a year after hearing her music for the first time. She opened with "You Belong With Me" and ended with "Should've Said No," which are, sonically and lyrically, two sides of the same dazzling coin. I can still picture the manufactured waterfall that came out at the end of the show, spelling out lyrics to the final song, and the picture (in my mind and easily searched on the internet) of her standing under the water, drenched in a black dress and boots, smiling and pointing to the sky. The spectacle of it all, the glittery guitars and an aura of the overdramatic that continues to this day. It was the beginning of something special.

Yo Taylor, I'm really happy for you, I'mma let you finish, but Beyoncé had one of the best videos of all time.

The 2009 MTV Video Music Awards and Kanyegate.

This early moment in Taylor's career is arguably some of the most well-documented media she has received and sometimes it's the one thing non-fans know, purely for the role it has played in pop culture. I have been quizzed on the topic multiple times. "What's the deal with the Taylor vs. Kardashians feud?" and "What did Kanye do that was so bad?" So, I wish I didn't have to, but yes, there's a whole chapter about this mess. Considering nearly 15 years later she has had to speak about it in interviews, it might be best to get some readers up to speed.

On the night of September 13, 2009, the third single from *Fearless*, "You Belong With Me" was nominated for Best Female Video at the MTV Video Music Awards. Taylor won the award, but as she began her acceptance speech, rapper Kanye West came on stage and took the microphone. He said, "Yo, Taylor, I'm really happy for you, I'mma let you finish, but Beyoncé had one of the best videos of all time! One of the best videos of all time!" referring to the music video for "Single Ladies (Put a Ring on It)." In the chaos, the live audience began to boo, and he returned the microphone to her and walked off stage. West was removed from the remainder of the show, and later on, when Beyoncé won Video of the Year for the aforementioned video, she called Taylor back to finish her speech. In 2013, *Rolling Stone* named it the "wildest moment" in the history of the awards show.

The backlash was swift and in Taylor's favour. The speech was embedded into the cultural zeitgeist and quickly became easily 'meme-able' in the early days of internet humour. Appearing on *The Tonight Show* with Jay Leno the day after the awards, Kanye attempted an unplanned apology. "I immediately knew in this situation it was wrong, and it wasn't a spectacle, and it was someone's emotions, you know, that I stepped on, and it was very, it was just, it was rude.

Period. And I'd like to apologise to her in person." Leno asks a follow-up question. "When did you know you were wrong? Afterwards, as you were doing it?" West replies, "As soon as I gave the mic back to her and then she didn't keep going." Almost a year later, as a guest on the *Ellen* Show in October 2010, West reappears in the US after living reclusively in Europe to escape the media. He addressed the event, describing it as a "moment of sincerity or alcohol," to which host DeGeneres replied almost jokingly, "Those don't usually go together, usually the alcohol rules out the sincerity," to the roars of the television audience.

On October 25, 2010, Taylor released her third album *Speak Now*. The album's title said it all. Speaking up is better than not speaking up. However, if it is not possible to express what you want to say in words, then put those words into songs. Her thoughts throughout the whole track list are presented as an open diary and an opportunity to take chances to say what was on her mind. Track 11, "Innocent," is a response to the VMAs incident described above. Chris Willman, writing for *New York Magazine* shares Taylor's response. "So there was this guy. "I think a lot of people expected me to write a song about him. But for me, it was important to write a song *to* him." Her lyrics allude to life being tough, maturity, and behaviour. Willman calls "Innocent" "a tricky piece of songcraft: Some viewers took it as deeply sympathetic toward West, others as patronising in its sympathy. But [it] clearly provides a turning point in which Swift gets the upper hand by casting herself in a mature, even maternal light." In the album booklet, the decoded secret message for "Innocent" is, "Life is full of little interruptions." It could be assumed that the legacy of that encounter would maybe not fade but fall into mild obscurity, referenced in only one song of hers, popping up on most of the countdowns of wild awards show incidents? You would be wrong.

In August 2015, the MTV VMAs saw a reunion between Kanye and Taylor, and this was Taylor's tasteful and uninterrupted introduction to Kanye presenting him with his landmark MTV Video Vanguard Award.

I first met Kanye West six years ago – at this show, actually! It seemed like everyone in the world knew about our infamous encounter at the VMAs. But something that you may not know is that Kanye West's album *College Dropout* was the very first album my brother and I bought on iTunes when I was 12 years old. I have been a fan of his for as long as I can remember because Kanye defines what it means to be a creative force in music, fashion and, well, life. So I guess I have to say to all the other winners tonight: I'm really happy for you, and I'mma let you finish, but Kanye West has had one of the greatest careers of all time! I am honoured to present the 2015 Vanguard Award to my friend, Kanye West.

To a rapturous applause Taylor does what only she can do best, makes a meme of herself, and cleverly repurposes the dramatic moment. Kanye's acceptance speech was less succinct and a little more on the confusing side, running for nearly ten minutes, and towards the end of the speech, he spoke a little about what happened at the 2009 VMAs, "After that night, the stage was gone, but the effect that it had on people remained...I fight for artists, but in that fight I somehow was disrespectful to artists. I didn't know how to say the right thing, the perfect thing." There was also a generalised conversation about the lack of recognition for hard-working artists that get overlooked with, "I still don't understand awards shows... people who work their entire life, sold records, sold concert tickets, come stand on a carpet, and for the first time in their life be judged on a chopping block, and have the opportunity to be considered a loser." It is delicate terrain to move across the platform of major viewership (MTV) and state such an honest opinion. There is a balance that has to be made between genuinely seeking change in the music industry for talent recognition and attention-seeking behaviour. He goes on to say, "I'm not no politician, bro. And look at that, you know how many times MTV ran that footage again [of his 2009 interruption] because it got them more views?" In my *very* biased opinion, here he almost sounds like he wanted credit for the popularity surge caused by him walking up on stage. During the Vanguard speech, he mentions Justin Timberlake being snubbed in February of 2015 for the Album of the Year Grammy, (as producer on Pharrell William's G I R L), and there is footage of Kanye pushing past members of the audience, walking up to the stage and then straight back down, generating first concerned looks and then laughs from the audience members (notably Jay-Z). In Brian Hiatt's 2019 *Rolling Stone* cover interview, Taylor re-explains the thoughts behind her Vanguard presentation speech and the aftermath, where Kanye says to her,

> I really, really would like for you to present this Vanguard Award to me, this would mean so much to me, and went into all the reasons why it means so much because he can be so sweet. He can be the sweetest. And I was so stoked that he asked me that. And so I wrote this speech up, and then we get to the VMAs, and I make this speech and he screams, 'MTV got Taylor Swift up here to present me this award for ratings!' And I'm standing in the audience with my arm around his wife, and this chill ran through my body. I realised he is so two-faced. That he wants to be nice to me behind the scenes, but then he wants to look cool, get up in front of everyone and talk shit. And I was so upset. He wanted me to come talk to him after the event in his dressing room. I wouldn't go.

Later in 2015, in an October *GQ* interview with Chuck Klosterman, Taylor explains there was pure confusion when Kanye joined her on stage back in 2009.

> When the crowd started booing, I thought they were booing because they also believed I didn't deserve the award...That's where the hurt came from. I went backstage

and cried, and then I had to stop crying and perform five minutes later. I just told myself I had to perform, and I tried to convince myself that maybe this wasn't that big of a deal. But that was the most happenstance thing to ever happen in my career. And to now be in a place where Kanye and I respect each other – that's one of my favorite things that has happened in my career.

That should have been the end of the story, but a few days prior to the 2016 Grammys, on February 12, Kanye held an extravagant double celebration with the launch of his Yeezy Season 3 line at New York Fashion Week. At Madison Square Garden, broadcast to theatres worldwide and on streaming service Tidal, his seventh studio album, The Life of Pablo, was heard for the first time.

With the events for fashion week locked in, West's production was so ambitious a spectacle that numerous designers rescheduled their shows so as to not clash with his launch. Julianne Escobedo Shepherd, writing for Rolling Stone, said, "He issued a clear reminder that he's so influential that no one can hope to ignore him and remain relevant...[and] ultimately clarified West's vision both as an artist and a cultural force at a time when fashion's desire to perch at the intersection of music has never been so acute." Immediately following the event, one controversial lyric line made its way into the spotlight. "Famous" the album's lead single, has an opening lyric that references Taylor and is conspicuous in its imagery, "I feel like me and Taylor might still have sex, why? I made that bitch famous (Goddamn!) I made that bitch famous."

It was clear that friends and family of Taylor weren't aware of the line. Rolling Stone reported that Swift's brother, Austin, posted a video on Instagram tossing his Yeezy's away, and Gigi Hadid, a close friend of Taylor's, attended the launch but tweeted afterwards, "My attendance somewhere does not mean I agree with everything being said in the music playing there. My friends know of my loyalty." Tree Paine, Taylor's publicist, released a statement the night prior to the album launch saying, "Kanye did not call for approval, but to ask Taylor to release his single "Famous" on her Twitter account. She declined and cautioned him about releasing a song with such a strong misogynistic message." Swift's rep also said, "Taylor was never made aware of the actual lyric, 'I made that bitch famous.'" That night, Kanye posted a series of tweets (see below) in the space of seven minutes that were almost-Trumpian in their tirade, unfiltered and nonsensical. Over the next few days, they were all very quickly removed. For clarification, in tweets 14 and 15, there are typos; 'seen' is supposed to be 'scene' from a movie and 'can stop us' should be 'can't stop us', referring to the Yeezy S3 line and album drop.

1 I did not diss Taylor Swift and I've never dissed her...
2 First thing is I'm an artist and as an artist I will express how I feel with no censorship
3 2nd thing I asked my wife for her blessings and she was cool with it
4 3rd thing I called Taylor and had a hour long convo with her about the line and she thought it was funny and gave her blessings
5 4th Bitch is an endearing term in hip hop like the word N*gga
6 5th thing I'm not even gone take credit for the idea...it's actually something Taylor came up with...
7 She was having dinner with one of our friends who's name I will keep out of this and she told him
8 I can't be mad at Kanye because he made me famous! #FACTS
9 6th Stop trying to demonise real artist Stop trying to compromise art
10 That's why music is so fucking watered down right now I miss that DMX feeling
11 7th I miss that feeling so that's what I want to help restore
12 8th They want to control us with money and perception and mute the culture
13 not just the famous people there but the kids the moms the dads

the families that came to share this moment with us
14 9th It felt like a seen from The Warriors ALL GODS ALL GODS ALL GODS in the buildin'
15 but you can see at Madison Square Garden that you can stop us

Responding in real time to Kanye's online chaos, Kristina Rodulfo writing for ELLE, wrote the same day (February 12), "We predict one of two things will happen after this: Either Kim [Kardashian] will call peace in a selfie with Taylor (her response after a similar Kanye-driven Twitter feud with ex-girlfriend Amber Rose and Wiz Khalifa a week before this on 2 February), or Kanye will join Taylor in her Grammys opening performance a la her MTV VMAs make-up with Nicki Minaj. What if it's all a ploy to get more viewers to watch the Grammys on Monday night?...Anyone else over it?"

The very next day after Kanye's album release, Taylor won Album of the Year at the Grammy Awards for her genre-shifting fifth album, 1989. At the time, it was the fifth instance an artist had won the award twice, Taylor being the first woman. Adele would follow suit the following year. Taylor's speech doesn't directly name West, but it very pointedly references the evolving situation. "There are going to be people along the way who will try to undercut your success or take credit for your accomplishments or your fame. But if you just focus on the work and you don't let those people sidetrack you, someday, when you get where you are going, you will look around, and you will know that it was you and the people who love you who put you there." Needless to say, there was no such predicted onstage reunion. TIME named "Famous" one of its best songs of the year, deciding "He uses all of that beauty to crack open his long-simmering spat with the biggest pop star on the planet. The court of public opinion won't ever reach a verdict on Taylor v. Kanye – did she consent to being mentioned? Did she double-cross Kanye? At least we can all agree that "Famous" captures West in all of his complicated, vital glory."

I think it's important to note another disturbing point

about this song: its music video. It begins with a stitching of sound clips together, and one of them is Taylor's voice, cut directly from the moment before Kanye took the microphone from her, where she says, "[giving me the chance]...to win a VMA Award." There hasn't been much done to hide or mask her voice, and it directly references the famous interaction between the two. The sound is disconcerting, and the visuals even more so, for most of the video, the steadycam wobbly quality moves through a bed, with recognisable faces in it. The end of the video zooms out to show 12 naked plastic models sleeping designed to look like famous celebrities, those featured are George W. Bush, Donald Trump, Anna Wintour, Rihanna, Chris Brown, Taylor Swift, Kanye West, Kim Kardashian, Ray J., Amber Rose, Caitlyn Jenner, and Bill Cosby. The video didn't do well, and there wasn't much spoken about it from the celebrities featured; though Taylor does call it "revenge porn" in a later Instagram post, it was really the lyrics that fans and Taylor's team had issue with. Here begins a third chapter in the Taylor v. Kanye epic. In Kanye's list of tweets, the fourth communication mentions a phone call between the two of them, where Kanye alleges consent and blessings were given about the reference to Taylor in the song. Taylor and her team disagreed, and the world picked sides. The gap in the six years between the interruption and the second VMAs meeting are filled in by the 2019 *Rolling Stone* cover interview. Taylor says to Brian Hiatt,

> The world didn't understand the context and the events that led up to it [the phone call]. Because nothing ever just happens like that without some lead-up. Some events took place to cause me to be pissed off when he called me a bitch. That was not just a singular event. Basically, I got really sick of the dynamic between he and I. And that wasn't just based on what happened on that phone call and with that song – it was kind of a chain reaction of things. I started to feel like we reconnected, which felt great for me – because all I ever

wanted my whole career after that thing happened in 2009 was for him to respect me. When someone doesn't respect you so loudly and says you literally don't deserve to be here – I just so badly wanted that respect from him, and I hate that about myself, that I was like, 'This guy who's antagonising me, I just want his approval.' But that's where I was. And so we'd go to dinner and stuff. And I was so happy, because he would say really nice things about my music. It just felt like I was healing some childhood rejection or something from when I was nineteen.

Kim Kardashian was featured on a *GQ* cover shoot in June 2016 and said this in her interview with Caity Weaver, "Kanye and Taylor (or Kanye and Taylor's reps) may both be telling the truth here – as they see it. Maybe the duo talked 'sex' but not 'bitch.' Maybe he misinterpreted her noncommittal politeness as implicit accord. Maybe they both hung up, pleased they were finally on the same page." There is an episode of *Keeping Up With the Kardashians* where Kris has a conversation with Kim about the possibility of apologising to Taylor.

> Kris: "How did this all start up again anyway?"
> Kim: "Just because I did an interview for *GQ*"
> Kris: "What would happen if you just called Taylor up and just say, what happened, how did this go so south? I don't understand the motivation to flip so quickly...Maybe she just took it the wrong way? My advice is that you give Taylor a call and try to make amends."

Kim responds with, "Thank you for your lovely advice, but I'm not going to take it." Kim maintains that Taylor is lying when she published that permission was not granted, and she has proof because they indeed recorded the phone call (which in the state of California, where Kim and Kanye resided, is not illegal, but in the state of New York, where Taylor mainly lives, it is a felony). Kim said to Caity Weaver, "I swear, my husband gets so much shit for things [when] he really was doing proper protocol and even called to get it approved...What rapper would call a girl that he was rapping a line about to get approval?"

On July 16, 2016, Kim uploaded a video to Snapchat that showed Kanye on speaker phone with Taylor, showing Taylor apparently giving approval to the misogynistic lyrics in "Famous." Kanye says, "As a friend, I want things that make you feel good," and Taylor responds with, "If people ask me about it, look, I think it would be great for me to be like, 'He called me and told me before it came out...joke's on you, guys. We're fine,'" Swift also says. After the video was released, Kim posted this tweet "Wait, it's legit National Snake Day?!?!?They have holidays for everybody, I mean everything these days!" Followed by 36 (yes, I had to count them) snake emojis. Kim's tweet and the video quickly went viral, with hundreds of users accusing Taylor as a liar because she had said that she hadn't consented to particular words used, but now there was evidence possibly suggesting the opposite. The internet began to re-use the snake emoji across Taylor's social media, tweeting the hashtags #KimExposedTaylorParty and #TaylorSwiftisOver.

Taylor posted on Instagram this statement; "I wanted to believe Kanye when he told me that I would love the song. I wanted us to have a friendly relationship. He promised to play the song for me, but he never did. While I wanted to be supportive of Kanye on the phone call, you cannot 'approve' a song you haven't heard. Being falsely painted as a liar when I was never given the full story or played any part of the song is character assassination. I would very much like to be excluded from this narrative, one that I have never asked to be part of since 2009." When GQ reached out to a spokesperson on Taylor's team, they didn't answer any clarifying questions, and instead provided a statement.

Taylor does not hold anything against Kim Kardashian as she recognises the pressure Kim must be under and that she is only repeating what she has been told by Kanye West. However, that does not change the fact that much of what Kim is saying is incorrect. Kanye West and Taylor only spoke once on the phone while she was on vacation with her family in January of 2016 and they have never spoken since. Taylor has never denied that conversation took place. It was on that phone call that Kanye West also asked her to release the song on her Twitter account, which she declined to do. Kanye West never told Taylor he was going to use the term 'that bitch' in referencing her. A song cannot be approved if it was never heard. Kanye West never played the song for Taylor Swift. Taylor heard it for the first time when everyone else did and was humiliated. Kim Kardashian's claim that Taylor and her team were aware of being recorded is not true, and Taylor cannot understand why Kanye West, and now Kim Kardashian, will not just leave her alone.

In March 2020, at the beginning of the global COVID-19 pandemic, a 25-minute uncut version of the video surfaced, establishing that Taylor wasn't lying, and Kanye did not in fact tell Taylor about the controversial line ("I made that bitch famous") which she had objected to. In the 20-minute leaked video, Taylor says, "You gotta tell the story the way that it happened to you. And the way that you experienced it…It doesn't matter if I pulled 7,000,000 off that album [*Fearless*] before you did that, which is what happened, you didn't know who I was before that, it's fine." Kanye says in the footage, "You've got an army," and that she does, easily mobilised and able to control the narrative. But in 2016, the damage had been done. Taylor responded on Instagram Stories with this,

> Instead of answering those who are asking how I feel about the video footage that leaked, proving that I was telling the truth the whole time about *that call* (you know, the one that was illegally recorded, that somebody edited and manipulated in order to frame me and put me, my family, and fans through hell for 4 years)...SWIPE UP to see what really matters. The World Health Organization and Feeding America are some of the organisations I've been donating to. If you have the ability to, please join me in donating during this crisis.

Kim tweeted on March 24, 2020, "To be clear, the only issue I ever had around the situation was that Taylor lied through her publicist who stated that 'Kanye never called to ask for permission...' They clearly spoke so I let you all see that. Nobody ever denied the word "bitch" was used without her permission." The most recent comments relating to this public duel were made by Taylor in her TIME 'Person of the Year' interview in December 2023. She called the feud and Kim Kardashian's comments, "a fully manufactured frame job, in an illegally recorded phone call, which Kim Kardashian edited and then put out to say to everyone that I was a liar," and added, "that took me down psychologically to a place I've never been before...I went down really, really hard." You only have to watch the middle section of Taylor's Netflix 2020 documentary, *Miss Americana* to understand the toll and hear it from the artist herself to fully understand the concept of being "cancelled." She says,

> When people decided I was wicked and evil and conniving, and not a good person. That was the one that I couldn't really bounce back from because my whole life was centred around it. #taylorswiftisoverparty was the number one

trend on Twitter worldwide. Do you know how many people have to be tweeting that they hate you for that to happen? When people fall out of love with you, there's nothing you can do to make them change their mind. They just don't love you anymore.

And so, her sixth album, *reputation* was born. Ever since the days of Taylor's rise as a solid cultural icon and an impressive figure in music, there have always been conspiracy theories created by fans that gain traction, whether or not they have varying degrees of truth. The potential is always there. One such is a fan theory that had this Taylor/Kanye/Kim feud not intensified, Taylor's sixth album *reputation*, would not have been made. It is speculated that an album perhaps sonically similar to her tenth album, *Midnights*, was planned for after 1989 and in the aftermath of 2015 was abandoned. Fans theorised that it was to be called *Karma*. In "The Man" music video, released in 2019, the names of all of Taylor's albums are seen as graffiti on a subway station wall, these as eagle-eyed detective fans would notice are in the same order as the re-recorded albums, forming a clock, but with 'KARMA' written twice, a sign that bans scooters on the subway and a poster that also says, 'MISSING: if found please return to Taylor Swift.' *Teen Vogue* wrote in 2022, that "there's a big 'MISSING' sign right in between 1989 and the word 'karma,' as if Taylor is trying to tell fans that there's an entire era *missing*." This is a double reference to both the 'Karma' missing album fan theory and the dispute with Scooter Braun and Big Machine Records about her master recordings. Twitter fans even believe that the presence of orange also could have been a colour palette for the album, and *Rolling Stone*'s Brittany Spanos confirms a theory that I personally believe is really strong, because it involves Taylor's new hair-do.

In 2016, Swift debuted a new look and seemed to be dropping hints that a new era was coming. That spring, she did a very un-Taylor Swift-like thing: She chopped off her long curly blonde hair and bleached it, an edgier aesthetic for her. She appeared on the cover of *Vogue*, at Coachella, and at the Met Gala with the new look...like other stars, Swift has frequently used a major hair change to indicate a new era. (She straightened her curls before *Red*, then touted a crisp bob for 1989). Her styling changed, too, and she went more glam than before.

1989 was released at the end of 2014. Taylor had a pattern of releasing albums every two years almost to the day. There was an album due at the end of 2016, however, that did not come, and it would not be until a year later, in 2017, that *reputation* arrived. If *Speak Now*'s "Innocent" was a reflection on moving forward, *reputation*'s lead single "Look What You Made Me Do," released August 24, 2017, makes no such attempt at forgetting the public feud, adding to the conversation.

I cannot begin to describe how many easter eggs (obvious and subtle), pointed references and hints there are in both this song's lyrics and music video, but this is the beginning of Taylor becoming very obsessed (and quite frankly unhinged) with hiding things in places for the fans to find. The video opens with a tombstone that says, 'Here lies Taylor Swift's reputation', and then a zombie-fied Taylor rises up to sing that she doesn't like games and tilted stages, a direct reference to Kanye's 2016 Saint Pablo Tour had a stage that floated 15 feet (5 metres) above the crowds. This metaphor of resurrection and the reclaiming of her music after taking an extended leave is obvious here. This video, Taylor said, "is a world that would exist if all of the ridiculous things were true that they were saying about me."

The last section of the music video is perhaps the most interesting. There are 15 Taylor's standing in an airport craft hangar, dressed in different outfits she has previously worn. This dialogue between versions of herself is a novel way of addressing the snarky comments, retorts or criticisms Taylor has faced during her career in music. "Stop making that surprise face, it's so annoying," "Yeah you can't possibly be that surprised all the time," "What's up with that bitch?" "Hey don't call me that," "Oh stop acting like you're all nice, you are so fake," "There she goes, playing the victim, again," "What are you doing?" "Getting receipts, gonna edit this later," "I would very much like to be excluded from this narrative." The dramatisation of these comments is done to poke fun, and more importantly it is an act of reclaiming her storylines and starting again.

"Look What You Made Me Do" isn't the only song on *reputation* that references this feud. "I Did Something Bad" uses its lyrics to weave reality into a fantastical narrative, implying that the Twitter backlash likens itself to a witch-hunt. In Track 13 of *reputation*, "This is Why We Can't Have Nice Things" there are clear and obvious connections to Kanye. Taylor appears to have softened towards West in the first few lines, almost forgiving him, before realising that there is no friendship as he has backstabbed her. She then meters out her own form of revenge with a symbolic axing of a mended fence.

As consumers of popular culture, we watch the media frenzy like sharks attacking a school of fish in the middle of the ocean, except here, there were only three fish and thousands of sharks. But being "innocent" bystanders in the age of online presence and social media followings dictates there will be sides taken and no lines drawn when it comes to unregulated online hate and harassment. As a die-hard Swiftie, I struggle to be unbiased and impartial, especially when it comes to a family like the Kardashians; some fans actively become angry at the mention of Kanye's name, will boycott his music and take to the internet to find others who share their anger and frustrations. It is a circus, and Taylor left that tent quite a while ago. The internet world of celebrity feuds will do its best to pit fan groups against each other when people's lives are quite literally at stake. What we see in the tabloids is only a quarter of the real story; there shouldn't be winners and losers. In-depth interviews like Taylor's *Rolling Stone* and Kim's *GQ* pieces share a clearer picture of each side, and at its core, journalism is a truth-seeking endeavour, but as we have differing opinions, so we have opposing truths, and that is where the stones start to get thrown. If you're invested, you read both and then make a decision. It is an age-old debate that has polarised society in the past: the ability to separate the art vs. the artist. I have permanently set up my tent in Taylor's camp. Kanye West, sadly, will always be a stain on Taylor's history that is hard to get rid of, but that is where the growth is, where moving forward happens...and Taylor has done that.

Speak Now era
2010 – 2012.

Having the courage to *Speak Now*.

I once had a writing idea (as of yet unpublished) where the title was, "Letters He Will Never Read." Confessional and self-explanatory, it centres on having one-sided conversations (a practice approved by my psychologist), which is almost identical thematically to Taylor's third album, *Speak Now*. We cannot fathom airing our worries in person, but we will do our best to write them down. In a deliberate move by the then 21-year-old as a response to critics of *Fearless* who questioned her songwriting ability, Taylor decided that every song on this next album would have a single writing credit: herself. This was unprecedented at the time because of her age and the lengths she would have to go to prove that she was worth paying attention to. The album was written alone whilst she was on the *Fearless* Tour throughout 2009 because "It just sort of happened that way," she explained to Bill Conger, who was writing for *Songwriter Universe Magazine*. "I'd get my best ideas at 3:00 am in Arkansas, and I didn't have a co-writer around, so I would just finish it. That would happen again in New York and then again in Boston, and that would happen again in Nashville…Some of the things I wrote about are things everyone saw me go through. Some of the things I wrote about are things nobody ever knew about. I'm beyond excited for you to hear these stories and confessions."

From my shiny new fan's perspective in 2010, the start of the *Speak Now* era is a little blurry because it is intertwined so much with the end of the *Fearless* one. Facebook wasn't a documentation device; it was a new privilege, and Instagram's grid wouldn't exist until October of that year, meaning I received my Taylor music news primarily via broadcast and print media. I watched the music videos on YouTube over and over and saw the concerts that made it into Australian headlines. My mother succumbed to the teenage girl magazines like *Girlfriend* and *Total Girl* where Taylor's face would move from the glossy pages and adhere to the walls of my bedroom and schoolbooks. The first time I saw her perform in my city was a week after she won her first four Grammys. On January 30, 2010, she won Album of the Year, Best Country Album for *Fearless*, Best Female Country Vocal Performance and Best Country Song for "White Horse." The record for the youngest artist, aged 20, to win Album of the Year would be a title she would hold for a decade, with Billie Eilish being 19 when she won with *When We All Fall Asleep Where Do We Go?* in 2020.

The theatrical release of *Valentine's Day* on February 12 was Taylor's feature film debut. Taylor's performance is comedic and dramatic, and if you're not a fan of her, you won't become a fan by watching this film, so please go and play her album *Speak Now*, her more successful release of 2010. She's not the greatest actress who ever lived; that title, in my opinion, goes to Meryl Streep, BUT Taylor is very funny. Critics were harsh in their reviews (not just of Taylor, but of the film in its entirety). British film critic Mark Kermode wrote in *The Guardian*, "Having invaded cinemas in time for the annual February 14 rom-com barf-fest, *Leap Year* and *Valentine's Day* now form a home-viewing marriage-made-in-hell, shipping up on DVD shelves together like a pair of vomit-encrusted greeting cards." Considering *Leap Year* is so ridiculous(ly good), I can only conclude that, quite simply, Kermode isn't the key demographic for either of these films. Peter Travers, writing for *Rolling Stone*, gave the film one star out of four. Travers' analysis of the film simply stated, "*Valentine's Day* is a date movie from hell." However, you cannot ignore the chosen demographic because the film won Choice Movie: Romantic Comedy and Taylor won the Choice Movie Breakout: Female at the Teen Choice Awards in August. With the exception of *The Lorax*, in which Taylor's voice role was the lead alongside Zac Efron's, the majority of her future film appearances were minor, her name alone driving fans to cinemas. Taylor had two songs on the *Valentine's Day* soundtrack, "Today Was a Fairytale," released on January 19, would debut at #2 on the *Billboard Hot 100*, breaking a record for highest first-week sales by a female artist, only her second time to feature on a soundtrack. She performed the song as part of a medley with Steve Nicks at the 2010 Grammy Awards, followed by "Rhiannon" and "You Belong With Me."

Taylor's *Fearless* Tour I attended wasn't the first time she visited Australian shores; it was a year earlier, and I like the coincidental timing – the first time she visited Australia was the same time I first heard her music at the beginning of 2009. It was her first official tour outside of the United States. She visited Brisbane's Tivoli, with a capacity of 1,500 on 5 March. The next show was the second headline act of 'CMC Rocks The Snowys' on 7 March, a country music festival in Thredbo, NSW, designed to encourage more tourists outside the ski season. She played two shows at Billboard, a Melbourne music venue of only 900 people, on 10 March and then travelled to Sydney for a 12 March show at Marrickville's Factory Theatre. Robert Moran, writing for *The Sydney Morning Herald* in 2024, saw that first Marrickville show (he mentions it couldn't have been more than 400 people) and wrote this,

> Taylor, in a sparkly dress, blonde curls falling like spaghetti, dramatically flicking her head back and forth like she was performing in an arena the size of the MCG rather than a small hall subdivided by a billowing black curtain. Cowboys, in cowboy hats and cowboy boots, slumped against the walls – appreciative but casual – leaving a cavernous empty space in the middle of the room...I'd like to say that, like a pop Nostradamus, I foresaw 15 years of Taylor Swift's cultural dominance from that room in Marrickville. But no, I did not predict that in 2024 I would be asked to write about what it was like to see Taylor Swift, Grammys record-holder and ubiquitous cultural juggernaut, perform on her first Australian tour. Maybe Stacie Orrico, but not Taylor Swift. But I remember thinking her performance was awkwardly big, too big for that stage – so I guess even at 19, Taylor Swift was already creating her destiny.

Ironically, a day later, she would perform at a bigger venue, the Sydney Cricket Ground, as part of 'Sound Relief', which was a large-scale charity concert organised as an aid initiative for Victoria's 2009 Black Saturday Bushfires (which I remember vividly) where 173 people were killed. The Red Cross announced that Sound Relief and donations in the lead-up raised AUD $245 million. The concert ran simultaneously in Melbourne and Sydney at the cricket grounds, and though not on the original bill, Taylor played four songs, closing with "Love Story." In the early days of her first two albums, many journalists perhaps expected Taylor to release one good album and a few radio hits and then disappear in the country genre. The underestimation of Taylor Swift is a beautiful thing. But who always expected her to be destined for great things? The fans. But maybe also TIME *Magazine*. The TIME 100 is a yearly list that looks at influential people in culture. Fleetwood Mac's Stevie Nicks, after their Grammy duet, wrote this entry on April 29, highlighting her established adaptability and correctly predicted the future.

> Taylor reminds me of myself in her determination and her childlike nature. It's an innocence that's so special and so rare. This girl writes the songs that make the whole world sing, like Neil Diamond or Elton John. She sings, she writes, she performs, she plays great guitar. Taylor can do ballads that could be considered pop or rock and then switch back into country... I still walk around singing her song "Today Was a Fairytale." All of us girls want that boy to pick us up and think that we look beautiful even though we're in jeans and clogs. We want it at 14, and we want it at 60. Taylor is writing for the universal woman and for the man who wants to know her. The female rock-'n'-roll-country-pop songwriter is back, and her name is Taylor Swift. And it's women like her who are going to save the music business.

The Thirteen-Hour Nashville Meet and Greet.

Taylor did something on Sunday, June 13, 2010, that would be hard to find another artist who had done this. As part of the CMA Music Fest in Nashville, she hosted a meet-and-greet in the Bridgestone Arena that ended up going for over fourteen hours. It began at 8 am, and for readers who work regular eight-hour days, that's almost the same duration as two days of full-time and would be more aligned with those who work long hours on their feet in the medical profession. I have met a few celebrities in smaller meet-and-greet situations, Rita Ora and Gretta Ray at album signings and Amy Adams and Tom Felton at the stage door of their West End productions, and while any time spent interacting with fans is appreciated and treasured, this kind of fan engagement is still unheard of. Joe Jonas "hosted" a pop-up merchandise store in Shoreditch in London last year. I was there; it ran for nearly six hours, and he arrived almost two hours late and stayed for 45 minutes. Oh, the joy to have been a Taylor fan living in Tennessee at the start of the new decade. Taylor said in a YouTube vlog,

> Every year that I've had an album out, I've participated in CMA Music Fest...It's a great way to meet fans, but I had an idea for doing it a little differently this year...One of the things that I wanted to do to make this year different than any other, was to sign for a ridiculous amount of time. I wanted to be there, showing the fans that I wasn't going to stop signing, and that this wasn't something that I just wanted to take up part of my day, this was an all-day thing and I wanted to sign for 13 hours, 13 is my lucky number so it's had a lot of great significance in my life so that's why I chose that number to sign.

The event was free and ran with a ballot system, whereby you would enter your mobile number and be chosen at random OR delegated members of staff would give you a wristband to enter a queue where you would meet, talk, take photos and interact with her. Halfway through the event, understanding that not all fans attending would have the chance to do this, Taylor gave an impromptu performance and sang "Our Song," "Fearless," "You Belong With Me" and "Love Story." While fans were waiting for their turn in line, there were a multitude of activities to pass the time and keep fans entertained throughout the day. The 20,000-capacity of Bridgestone Arena meant that Taylor's tour bus could be inside, positioned on the floor, where her mum ran guided tours. Band members stayed most of the time and walked around taking photos. Her father, Scott, engaged with fans for the opportunities to hold and take photos with THE sparkly guitar she uses on tours and awards shows whilst handing out guitar picks. There were pop-up stalls of American Greetings cards (for which Taylor had curated a collection), make-up stands from brands Taylor had worked with and home videos and behind-the-scenes clips from the tour, and Taylor's life was playing on the jumbotron in the middle of the arena. Taylor said in her video blog,

> I didn't take any breaks throughout the day. The only break that I took was to go grab my guitar so that I could play the performance. I didn't sit down. And somehow, I was wearing painful heels. You know, the fans weren't sitting down, so why should I? But it was so much fun! The fans kept my energy high all day because every time I turned around a beautiful emotion was shown to me.

At the end of the event, when there was a small number of fans left, instead of doing what any normal person would do at the end of a 13-hour working day and saying, "That's it, thanks for coming, bye," she stayed for another hour and made sure that every fan with a queue ticket had their chance to spend time with her. Part of her widespread appeal to her audiences is gratitude, an understanding that without the fans, none of the record-breaking record sales, sold-out tours, and immense wealth now accumulated would be possible. This incredibly scaled meet and greet was her way of giving back to the country music community of teenage fans who had treasured her from the beginning. A news writer for *Sounds Like Nashville* wrote on June 16,

> During the meet & greet, Taylor rarely looked down at the items she was signing; she made a point to pay attention to the fan she was with and to make that person feel as if he or she was the only one that mattered at that moment. You can see that she genuinely cares about each and every one of her fans, and no matter what some may say, she hosted this event to say 'thank you' to them, not as a marketing ploy.

In the video blog, you can see thousands of fans, but Taylor points out one young girl in particular. You can see a 17-year-old Kelsea Ballerini attending the meet and greet with her friends two years before being signed as a country music artist with Black River Entertainment. In 2014, she released her debut single, "Love Me Like You Mean It" and a year later, with the release of her first album, *The First Time*, the single reached #1 on *Billboard* Country Airplay chart, which made Kelsea the first solo female country music artist to score a number one hit with her debut single since Carrie Underwood's "Jesus, Take the Wheel" in 2006, (only the eleventh in history). They interacted with each other on Twitter in 2015, where Taylor posted, "Driving around with @KelseaBallerini EP on repeat," and Kelsea replied with, "You are one of the main reasons I started writing songs and being fearless (ay?) enough to do this. That just made my year." Taylor brought Kelsea on stage during the 1989 World Tour in Nashville in September of the same year to sing Kelsea's debut single. Online publication *Taste of Country* wrote about the pair in 2016, saying that Taylor has been a mentor to Kelsea, who said,

> I was trying really hard to be very polished, give the perfect answer and use my media training and all that stuff, and

that's just not who I am. I'm 22 years old…She [Taylor] told me, 'It's going to feel like too-cool-for-school wins sometimes. Just know that in the long run, being warm and human and you are going to win. It might take longer, and it might not seem recognised sometimes, but that's what's going to win.'

They have kept in contact over the years and recently sat next to each other at the 2024 Grammys; their friendship is truly the gift that keeps on giving.

Speak Now was announced on a live stream on July 20, 2010, with the first single, "Mine," being released to US Country radio and digital sites on 4 August. It peaked at #3 on the *Billboard* Hot 100 and was certified triple platinum. It reached #6 in Japan, #7 in Canada and #9 in Australia. The album cover was released on August 18 and has two variants, the first where she is wearing a beautiful purple ballgown and the second identical to the first, but the gown is instead red. It was released as a US Target-exclusive deluxe edition. This album is the first that features an almost full body image of Taylor, filling over half the photograph, curls cascading down her back. There's an artistic quality to the image, similar to her first album, with splashes of paint melting into the material of the dress.

The new cover art for *Speak Now (Taylor's Version)* in 2023 evokes the reinvention style of all of the re-released albums, where the image feels reminiscent but updated. The direction of her body has changed; she is surrounded by purple tulle with bare shoulders. She has tried to push her hair off her face and replicate the trademark curls, a lá 2010. She stares down the barrel of the camera without smiling. In preparation for the album release, three digital singles were released weekly to the iTunes store as part of a countdown. "Speak Now" was on October 5, "Back to December" was on October 12 and "Mean" was on October 19. On October 22, "The Story of Us" was previewed, and as with all singles, they have accompanying music videos. The album was released on October 25, 2010.

Track 3, "Back to December" is hands down one of the saddest songs Taylor has written and yet one of my favourites. To me, it could have pushed "Dear John" out and taken place as the Track 5 sad-girl-song of the album. More on that in the next chapter. It is a rarity in Taylor's songwriting, as it exists as the only song in her catalogue that contains a sincere apology from the narrator. She hasn't been wronged; in fact, this time, it's her doing the hurting. This song is about regret; she wishes she could go back and change what happened in December, but she knows this is impossible.

I cried so much to this song in the aftermath of my break-up because, just by coincidence, the month she talks about was significant as both the end and the beginning of my first and greatest love. As I've mentioned before, I've only had one long-term boyfriend, so as you can imagine, I loved him a lot. When our relationship was ending, it was made even more sad by the understanding that both of us knew there was an end date coming, we just had to agree on it mutually. And then the end date came, the dams opened, *and* at the same time, my grandma died. We broke up four days before her funeral, and I didn't tell my parents for two weeks because they went to India for a wedding. I don't know how I functioned in those weeks, holding it together and pretending everything was okay, it clearly wasn't.

I am strong-willed and love people wholeheartedly, but I didn't realise that love can cause the same pain with paradoxical intensity. Almost a year to the day that he and I started becoming more than friends, we had a few long and hard conversations about our future together, and it started to unravel. I can remember where we were when we had talked, where he'd parked his car in Terrigal, and the exact moment when he drove me home; I was crying and angry, and I got out of the car, slammed his door and stormed up the path to my house. With words echoing in the silence that I can never take back, I turned around and saw he had his face in his hands in the front seat, crying. I wish I could tell him how sorry I was, but I think he already knows. Had my mind not been set on trying to have both things that were good – long travel plans and the immense joy and comfort I found in his presence – we would have been together for longer. I often tell people it felt like so much more time than just 12 months, but the length of a relationship doesn't always equal the magnitude of which you love them. We've both moved on (it took me years longer), but it was that moment that still haunts me into understanding how much I was capable of hurting people, and that's why "Back to December" still brings up hard feelings.

It was the same month, and it was the same apology that I desperately needed him to know. I still cry, but I cry because, with this song and that lyric line, I'm remembering how much someone loved me and how much I ruined what we had. The song speaks of past memories; of reliving the happier times and then thinking about the times when one person in the relationship hurts the other and has to live with that regret. There is a juxtaposition of beautiful and painful memories; great times in the summer and a birthday that went by without a phone call, not being able to sleep and remembering the laughter in the car.

In the bridge of Track 9 "Enchanted," Taylor begs the person she loves not to be in love with anyone else. I cry-sang this like a motto until I found out that wishing on stars for someone doesn't always come true. She would write similar lyrics years later in "New Year's Day" in *reputation*, but this time she talks about recognising familiar laughs, and going from being together to being friends. This resonated with me as it isn't as cruel, because my ex is still a friend and his laugh for a long time was my favourite sound. He's the reason why I can't watch rom-coms without being a cynic because I know what I gave up, hence the hopeless in hopeless romantic, and why I broke down crying whilst reading Sally Rooney's *Normal People*.

Track 6 "Mean" is another meaningful song because it has always had a beautiful sense of foreshadowing. Taylor's lyrics respond to music critics who wrote nasty things about her because of her age and supposed naivety entering the music world. She says in an interview, "I had a lot of people who would say, 'Oh, She is an eighteen-year-old girl. There is no way that she actually carried her weight in those writing sessions.' And that was a really harsh criticism I felt because there was no way I could prove them wrong other than to write my entire next record solo. So, that's what I did."

I had a very toxic friendship breakdown right after I finished high school; the girl in question and I always went to concerts together. We went through school together, becoming closer in our senior years. Something snapped, and she became rude, aggressive and emotionally manipulative. It hurt me that someone could flick a switch and become someone I didn't know. Over the years, I slowly, slowly forgot about her except in random moments of joy that would remind me of her because they were musical memories, and I would quickly recollect. When I moved to London in 2022, into the little apartment that I share with a lovely friend, I rarely thought about this girl until one night when I played the Speak Now album, and as always, the song was upbeat enough to dance to in the kitchen, but the lyrics cut like the knives I was using. In "Mean" Taylor explores what it's like to be bullied, to feel humiliated and to have lies told about you. She knows she is not perfect, but she doesn't need others reminding her of her flaws. Walking with your head down is not shameful; it's a moment to understand that not listening to painful opinions or hurtful comments sometimes works.

The older, quieter sister to 2014's shouty "Shake It Off" finishes with the line that did make me tear up in my West Hampstead kitchen (and I wasn't cutting onions) because I remembered the girl I was friends with and wondered why her behaviour to me was cruel. She means nothing to me anymore. Track 8, "Never Grow Up," is also an emotional song (that isn't about a break-up). Taylor sings it as a letter to her younger self, not as a 'these are the lessons you should learn' instruction manual but simply as a reminder to younger fans and people surrounded by children never to wish away the special time that being a child is. Taylor did say once in an interview, "Adulthood is like looking both ways before you cross the street and then getting hit by an airplane." When I was a kid, I was part of the world that my parents built, and I adored every minute of it; as a teenager, all I wanted to do was see the world; now, I've seen the world, and all I want is my family. This song explores the passage of time, the stages of childhood, growing up and living in the world with the responsibilities that make us yearn for a time that was simpler. Taylor doesn't want us to grow up too fast. She asks us to keep the memories of childhood because time passes quickly. We will never get that time back and there are times when life gets too hard. At those times, sometimes we wish we'd never grown up.

I think about my little cousin Greta when I listen to this song. She was born two and a half years after I heard this song for the first time when I was starting my final year of high school. I mourned being older; I didn't want the expectations and the crippling sense that everything from now on would be my choices. I also didn't think about the opportunities that would be coming. Her older sisters, the twins I mentioned in the *Fearless* chapter, were my little shadows and copied everything I did. I raised them listening to Taylor as their mum raised me listening to Britney and Michael Jackson. Greta is 11 now, no longer that tiny little bundle I once held in my arms, and I would fight demons to make sure she doesn't get her heart broken; the sense of protectiveness I have with my younger family members only intensifies as we all get older. And at the end of this song, I come to an understanding that adults possess the same vulnerability that we had as children. We still need comfort when we are alone and afraid, and we remember everything as it was, back when were the children who thought everything was permanent and we were invincible.

Lizzie Widdicombe profiled Taylor for *The New Yorker*, published on 3 October, 2011. Taylor is 21 in this interview, almost 22, and according to Widdicombe, "She has an Oprah-like gift for emotional expressiveness." I think this article is important to mention purely because of the writer's ability to see into the future and predict the stardom that would await Taylor, but also, I can criticise it in ways that don't stand the test of time. One of those ways is the unfair comparison of other female artists in this essay, battling off the popstars of the time with the squeaky-clean image Taylor showed her audiences. Widdicombe says,

> Swift has the pretty, but not aggressively sexy, look of a nineteen-thirties movie siren. She is tall and gangly, with porcelain skin, long butterscotch hair that seems crimped, as if from a time before curling irons, and smallish eyes that often look as if they were squinting. She loves to wear make-up, but it tends to resemble stage make-up: red lipstick, thick mascara. In a world of Lohans and Winehouses, Swift is often cited as a role model, a designation she takes seriously. 'It's a compliment on your character,' she told me. 'It's based on the decisions that you make in your life.' She is in the midst of her second world tour, and every show begins with a moment in which she stands silently at the lip of the stage and listens to her fans scream. She tilts her head from side to side and appears to blink back tears – the expression, which is projected onto a pair of Jumbotron screens, is part Bambi, part Baby June.

The mention of a siren intrigues me. Could you have told 22-year-old Taylor that she would indeed release a song in 2024, off her eleventh album titled "Clara Bow" in reference to the silent movie star who rose to prominence and have yourself compared to her here? Having only released her third album at this point, we would have to wait for three more albums and seven years until *reputation* and with its dark, sexy, grown-up themes.

> Early adulthood is an awkward time for teen stars, but Swift's has been free of embarrassing incidents. She doesn't drink or go to clubs, and she has avoided the trip to rehab that marked the coming-of-age of the former Disney star Demi Lovato. She also hasn't made the jarring transition to the darker, sexier material embraced by former teenyboppers Miley Cyrus and Britney Spears. Swift describes this decision as an artistic rather than a moral one. 'I don't feel completely overcome by the relentless desire to put out a dark and sexy "I'm grown up now" album,' she told me. Still, her most recent record makes subtle references to more adult relationships, including lines such as 'There's a drawer of my things at your place.'

The article also talks about the parasocial relationship Taylor nurtured from a young age (the 13-hour meet and greet) and the way her website evolved over the years from an open online message forum to a nicely presented simplistic shop. The inclusion of the arm lyrics was an era-defining contribution that allowed us to decode more of what Taylor was expressing in her live shows, not just her lyrics. Most of the time, they weren't her lyrics. They were linked to artists based on the locations of her shows. The Myspace days were soon replaced by Tumblr, preparing for Taylor's generous fan experiences in the 1989 era, and I am sure that Lizzie Widdicombe, re-reading this article in 2024 (if she ever did), would also laugh at her accidental and anachronistic *Saltburn* reference.

> More recently, she has been scrawling lyrics, such as U2's 'One life, you got to do what you should,' on her left arm; deciphering the references has become another fan activity. Swift's ability to hold her audience's interest reflects, in part, a keen understanding of what fuels fan obsession in the first place: a desire for intimacy between singer and listener. [Taylor] told me that the best musical

experience is 'hearing a song by somebody singing about their life, and it resembles yours so much that it makes you feel comforted.' Her Web site includes video journals and diary-like posts to her online message board, which Swift does not outsource. Her fans, who call themselves Swifties, respond with passionate testimonials – 'I would drink her bathwater.'

In February 2012, *Speak Now* was nominated for Best Country Album at the Grammy Awards, and the album's third single, "Mean," won awards for Best Country Song and Best Country Solo Performance. Taylor said, "This one really means a lot to me, because this is for a song called "Mean" that I wrote, and there's really no feeling quite like writing a song about someone who is really mean to you, and someone who completely hates you, and makes your life miserable and then winning a Grammy for it."

Later in the same month, in connection with the first *Hunger Games* film adaptation, Taylor released two songs on the soundtrack; the first promotional single was "Safe and Sound" featuring Nashville country duo The Civil Wars, and the second was "Eyes Open." The first time "Eyes Open" was played live was her closing night of tour a month after its release, on tour in Auckland. I began my penultimate year at school and decided I wanted to learn "Safe and Sound" on piano and as it turns out, for a music assessment. I had done six or seven years of lessons at that point and was happy to accompany the singers in my class, so when I asked a couple of them to sing for my assessment, we practised a few times, but then my teacher decided I was going to do it alone. Play and sing? Very funny, a nice joke. The fear of the whole ordeal, ahem, performance means I can't remember the day it happened, probably sometime in May or June, but because it was just for an in-class mark, no one watched, which was wonderful. So, I have technically performed a Taylor song for one person, or three, if you count my parents, who were very gracious with turning their listening ears off while I was rehearsing.

Taylor told MTV upon the single's release, "I had this title that I had been working with called "Safe and Sound," and I just knew that I wanted it to deal with the empathy, sort of the more sensitive side, the bittersweet side of this story," she said about the sullen track. "Never imagining that this would ever be picked or a single, 'cause it's a lullaby. This song was such an amazing experience, because it's like it just happened...We wrote this song and recorded it one day. When we got the track back, I was so surprised by the restraint," she said. "He created this ethereal sound without making it this big battle anthem."

When you watch *The Hunger Games*, it would be fair to say that you would not expect a Taylor Swift lullaby to feature, but it does appear in the second half of the closing credits. The soft picking of the guitar is a harsh contrast to the violence you've just seen, which is part of the song's beautiful juxtaposition. Both of these were re-released in 2021, at the same time as *Red (Taylor's Version)*. They weren't part of the original track list, but it was essential to release them so that she could own the masters to these songs.

My *Speak Now* show, and the hug that changed the course of my life. March 9, 2012.

The *Speak Now* World Tour started in Singapore in February 2011 and ended with the New Zealand shows in March 2012. Every date was sold out. After performing for over a year, Taylor brought her shows down under. Social media hadn't developed enough to give us the crisp videos and images that we are used to by today's standards and Instagram was still in its infancy. It was her second arena tour of Australia and New Zealand, performing in Perth, Adelaide, Brisbane, Sydney and Melbourne with her final shows of the tour being three nights in Auckland. I went to the first of the two Sydney shows with my cousin Claudia, who I have shared many concert memories with. Two years had passed since being in this very room with my mother and high school best friend, seeing Taylor for the first time. The opener, Hot Chelle Rae started playing,

I knew some of their songs and everyone around me was screaming, the same as me. We were seated on the side of the arena with a great view and there wasn't much longer to wait. The three girls next to us were beside themselves with excitement and anticipation when suddenly a woman appeared and beckoned them to follow her. My cousin, Claudia, pushed me in their direction because she knew what was going on and said "go, go, go." "Are they with you guys?" the usher started to say, irrelevant because we were coming anyway. She turned to us and grouped us together with the others, Claudia pushed me forward and we walked onto the arena floor. We left the seats reserved on our tickets, unsure of where we were headed. It could have been anywhere. We were stopped at the back of the arena, on the other side of the barricades, and some people were giving us confused looks, because we were in front of them. We were looking at a small circular stage with a large, white tree as the centrepiece. The B Stage. "You're happy to be here for the whole show?" the lady who brought us down asked, and we obviously agreed.

Before The Eras Tour, Taylor's shows were characterised by a chosen movement, a specific amount of time on the main stage before moving through the crowd (on 1989 and *reputation* she would fly over) to a second smaller stage, (for those not in the know, sometimes called a B stage) towards the back of the stadium or arena floor, and then back again. She made sure the whole crowd was participating in the show. That's where we ended up on a sparkly night in March, centimetres away from the tall curly superstar with a 13 on her hand and lyrics written all the way up her arm. We were told to wait, alongside about 20 other young fans, little girls and older teenagers, boys included. Claudia turned to me and said, "Caitlin. I think you're going to meet her." I didn't need to ask who. When you talk to fans who have been given that chance, they will tell you things like, "The whole night was a blur" and truly it was. The house lights of the arena came up after the opener, Hot Chelle Rae left. We were waiting now; two years since the album had been released and now, we would hear it live. Then the red curtains parted and she came out. Before she appeared, a recording of her voice echoed around the arena, saying,

> Real life is a funny thing, I think most of us fear reaching the end of our life and looking back regretting the moments we didn't speak up, or we didn't say I love you, or we should have said I'm sorry. So, there's a time for silence, and there's a time for waiting your turn but if you know how you feel and you so clearly know what you need to say, you know it, I don't think you should wait, I think you should speak now.

Then she started singing and all the words I knew, and I sang them loud. The costumes were new; big ballgowns, short fringe dresses in black and gold, still sparkly. There is no greater feeling than when the songs that you play in your bedroom alone, or from your headphones on the way to school, are played to an audience of 30,000 people and you scream them louder than before with the people you love. I wore a dress that I had bought in America a few months earlier, that made me feel like Hannah Montana. It was cherry blossom pink with glitter and frills, like some of Taylor's. I wore my trademark sparkly Converses that matched Taylor's guitar. After about 40 minutes of singing, doing cheeky introductions, banging on huge drums, and playing her sparkly guitar, there was a dramatic stage production of a wedding. Taylor played a 'wedding guest' at the ceremony where her dancers are the characters; including a groom who leaves his bride at the altar. This was her album-titled song "Speak Now." Her costume for this number, and a few other songs, was a purple halter short prom dress with white gloves and vintage-style heels with her curly hair in a ponytail. A blue 13 was drawn on her hand, lyrics written down her arm in black permanent marker read, "Go cut through the noise so you can know what love sounds like" from "Neon Lights" by Natasha Bedingfield.

    Then the band played an extended outro and there was movement around us. Security was preparing the space between the barriers and the little stage. There were excited murmurs and I looked around me and saw little girls, teenage boys, parents and every kind of demographic present around me. I heard Claudia say to me, "She's coming!" The girl next to me was crying, and then I was crying too. We were in front of the barrier where the other fans were stretching their hands out, and Taylor walked through the crowd circling the stage and saying hello to people and I saw her hug the girl before me.

Taylor was in front of me. I stretched my hands out, and she pulled me into her. She is so tall (180cm – not including heels, and I'm 159cm) and I remember trying to not appear so tiny. In one sparkling moment, we locked eyes and she spoke to me. "Thank you for listening to my music, thanks so much for coming." Through the tears, I hope I said something profound back, but I was probably too shaken to remember how sentences work. Then she did the same for the next person and the person after that, making sure we felt special. She sang three songs, a mash-up of "Fearless," "Hey Soul Sista" by Train and "I'm Yours" by Jason Mraz and then went back to the main stage for the second half of the show. They didn't make us go back to our old seats and we stayed on the main floor at the back with a wide-open space to dance as we watched the confetti fall at the end. That was it. The same sentence when retold now, still feels surreal, "I hugged Taylor Swift at her *Speak Now* concert."

All of these memories are the reason that my eyes well up with tears every time I hear the opening to Track 14 on *Speak Now*, "Long Live" because even though she had been writing songs *for* us for a few years, she had written a song *about* us; about how the fans make her feel, the way we make each other feel and the electricity that is made when we spend a night at one of her concerts. It was a love letter. Her final song of the set, (before the encores) was "Long Live." I knew this was the time and place for this exact song. It didn't belong in my bedroom with my hairbrush or in the car with my dad who always turned the volume down. It belonged here with her and the rest of us in the purest outpouring of love and appreciation.

And she took the time to thank some of us in a way that we will carry through the rest of our lives. The lyrics ask her fans to make a promise, "Will you stand by me?" Yes, we will. The rest of the song is a helpful recount of that night; when my little brain was too filled with emotion to remember all the details.

The part of the song that mentions memories breaking the ground when we fall, couldn't be more poignant for me. I went home that night from one of the best experiences I have ever had and woke up the next day in a very different world. In the morning before work, the vet visited our house and we said goodbye to Tilley, our 11-year-old golden Labrador. She was my first best friend, and Christmas present when I was five. I cried for every night for weeks, wrote letters and kept her toys and her lead, but in the midst of it all, these concert memories that flooded back did their best to stifle the tears. I wouldn't know that kind of sadness again for at least a few years. But there was dancing and joy amidst immense pain. When the house lights come up after the end of any concert it is dizzying. The spell cast by the music is broken, your real life has to continue now. That March night is truly one that I will never, ever forget. They tell you to never meet your idols? That could never apply to her. Taylor Swift gives the best hugs.

Speak Now (Taylor's Version) was announced in Nashville on The Eras Tour on May 5, 2023 and released on July 7. It was the third in line of her re-recorded albums. After the on-stage reveal, Taylor wrote on socials,

> It fills me with such pride and joy to announce that my version of Speak Now will be out July 7 (just in time for July 9th, iykyk) I first made Speak Now, completely self-written, between the ages of 18 and 20. The songs that came from this time in my life were marked by their brutal honesty, unfiltered diaristic confessions and wild wistfulness. I love this album because it tells a tale of growing up, flailing, flying and crashing...and living to speak about it. With six

extra songs I've sprung loose from the vault, I absolutely cannot wait to celebrate Speak Now (Taylor's Version) with you on July 7th.

The added vault tracks were "Electric Touch (feat. Fall Out Boy)," "When Emma Falls in Love," "I Can See You," "Castles Crumbling (feat. Hayley Williams)," "Foolish One" and "Timeless." Inside the sleeve of the newer vinyl release, Taylor writes,

> I had the nagging sense that in the most intense moments of my life, I had frozen. I had said nothing publicly. I still don't know if it was out of instinct, not wanting to seem impolite, or just overwhelming fear. But I made sure to say it all in these songs. I decided to call the album Speak Now. It was a play on the 'speak now or forever hold your peace' moment in weddings, but for me it symbolised a chance to respond to the chatter and commentary around my own life. Some of these emotional revelations were surprising to people. Some expected anger and instead got compassion and empathy with "Innocent". Some expected a kiss-off break-up song but instead got a hand-on-heart apology, "Back to December".
>
> It was an album that was the most precious to me because of its vast extremes. It was unfiltered and potent. In my mind, the saddest song I've ever written is "Last Kiss." My most scathing is "Dear John", and my most wistfully romantic is "Enchanted" These days, I make my choices for those people, the ones who thought I had been good enough all along. I try to speak my mind when I feel strongly, in the moment I feel it. I'm still idealistic and earnest about the music I make, but I'm less crushed when people mock me for it. I know now that one of the bravest things a person can do is create something with unblinking sincerity, to put it

> all on the line. I still sometimes wish I was a little kid again in a tiny bed, before I ever grew up...I always looked at this album as my album, and the lump in my throat expands to a quivering voice as I say this. Thanks to you, dear reader, it finally will be. I consider this music to be, along with your faith in me, the best thing that's ever been mine.

Annabel Nugent, writing a review for *The Independent* says of the re-recorded album,

> To listen to *Speak Now*, written entirely by a then 20-year-old Swift, is to hear an artist in transition – both in her music (Swift cleaves closer to pop here than she had ever done previously) and her profile, which was rising rapidly and dizzyingly...the past typically isn't the most comfortable place to inhabit, but Swift embodies her younger self fully, imbuing these tracks with the same immediacy and emotional heft as she did all those years ago. Country twang or not.

The *Speak Now* era will always hold a special place in my heart. It is often what non-fans might come to remember as quintessentially Taylor, filled with fireworks, arm lyrics scrawled in permanent marker and sparkly ballgowns. The long, trademark country curls were about to disappear; she had already started her ascent into the pop music celebrity universe. For many Swifties, *Speak Now* was the ethos that defined a decade. The soft lilacs would make way for a darker rouge. By then, the year was 2012.

Red era
2012 – 2014.

What colour is love?

I have one specific memory about *Red*'s release in Australia. October 22, 2012 was a Friday, and my friend and I went to the shops after school, driven by her mum or mine. We walked straight into the music store (shout out to Erina Fair's JB HI-FI) and out with the deluxe album. This was significant because *Fearless* had a delayed release in Australia. I had only a digital copy of the album *Speak Now*, and so it felt like I had finally achieved something as an international fan: listening to the album at the same time as everyone else. Taylor's debut appearance on my Instagram was my twenty-fourth photo ever (I have over 500). It is a picture of Taylor's blunt fringe and dead-straight hair from the November 2010 AMA Awards, a night where she picked up the award for Favourite Country Female Artist. I posted it on September 27, 2012, only a month before *Red* was released. I wrote, "I think I want hair like this #taylorswift #bangs." Who could predict that that hairstyle would follow me around for a few years yet? I remember it was around this time, my penultimate year of high school, that I decided I wanted a fringe, and this could have been a choice of mimicking greatness. Every Taylor friend I know has tried their luck with a fringe, and I am no different. I loved my fringe, but my parents hated it, and it meant I finally had to pay attention to looking after my hair instead of being lazy. Taylor's corkscrew curls were officially gone, and they have yet to return to their original state. Taylor wrote in ELLE in 2019, "From birth, I had the curliest hair, and now it is STRAIGHT. It's the straight hair I wished for every day in junior high. But just as I was coming to terms with loving my curls, they've left me. Please pray for their safe return."

The central theme of this album was significant: a clear statement that love was a colour. The lyrics of the title track, "Red," explain and encapsulate many songs on this album. Taylor assigns a colour to each phase of a relationship; losing him was blue, missing him was dark grey, and loving him was red. In your early twenties, there's a feeling of being invincible until you're not. Something happens that will rock you to your core, and for Taylor, like the albums beforehand, that was heartbreak. Taylor was 22 when this album was released, and it became clear that the music had shifted from songs about romances in a general sense. They were deep, raw and fragile; they were her own memories. The end of the original album booklet of *Red* says this,

> My experiences in love have taught me difficult lessons, especially my experiences with crazy love. The red relationships. The ones that went from zero to a hundred miles per hour and then hit a wall and exploded. And it was awful. And ridiculous. And desperate. And thrilling. And when the dust settled, it was something I'd never take back. Because there is something to be said for being young and needing someone so badly, you jump in head first without looking. And there's something to be learned from waiting all day for a train that's never coming. And there's something to be proud of about moving on and realising that real love shines golden like starlight and doesn't fade or spontaneously combust. Maybe I'll write a whole album about that kind of love if I ever find it. But this album is about the other kinds of love that I've recently fallen in and out of. Love that was treacherous, sad, beautiful, and tragic. But most of all, this record is about love that was red.

And a section of her updated prologue for *Red (Taylor's Version)* in 2021 says this,

> Musically and lyrically, Red resembled a heartbroken person. It was all over the place, a fractured mosaic of feelings that somehow all fit together in the end. Happy, free, confused, lonely, devastated, euphoric, wild, and tortured by memories past. Like trying on pieces of a new

life, I went into the studio and experimented with different sounds and collaborators. And I'm not sure if it was pouring my thoughts into this album, hearing thousands of your voices sing the lyrics back to me in passionate solidarity, or if it was simply time, but something was healed along the way.

At the 2014 Grammy Awards, Red was nominated for Album of the Year and Best Country Album but didn't win either. But MTV News in 2022 cited the album as influential for a generation of songwriters. Olivia Rodrigo, Billie Eilish, Kacey Musgraves, Conan Grey, Halsey, and the Chainsmokers have all adapted "her country-honed knack for seasoning her songwriting with glimpses of her personal life." MTV News wrote,

> By letting us into the most vulnerable corners of her heart, Swift spoke in a way that allowed us to see ourselves, a skill she's continued to flex in songs like "Cornelia Street" [from Lover] and "Invisible String" [folklore]. Her devotion to detail created a unique bond with her loyal Swifties and inspired other artists to utilise the same candidness to connect with fans…It should come as no surprise that a decade later, Red (Taylor's Version) has been just as successful as its septuple-platinum predecessor. The intimacy Swift brought to pop music is here to stay as we seek out lyrics that speak to the lucid recollections we hold tightly ourselves.

In the United States, Red debuted at number one on the Billboard 200 with its first-week sales of 1.208 million copies, surpassing Garth Brooks' Double Live (1998) as the fastest-selling country album of all time. In the same format as Speak Now, she released a promotional single each week from the four weeks leading up to the album's release; they were "Begin Again," "Red," "I Knew You Were Trouble," and "State of Grace." One of Taylor's

Red-era non-album singles was "Sweeter Than Fiction," and it is credited as the first song she and Jack Antonoff worked on together. It was released as a single to the soundtrack of the film *One Chance* on October 21, 2013. It was also the second consecutive Golden Globe nomination for Best Original Song, having also been nominated in the previous year for "Safe and Sound." A decade later, she re-released the song to be exclusively available on the physical *Tangerine Edition* of *1989 (Taylor's Version)* on October 27, 2023. In November 2013, she performed at the Victoria's Secret fashion show in London with Ed Sheeran and Fall Out Boy.

    The *Red* era introduced me to an important person: Ed Sheeran. In an eerily similar way to Taylor, I first heard Ed's breakout single "The A-Team" when it started to gain popularity in Australia in 2012, a year after its UK release, and my friend Bec was again the one to introduce me to him. When it was announced that Ed would be the tour opener for all North American dates of the *Red* tour in the US, for us, it seemed like a match made in heaven. Taylor is four years older than him, so the little brother/big sister dynamic between them felt natural and appeared so to the media and journalists. Ed was new to fame, and Taylor felt like a seasoned professional at this point, with four albums, so to have such an important friend guide you through touring, dealing with fans, and supporting each other's songwriting is something many people might not draw connections to. With Taylor's Ed-orsement, his music gained popularity with US audiences, assisting him greatly with exposure and, most of all, employment. Every night they were on tour together, they sang their first collaboration, "Everything Has Changed," Track 14 on *Red*. It is still one of my favourites, mainly because seldom do your two favourite musicians join together to create something magic. It documents the sparks-flying time in a new relationship when sentiments like memorising what someone looks like when you are not with them happen and learning to open up to someone new is really special. Everyone knows what this feeling is like.

Ed credits Taylor for creating his family; his wife, Cherry Seaborn, was a school friend. He lost contact with her, and whilst he was touring, they reconnected when Cherry was working in the US, and they started seeing each other. At Taylor's Fourth of July party in 2015, held at her Rhode Island home, Taylor invited Ed, and Ed asked if he could bring a plus one. A marriage and two daughters later, the rest is history. Talk about using your friends to impress a girl; it's fair to say that the flex worked. Taylor's endorsements of any artist are taken seriously, and Ed is a testament to that, so after working with Aaron Dessner on *folklore* and *evermore*, Taylor connected Aaron with Ed, and Aaron produced Ed's sixth album, - (*Subtract*) released in 2023, co-writing 11 out of 18 tracks on the deluxe edition. Since 2012, they have released two songs as co-writers together. "Run" was written during the same writing session as "Everything Has Changed" and released as a vault track with *Red (Taylor's Version)*. Ed features in "End Game" released on *reputation* and Taylor features on a duet version of "Joker and the Queen" released as the fourth single from Ed's fifth album, = (*Equals*) on February 11, 2022. Most recently, Ed and Taylor performed "Everything Has Changed," "End Game" and "Thinking Out Loud" together on night four of The Eras Tour in London on August 15, 2024.

I found this diary entry in my phone's Notes, written almost exactly a week after I arrived in the UK to start my visa. A whole decade after the original release of *Red*. The end of the note says I have seen him eight times, but three months later I flew to Munich to see him for my ninth time in Olympiastadion, and being there with my cousins was like being home with my family because I really was.

June 23, 2022, 4:30 pm
Little girl in the biggest stadium in the world. People ask me why I love Ed Sheeran. He and Taylor write the love stories I believe wholeheartedly in but might never experience. I get to see love in my best friends and their relationships and in

my parents and my family, and in love songs and lyrics. And now, at Wembley tonight. This feels like coming full-circle when I am screaming about the world hurting less when I'm by your side into the universe. Even when the people I love are far away, I know that when someone thinks of Ed Sheeran, there's a chance that they will think of that weird friend of theirs who's seen him eight times.

Stand Up to Cancer is an American charity that has run music fundraising telethons every year since it was formally launched in 2008. On September 8, 2012, Taylor released a single titled "Ronan" in support of this cause. Ronan Thompson was a little boy diagnosed with neuroblastoma when he was three, who sadly passed away nine months later, three days before his fourth birthday. I posted a photo of Ronan on my Instagram on the day of the single's release, and my caption read, "This is Ronan. He was four when he died of a rare cancer called neuroblastoma. Taylor Swift decided to write a song about him. I cried. #RED #taylorswift #standuptocancer." Taylor discovered a blog called 'Rockstar Ronan' written by Ronan's mother, Maya, and after inviting her to her concert in Glendale for the *Speak Now* tour, she asked permission to use excerpts of the writing in her song. Because of this, Maya is credited as a co-writer on the single. She has performed this single live only twice, in a performance for Stand Up to Cancer at the live telethon event in September 2012 and on the 1989 tour in Glendale, Arizona, on 17 August 2015, when Maya was in the audience. The song was downloaded 220,000 times in its first week, debuting at #2 on the Digital Song Sales chart. The #1 song was her own, "We Are Never Ever Getting Back Together." It peaked at #16 on the *Billboard Hot 100*. Ronan was re-released as a vault track on *Red (Taylor's Version)* in 2021.

The *Red* tour dates began in the US on March 13, 2013, in Omaha, Nebraska, before going to New Zealand and Australia, and then on to Europe and Asia and ending on June 12, 2014, in

Singapore. In total, there were 86 shows across five continents, and when it concluded, it became the highest-grossing tour of all time. The tour included special guests who performed duets of their songs with Taylor, including Ellie Goulding, Nelly, Carly Simon, Jennifer Lopez, Rascal Flatts, Luke Bryan, Emilie Sandé, The Script, Sam Smith and others; Ed Sheeran appeared on 1 February, to play "Lego House" in London and on February 7, in Berlin he played "I See Fire." Gary Lightbody from Snow Patrol appeared in Sacramento to play the duet featured as Track 10, "The Last Time." Sadly, I did not attend this tour; it is her only album tour that I have missed. When the tour dates were released, Sydney's stop in December 2013 clashed with a family holiday in Hawai'i to celebrate my high school graduation. I told my dad I would fly to Auckland in New Zealand, to watch the show and meet them in Honolulu a day later. An ambitious thought for a freshly 18-year-old, but I saw the vision.

  Red has a perfect combination of melancholy and joy. Both are important in Taylor's songwriting. Songs like "Treacherous" are counteracted with "22," and the optimism in the storytelling of "State of Grace," "Starlight," and "Begin Again" are balanced with the sadness of "The Last Time" (featuring Gary Lightbody of Snow Patrol), and "Sad Beautiful Tragic." Even the negative surety of the title "We Are Never Ever Getting Back Together" contrasts with the bouncy melodies. When you try to categorise Taylor's albums by feelings, Taylor's albums up to 2012 are all very different, demonstrating her versatility. Her debut is bouncy, joyful and imaginative; *Fearless* is nostalgic and pulls you straight back to high school; *Speak Now* is fervent, urgent and outspoken. I refer to *Red* as her heartbreak album, an opinion I know I do not have alone.

The Phenomenon of the Track 5: validation and the power of remembering.

When you are a fan and meet a new Swiftie, one of your first conversations will be about "All Too Well." For those unaware, welcome; you have now entered the realm of the "Track 5 sad girl songs." In January, I pitched a chapter abstract for a book of essays about Taylor. Had it been published, I would have titled it "Never Underestimate the Cultural Power of a Broken-Hearted Woman: An Analysis of Taylor Swift's Track 5s" and what you are about to read is the continuation of the idea. Harrison Brocklehurst, writing for *The Tab*, explains that "To know Taylor Swift, to be a card-carrying Swiftie, is to know that every single Track 5 on her albums is famous for being the killer blow. It's where she puts her devastator – the track that smacks you round the face, punches you in the gut, and leaves you weeping on the floor." These songs speak to the complex psychological experience of the fandom, where we aggressively choose to exist in a melancholy state, the act of which is validated by the master herself. I went to a dedicated Taylor Swift club night in east London in March called 'Swiftogeddon' where the host DJs said, "We're going to do something that we've never done before," and then played "Cold As You" and I knew immediately what nine songs were to follow. Taylor, as of *The Tortured Poets Department* release, has 11 Track 5s. She has been singing about the glittery ecstasy of falling in love and the deep blue earth-shattering pain of its aftermath for nearly two decades, so we know, when romance comes, to expect both sides of the coin. I strongly suggest you find one of these playlists with all the Track 5s in a row, so it's not just a reading experience; it's a musical journey, too.

1. "Cold As You" is, first and foremost, about not being on the same level of commitment, connection or caring as that person with whom you want to start something. I will speculate, because of Taylor's age, that it could be one of those burned-hot-way-too-fast kind of moments that happen the most when

you're a teenager but pop up again where, despite their actual age, immature boys will pretend that they are men. We want any person we spend time with to care about us, developing after the stages of getting to know someone, trusting them, and then, deeper still, caring about whether our feelings were hurt because of something they might have done. Here, in this song, that person doesn't exist. The song tells of unspoken apologies, The juxtaposing sides of relationships that can at once be a great conversation starter and the beginning of something breaking inside. This song was written with Liz Rose, an early songwriting collaborator responsible for three Track 5s. The album booklet's secret message is, "Time to let go." These are not quite the stories we will tell our grandchildren about, but they are the kind that keeps us up at night sobbing quietly into our pillows. They are the trademark emotions that resurface in albums to come.

2. "White Horse" is about timing. If *Fearless* was the album constructed around mythical and storybook love, this song quickly dismantles that theme. This is what happens when the prince charmings don't show up. As sad as the lyrics are, I don't find the musical quality sad, as opposed to something like "Dear John," which doesn't necessarily become more upbeat; it just builds in its sadness. There's self-deprecation in the lyrics of "Cold as You" but there is honesty as well in describing the rush of infatuation and every sensible thought leaving your brain in the early days of being close to someone new. It is not just a Taylor Swift phenomenon that she "got lost" in his eyes. That happens to everyone. White Horse examines a fairytale romance that starts to fall apart when real life happens, and there is a growing awareness that behind the fairytale is harsh reality. We know the truth is that happy endings don't always exist, and it is only with hindsight that we understand that. Another Liz Rose co-penned song, the production value is still

country with soft guitars and backing piano. The album booklet's secret message is, "All I ever wanted was the truth..." and the authenticity of that is it's often not the truth that we want.

3. "Dear John" has one of my favourite opening lines to a Taylor song. This song is about perspective. Historically, a Dear John letter is a break-up note posted by women to their husbands in active military service, which is mostly an American tradition, but the title bears no similarities to those sentiments. At its core, this song emotionally reflects the analysis that some people only experience once they are out of an abusive relationship. And it sounds like it, too. Of the ten Track 5s, I think this song and "tolerate it" are the saddest. The vocals are soft, like she's telling a bedtime story with a special message that could have been something like, "Have your walls up, sweetheart, protect yourself." While fans speculate that the title and the music were inspired by Taylor's brief romance with singer John Mayer, she never confirms her sources; everything is speculation. In this song her lyrics reference a chess game, which is repeated over a decade later in her song, "Mastermind" from *Midnights*, Taylor plays with metaphor; chess representing the game of love, but if you're losing all the time (like in this song), the joy disappears. The pre-chorus speaks of wondering which version of her lover she might get on the phone. The lyrics hark back to the modus operandi of the *Speak Now* album, putting words into songs that you can't say in normal conversations, because you either missed the opportunity or couldn't bring yourself to say it out loud. I love the realisation that in the end, she says she's shining like fireworks over his sad, empty town.

5. You wouldn't guess that "All You Had To Do Was Stay" is a Track 5. The takeaway from this song makes it very clear that sometimes (and Taylor understands this), it is absolutely necessary to dance your way through the heartbreak. I would know; it's the only

form of medicating that I do with mine. I created a playlist for myself whilst writing this book of her Track 5s only, and it is a harsh jump between "All Too Well" and "All You Had To Do Was Stay", where she resents the phone calls after a break-up. This reminds me of the phone call in "Dear John", where the other end of the line is dead, so the trying is one-sided. That is a recurring theme through all of the devastator tracks. Since 1989 is one of my favourite albums, I gravitate towards this track, and again, the catchiness of repeated phrases that are very slightly changed in each song works very well. This could be an anthem full of instructions, similar to "Should've Said No," but also there are parallels with this and "The Archer," where the yearning and questions of "what-ifs" are never fully answered, but they still keep coming. The shouty falsetto that builds into a reverb throughout the song symbolises the desperation that comes with the finality of consequences with "All you had to do was STAY!"

6. "Delicate" is about having a love filled with insecurities, walking on tightropes, treading on eggshells, and doubts. It's not a trust-filled love, and it's not the right kind of love. This song doesn't promise anything. It doesn't say, "I vow to support you and love you always, in sickness and in health." It is something more along the lines of, "I solemnly swear that I am up to no good." Then there is the constant checking if the behaviour is okay, whereas in a solid relationship, these niggly uncertainties are the furthest thing from your mind. There are desperate-sounding questions that don't need answering. They're extremely relatable when you're trying to get to know someone. The sound of the bridge in this song is the sound of delusion, where the musings sung out could sound like quiet pleas for attention. I don't think "Delicate" is sad with a capital letter; instead, it is filled with doubts, and we know that being unsure is almost as torturous as being let down by someone. It is a fun song, singing of situationships long before I knew what they were.

7. "The Archer," Track 5 from Lover, has almost the opposite effect of "All You Had to Do Was Stay," from 1989. In an album filled with happy, joyful bangers, it doesn't replicate the upbeat, joyful sound. It drops tempo, pulling the listeners into a space of uncertainty. We hear a softness and subdued tone to the fighting happening in the lyrics because the music doesn't match the aggressiveness of the words, which are sung in a tone of defensiveness, as though she is preparing for a fight. Here, Taylor faces her fears about love, identity, and the scars we are left with when we confront our internal struggles. "Death By A Thousand Cuts" has devastating lyrics and could have easily been Track 5, but "The Archer" is softer in tone with its desperate pleas of what *could* have been. There are direct similarities with the drawn-out note of this song with, "All You Had To Do Was Stay." The elongation of the sound "you could stayyyyy" at the end of the song helps it build to nothing before it fades out, a sonic memory of the relationships left out in the cold.

8. The first time I listened to "my tears ricochet," I was speechless. That's not an exaggeration. The song speaks of being hurt by someone so much that you die a metaphorical death. There are references to funerals and wakes, and I am still haunted by the harmonies that start this song, and I could confidently say it's in my top five of Taylor's songs. In the *folklore: long pond studio sessions*, her 2020 film, Taylor shares that this Track 5 was chronologically the first song she wrote for the album, adding, "Picking a Track 5 is a pressurised decision." The lyrics about going anywhere she wants, but just not home, are difficult to sing as an Australian living in London with Europe on her doorstep but with her parents and brother on the other side of the world. When my emotions get the better of me, I think of 'dead' friendships, and I mourn them with lyrics from this song that perfectly fit the situation. Taylor always has a very specific and personalised line for each common situation.

9. "tolerate it" is about a fictitious ambivalent love. The inspiration for this song comes from the novel *Rebecca* by Daphne de Maurier. This is a direct result of the songwriting shift that occurred with *folklore* and, *evermore*, moving away from Taylor's autobiographical style and having an imaginative focus on the stories in her songs. It doesn't surprise me that Aaron Dessner, Taylor's co-writer on the track, told *Rolling Stone* when he heard the demo for the first time, he cried, describing the song as "crushingly beautiful." As in the literature that inspired this song, there is glorification of the partner where none is due. The sadness in this song is that despite imagined origins, the reality is that relationships like this certainly do exist.

10. "You're On Your Own, Kid" is about feeling alone. The first line of the song shatters expectations of hot season romances continuing after the temperatures drop as Taylor laments the end of a summer love. The alliteration in the line containing "sprinkler" and "splashes" sets the tone for sunshine and fun with the upbeat track, but the lyrical melancholy provides a harsh juxtaposition. One single lyric in the song is the catalyst for the presence of friendship bracelets at Taylor's concerts. And yet it is the labelled the saddest song on *Midnights*. I am a member of (I can't remember how many) Facebook groups trying to sell concert tickets, looking for outfit inspiration, and asking other online Swifties to post their daughter some confetti that fell from the ground in the final song. They ask strangers on the internet what they think of their homemade friendship bracelets. If tasting the moment is what the culture is currently talking about, then right now, that is The Eras Tour, and these practices have taken the fandom to a whole new level. Back in the *Speak Now* era, Taylor used to fill up her wrists with fan-made bracelets given to her, and now we give them to each other. This is the joy found in collective sadness; the most devastating track has sparked it. This message is for everyone who has wondered about, seen them in the flesh, traded, or

even given Taylor a friendship bracelet, contrary to the title please remember you're not on your own.

11. The harmonies at the beginning of "So Long, London" made it clear: this one is about the city and the boy that nearly broke me. The abrupt change in the backbeat made me question what I was anticipating. Anxieties were high on my first listen, but the trick with every Track 5 is that those anxieties actually begin the minute one is played. We give ourselves fair warning; we know what we are in for. Five years later, *Lover*'s "London Boy" has met its depressed cousin. From the first lines, you know the joy has disappeared as Taylor describes the pain of a relationship that is slipping away. My fingernails attach themselves to the palm of my hands, recoiling in remembrance of how intense my infatuation was. There are questions raised here about how much pain our bodies are capable of. Taylor sings about leaving what she knew and her lover leaving her at a house This hurts immeasurably because that's what where I live (Hampstead is referenced in the song), what a boy did to me, and it happened in England. Something as simple as stitches being "undone" is enough to unravel me, and the concept of remembering to breathe and relax when the relationship is hanging by a thread is also touched upon here. But there is a passage of time hiding in this song, too, where a sense of moving on is a physical adjustment (the colour returning) and then a stage of anger replaces it as she sings about having to leave London. Once, I wrote a journal entry starting with, "Everybody has somebody else," and Taylor knows that too.

4. If you wondered where in the numbered list number four is, you've found it; and there's a reason it is last.

I wish I could go back to when I heard the song "All Too Well" for the first time. Swift's fourth album, *Red*, is important in many ways. It signals the return of co-writers, having independently written all the songs on her third album to prove a point to an industry that questioned her craft, skills and integrity. It was another move forward in songwriting and craft for the artist, who at this point had already won Grammys and countless other awards before she turned 22. "All Too Well" was co-written with Liz Rose while Swift was touring with her *Speak Now* World Tour in February 2011 and released as Track 5 on *Red* on October 12, 2012. She performed it at the Grammys in 2013, and in the 11 years since its release, this ballad has become beloved by fans. On the *reputation* Stadium Tour film released to Netflix, she performs it as the surprise song filmed at AT&T Stadium in Arlington, Texas on October 6, 2018, the final North American show, saying this to the crowd,

> It's weird because I feel like this song has two lives to it in my brain. In my brain, there's the life of this song, where this song was born out of catharsis and venting and trying to get over something and trying to understand it and process it. And then there's the life where it went out into the world, and you turned this song into something completely different for me. You turned this song into a collage of memories of watching you scream the words to this song, or seeing pictures that you post to me of you having written words to this song in your diary, or you showing me your wrist, and you have a tattoo of the lyrics to this song underneath your skin. And that is how you have changed the song "All Too Well" for me.

The first lesson "All Too Well" (ATW) teaches us is patience. Whilst Taylor was promoting the release of *Red*, she spoke about the difficulty in preparing it for the album, and at five minutes and thirty seconds, it is the longest of the original 16 tracks. On *Good*

Morning America before the album's release in 2012, she said that it was "the hardest to write...it took me a really long time to filter through everything I wanted to put in the song without it being a ten-minute song, which you can't put on an album."

I would argue that never has there been more anticipation for a Taylor Swift song than for the ten-minute version of ATW. If you read tabloids and see her name and know nothing of her discography, there would have come a time in 2021 when all you would have seen were mentions of Taylor, a red scarf, and a really long song with quite a few verses. Maybe you were confused. On June 18, when Swift posted on socials that the second of the re-recorded albums after her master's dispute would be *Red (Taylor's Version)*, the last line of the announcement read, "This will be the first time you hear all thirty songs that were meant to go on *Red*. And hey, one of them is even ten minutes long." For fans like me, it immediately sent our group chats and social media platforms into a frenzy, a long-awaited tease had been confirmed.

The second lesson that ATW teaches us is that romance is not without its bruises. This power ballad joins the ranks of the strong female-driven iconic songs that have come before it, where the power lies not in the production of the song but in the lyrics. Some that come to mind are "The Chain" by Fleetwood Mac, "Total Eclipse of the Heart" by Bonnie Tyler, "I Have Nothing" from Whitney Houston and "Best Thing I Never Had" by Beyoncé. Women's heartbreak is the backbone of popular music, and with each new decade comes a song that encapsulates the melancholic human experience.

Critics and fans agree that ATW is some of her best words, bringing a musicality to the experience of love and a relationship that burned very bright for a short amount of time. *Rolling Stone* put it at #69 in their 2021 revision of '500 Greatest Songs of All Time.' Speculation about the 'who' in the story always will be a guessing game for fans, never confirmed (or denied) by Taylor herself, and this song is not any different.

This mystery over the 'who' is part of the magic. It transfers to the fan experience in that fans have different ideas about the 'who.' To know about this song is to know about the scarf. The scarf has become a motif and metaphor for the things we lose when love disappears, mentioned in the first, and one of the last verses. The timeline of this song's release parallels Taylor's brief relationship with actor Jake Gyllenhaal. The fans and then media's obsession with Taylor's songwriting has meant that the actress and director Maggie Gyllenhaal, Jake's sister, has been asked to confirm or deny the existence of the scarf in her house in interviews. She had no idea what the interviewer was talking about until it was explained. The scarf appears in the *All Too Well: The Short Film* starring Sadie Sink and Dylan O'Brien, and was sold as a merchandise item on Taylor's website, and yes, I own it. In 2021, following the release of the film and *Red (Taylor's Version)*, Google searches for "Taylor Swift red scarf meaning" surged by 1,400 per cent. The short film premiered on November 12, 2021 in Times Square, with a limited cinematic release in select locations, and had special screenings at both the Tribeca (June 11) and the Toronto International Film Festival (September 9, 2022), with the latter being shown in 35mm form. In Toronto, after the showing, she had a Q&A with the CEO of TIFF, Cameron Bailey. Taylor said during their conversation,

> One of the reasons I wanted to make a short film and not a music video for this song is because I've been fascinated with the dynamic of the age of the character that Sadie is playing, and what a precarious age that is, when you could fit back at your family home sort of, but you sort of don't, you could fit in an adult's cultivated apartment where they have a French press and they have all the things that adults have but you kind of don't, so you kind of fit everywhere but you kind of fit nowhere.

This is the age that Taylor was when *Red* was originally released: 21 and 22; on the cusp of being an adult but still very much a teenager. There is a taste of independence from your parents but also a need for them to still cushion you when you make the wrong decisions. On *Variety's* YouTube channel, there is a series called 'Directors on Directors' released on December 12, 2022. Taylor is in conversation with Martin McDonagh, esteemed and decorated British Irish filmmaker, writer and director of films like *Three Billboards Outside Ebbing, Missouri* and *The Banshees of Inisherin*. He has also had many plays on London's West End. She says,

> I wanted to treat it completely differently than I'd ever treated a music video. It was something that the fans wanted, this song was very grassroots, it was never made into a single, it was always just a song on the album that I loved. And over the years the fans made it very clear that it was their favourite song of any song I've ever done…I think there's a moment when you're nineteen or twenty, where your heart is so susceptible to getting broken, getting shattered and your sense of self goes out the window so quickly. It's such a formative age. I wanted to tell that story too, about girlhood calcifying into this bruised adulthood.

Each fan will tell you they have a special "All Too Well" lyric that hits them the hardest. Sadly, I can't write the lyrics directly into this book but for me, it is when she sings about being paralysed by time because it won't pass quickly enough. She sings about wanting to be her old self again but has difficulty doing that. Other lines suggest there is a sense of time moving nowhere in times of heartbreak because Taylor sings as though she is still in that space of time, highlighting the present; the tense hasn't moved and somewhere in time, and she is still in the relationship. When the ten-minute version was released, and we were greeted with newly released lyrics to an old song. She asks if an affair maimed her lover. This resonated with me because of the idea that no one leaves the end of a relationship without being stained with joyful memories that hurt more than the breaking apart does. "All Too Well" shines in its lyricism and expert pastiche of heartbreak and remembrance, and it is one of the first songs I share with fans who are beginning their musical journey after *Fearless'* break-out singles. The hype around this song, the heartbreaking majesty of all ten minutes, is real. I do, in all honesty, feel like a crumpled-up piece of paper after listening.

So, there they are – all of Taylor's Track 5s. These tracks allow us to dive into Taylor's psyche, into the depths of her soul, as she unpacks the many stages of grief present in these songs: first loves, situationships, relationship breakdowns for reasons known and unknown, and, of course, the realisation that the sadness does indeed end. Listening as a youngster, you will not have experienced what she sings about until it happens. Then, as a teenager, love appears and then stays or goes away, but we've already been given the tools to sit in heartbreak, knowing we will get through the drama, the screaming, and the tears because she has felt the same feelings, and immortalised them in song. Taylor may not be known as the queen of building bridges, but she certainly is the duchess of writing them. The musical journey that fans take when they come across a Track 5 is one that they do not take alone. You can feel and hear a single lyrical thread with plenty of repetition tying these eleven songs together. Through our growth and rebuilding, Taylor is there.

Okay, since we've made it out of our psychologist couch session, welcome back to the HAPPY side of this album. "Everything Has Changed," "Stay Stay Stay," "22," and "We Are Never Getting Back Together" were the soundtracks for my last year at school, and they bring back so many positive memories of the giddiness that comes from waiting and receiving new music. Taylor has often said of her early albums that she was writing about experiences that she saw around her, having to make up the feelings of first loves that she sang about because she hadn't experienced them yet. I was the same.

When *Red* came out, I was 17, enjoying being at school with my friends but never becoming one of the overtly flirtatious girls that I saw walking arm in arm with their high-school boyfriends. I was perfectly happy to wish the boy up the road would walk me to school one day, and then I'd go home and sing about imaginary relationships blasting through my bedroom speakers. I didn't know yet what these words meant; they weren't stories about me, but I still sang "Stay Stay Stay" at the top of my lungs. Music critics got a taste of Taylor's potential move to the pop genre with bouncy singles like "22" or "I Knew You Were Trouble." On *Late Night with Seth Meyers* in 2021, promoting *Red (Taylor's Version)*, she says, "There are like 14 different genres on this album; it's a real patchwork quilt of genre, I was really experimenting." When she said that I realised what she meant. *Red* is a testament to a few things: musical versatility being one, but also letting everyone know that genre shouldn't be a limitation; it is, in fact, a wardrobe choice.

Country-singing Swiftie sweethearts: Sarah and Bryce Sainty.
When I think about my friends who have liked Taylor as long as I have (aside from Bec), my friend Sarah comes to mind. Sarah and I met when we were selected to be on our high school council. I was in Year Seven, and she was the year above. When I started high school, I was terrified when I watched my friends from primary school find other friends, so I started to befriend the older kids because they were nicer and a bit more inclusive. Sarah's nieces are called Betty and Daisy Mae, whose names have both been mentioned in lyrics, *folklore*'s "betty" and "You're On Your Own, Kid" from *Midnights*. The matching of the children to the songs was coincidental ("She didn't know, I said to my sister, literally you've named your children after two Taylor Swift songs!"), and since talking to her, with *The Tortured Poets Department* release, Sarah's name has also been included in the new song, "But Daddy I Love Him." I called Sarah on Zoom so she could tell me about her and her husband Bryce's shared joy of Taylor, exploring the intricacies of being a fan, but also with a

unique perspective of being country music singers and performers who see Taylor and think, "Imagine if...that was us?" I asked about her early listening experiences, and she shared, along with her holy trinity (top three) Taylor albums.

"My first experience of Taylor wasn't until *Fearless*, when someone else sang "Love Story" at a singing competition that I was at, and it being obviously country music, this girl was much older than I was, and I think she actually won the competition, and immediately I was like 'damn, what is that song? I love that song. I had never heard that song before, and as soon as I got in the car, it was played on the radio probably ten times on the way home from Sydney, and I remember thinking, 'Oh okay, who is Taylor Swift?' and then the obsession began, and then I delved backwards from there, listened to the first album, watched all the film clips, they were very iconic at the time."

"I have a deep love of *reputation*. It's probably the most controversial of albums, a lot of people dislike it, but I am obsessed, and it's definitely my most-played album. *Red* is there for sure because it is reminiscent of such a pivotal time in my life, right at the end of high school and into my few years of university. It was the background of falling in love for the first time with my husband and feeling all the 'Red' feelings like the emotional rollercoaster of songs like "Stay Stay Stay," "All Too Well," "Red" and "Everything Has Changed." 1989 is where I feel most nostalgic because I was in America at the time, and we listened to it everywhere we went. It was just after it was released, and I remember going to New York. I took a photo of myself next to the sign at the airport that said, "Welcome to New York" and it would have been in the first six months of it being out that we went to New York for the first time, you could hear the start of the song playing in my head as you were leaving the plane. If you think about how much she's shaped pop culture, that's a pretty big thing for people to align a city to her music. It's this generation's rendition of Frank Sinatra's "New York, New York" or Alicia Keys and Jay-Z "Empire State of Mind." Bryce's favourite three is almost the same, swapping out reputation for Speak Now, a testament to his matching skills as a songwriter. "I think we are just both so in awe that she wrote the entire album solo."

Sarah is married to Australian country music singer Bryce Sainty, there are certainly elements of their high school romance that scream Fearless, and she mentioned that "Bryce and I met through singing, and through country music and honestly through a love of Taylor Swift because he was probably more of a Taylor Swift fan than I was." Bryce remembers watching Taylor perform on the television broadcast of the 2008 CMA Awards a few months before Fearless was released. "Because I was just beginning my songwriting and country music performance career, I very quickly became a fan." Sarah laughs as she tells me a funny story about the two of them in the early days of their relationship,

"Bryce actually took a different girl to the Speak Now concert [in 2012] even though we were dating, it was right at the start of our relationship, and obviously, you have to buy tickets so early – and then she refused to give up her ticket, and Bryce also refused to give up his ticket, and said 'no, I'm going to Taylor Swift, I love Taylor Swift so give it up, I have a new girlfriend, let her go instead' but I didn't get to, even though they weren't together they went but he brought me back a poster."

Bryce was hailed as 'artist to watch' by Spotify with over 3.5 million streams, his debut single in 2012, "Message in a Bottle" which reached the top 10 on iTunes charts. He has written songs with Morgan Evans and recently toured with Andrew Farris from INXS and The Whitlams' Tim Freedman. This year in January, Bryce had his first headline show at Australia's internationally renowned Tamworth Country Music Festival. "It was incredible, and it was something I had been dreaming about and working towards for a very long time and honestly, I don't feel like it could've gone better."

This pairing inevitably changed Sarah's listening and singing habits, "I had always sung pop music, and then meeting Bryce, and then working with Gina Jeffries made me transition into country music because I explored it a little bit more, I had listened when I was younger, to Dolly Parton and Shania Twain, so when Bryce and I got together and started singing together, so the genre just naturally shifted to country music, and it opened up a whole new world for me because I'd never really listened to contemporary country."

"We go to Tamworth every year, and we went to Nashville a couple of years in a row, and we're going again this year, and that is the home of country music and was Taylor Swift's base, and obviously where she made her mark, so we would drive down Music Row and be like, 'Oh my gosh, this is the same street where Taylor Swift drove down with her mum, and took her CDs to record labels.' It's so wild. Bryce has played at the Bluebird Café, and that was iconic because it was where Taylor was somewhat discovered, and so that was our background and obviously, just performing everywhere and wherever we can, and we still do it now." Bryce said the experience performing there was "very surreal, and definitely a much smaller venue size than I had originally thought."

Sarah explained to me the turning point of her decision not to pursue a full-time singing career, and she mentioned her other big love and passion: her job as a school teacher. "My first year of teaching full-time [Sarah is currently an assistant principal at a primary school], I had laryngitis, I think, three times so that I would lose my voice really easily. We were still doing gigs on the weekends that were about four hours; we would do weddings that were a couple of hours, so I just had no voice. So that was a big part of it. And also, the music industry is cooked, especially in Australia.

It's incredibly hard to make money from it, but also, to have any kind of success, you have to be doing it almost full-time, but then you have no money behind you to do it, unless you've got a second job. So it's just incredibly hard, unless you're going to go all in. For me, I wasn't all in, and there are parts of me that regret that choice; because it wasn't necessarily my talent holding me back, it was my sense of self, thinking 'I'm not going to be successful because this industry is too harsh, and I don't know if I'm equipped to take on this many setbacks and criticism for something I hold so dearly."

"I watched Bryce absolutely go all out at pursuing music full-time and knowing how much money and time goes into it and to see, whilst he's had success now, that took ten years. He's getting incredible amounts of Spotify plays, but that also doesn't translate to money, so sometimes you can't afford to do your next lot of music, unless you're signed. He's definitely pursued avenues; labels have had interest and he's had offers but he isn't yet fully on a contract on a record label." When it comes to choosing to be an independent artist or signed Bryce says, "For me it's more about working with people that I want to work with, not so much the company that it's with I want to build a team that aligns with my vision and is as loyal as I am."

I asked Sarah and Bryce what the difference is between being a singer and performer, while also being a Swiftie as opposed to being a regular, average audience member like me. Her answer I think is relevant to every era and album Taylor has presented up until 2024.

"I think we just know how much goes into shows, and we also see it from a business point of view, because her marketing is insane. The key is in the subtlety because she is almost doing so little marketing and yet still having an impact, because she's nurtured these fans for so long that they are obsessed with everything she does. She's given so much but also so little. Any photo she posts or a line in a song, obviously the easter eggs part, is a huge part of her marketing tool. People are constantly talking on Reddit threads, on Tumblr and YouTube, dissecting every song and every move she is making and there's so much talk about it without her having to talk about it. So, it is very clever from a music business standpoint."

"But also, just the machine that is Taylor Swift, we think about how much money she must make off merch, how big her team would have to be to load in her stage, and things like that we think about it in awe of 'imagine if?' But also, from a songwriting perspective, she's so clever. She's the original storyteller and has completely encapsulated so many people's experiences over ten albums. So, we're just in awe of that, too. That's Bryce's main occupation, so she's also a huge influence in that way. Bryce writes all of his songs himself and for other people."

From a singing perspective, people have mentioned to me that Taylor's lack of vocal range has turned them off her. For Sarah, that's not hugely important because Taylor *can* sing, but even though she is not at that elevated vocal level of other performers, she doesn't need to be.

"I think it's not fair because we're expecting her to have all the things, to have the vocal range of Beyonce or Adele, but also do all these other things. Her music would be incredibly different if she only sang songs like that, but her songs are for the pop-machine radio. If you think of someone like Adele, who has a crazy range, but all of her songs are pretty much ballads, it would be such a different experience; you wouldn't have the dancers in the background, there wouldn't be so much going on, you would have a completely different vibe."

"Musicians have different strengths in different things. I think Taylor sometimes gets a bad rap for her vocals, but [as fans], we like that because it works with her songs. If she sang like a more mature person with a crazy vocal range, it wouldn't work. She has never traditionally been what many people describe as a good vocalist. I don't know if many people say Taylor's strength is her vocals. You could say her songwriting, her entertainment value, how clever she is, her visuals, her outfits…there would be a lot more that people would say as opposed to her vocals."

Red was a defining album for Taylor, not just with a change in sound but also a change in fashion. Gone were the cowboy boots and curls, and she had a significant preppy style change to mark the change for herself, but it was clear she was starting to move away from country. Sarah and I are part of the generation that (even now still subconsciously) models what we wear off Taylor's style. We both had fringes at similar times, and part of being a fan meant that we always attempted to *look* like our role model.

"So much of her *Red* time, my last year of school and then into uni, was me every night looking on Tumblr, and on Taylor Swift Style to see what she wore that day, because then I would try and recreate her outfits. I liked it because it was around the same time and had a very similar vibe to Jess Day from *New Girl*; it was ballet flats and fit and flare dresses, a little bit vintage, but not hardcore, lots of stripes, lots of red, little skirts and tops. Because she was photographed nearly every day, I would go home and check online and try to copy them. And then that pivoted to the 1989-era, with more sets, less vintage and a change in colour scheme and I was very much trying to wear those outfits every day at uni because I thought I was so cool… all my friends too at the time were very Taylor Swift-influenced."

Sarah and Bryce went to The Eras Tour in Sydney, "It is next level, and such a huge moment in time. We got a really good night; our secret songs were "Is It Over Now?" mashed with "I Wish You Would" and "Exile" mashed with "Haunted." It was crazy, like something out of a movie, going through each era is like being transported back to old concerts, she also doesn't age; even some of the choreography was a nod to the old choreography, so that was cool to reminisce like that."

What neither the Sainty's nor I had on our 2024 Taylor Swift bingo cards is that three months after this interview, their Nashville holiday would hold an incredible moment. Bryce played at the Green Light Bar in a singing showcase on 13 June, and the next night, they went to a songwriting show at the Listening Room Café as part of CMA Fest, where Bryce has sung before. It's a cool event where famous writers share stories behind the songs. That night, their featured guests were Liz Rose and Phil Barton, who also sang. Liz Rose wrote extensively through Taylor's debut and *Fearless* albums, and Sarah posted an Instagram Reel detailing her surprise.

"If you don't know who Liz Rose is, she wrote "All Too Well," "Tim McGraw," and Little Big Town's "Girl Crush." She is a lyrical melodic genius…so last night, I sang with Liz Rose on stage with a bunch of other people; I am not okay. I sang "You Belong With Me" with Liz Rose; it was an iconic experience, something I never would have dreamt of doing, and I can happily die now, knowing that I sang on stage, "You Belong With Me" with Liz Rose, the writer of "You Belong With Me," so yes, this Nashville trip has been incredible." Bryce was also on stage, and honestly, this being icing on the cake for their amazing trip, couldn't have happened to a pair of more deserving Swifties.

In an age where the music industry is so polarising towards artists like Taylor, it is important to remember to listen to talented artists like Bryce, who have been in the game for a long time. How many young artists like Taylor are out there today doing an amazing job building their careers? They all start somewhere. How many incredible performers are smashing it every day and not able to crack the system because the algorithm is against them? Having a career in music is an incredible achievement, but it is also a constant fight for recognition for artists who always are working their hardest to keep succeeding. That's a lesson I learnt from Sarah and Bryce, and I have to be better about widening my listening habits, too.

Red (Taylor's Version) was released on 12 November, 2021. Similarly to Fearless, the songs from the vault were released with jumbled-up titles in a video to social media to entice fans into immediately decoding the cryptic clues. There were ten vault songs, "Ronan," "Better Man," "Nothing New (feat. Phoebe Bridgers)," "Babe," "Message In A Bottle," "I Bet You Think About Me (feat. Chris Stapleton)," "Forever Winter," "Run (feat. Ed Sheeran)," "The Very First Night," and "All Too Well (10 Minute Version)." It truly is a brilliant business loophole and a treat for her supporters that nearly a decade after the album's first release she gets to share the cuts that everyone thought would be left hiding on a hard-drive somewhere. They are where they belong: out in the world.

The Red era was FUN. The red lips and immaculate bangs were here to stay, her tradition of a concept album would re-emerge later on with Midnights, and the phenomenon of copying her style well and truly exploded. Her music was becoming more grown-up, and so were her teenage fans. But for a lot of people, Red would signify almost the end of their appreciation for Taylor, with the shedding of her country music meaning that she now slipped into the cookie-cutter pop grind that reduced their enjoyment. Taylor won NSAI's 'Songwriter-Artist of the Year' Award seven times between 2007 and 2015, and after moving into pop with 1989, it is fair to say that without the clear and defined focus that country music gives to songwriters, she would not have been confident to make the jump.

I have a lifelong friend, Erin, who is a hardcore country music fan, and she doesn't listen to "new" Taylor Swift songs. She messaged me this year and said, "You'll be pleased to know I listened to a Taylor Swift album for the first time in about five years." When I questioned further, knowing this was a huge step for her listening habits, she said, "She turned into just another typical pop star. She ruined what made her original." I could hazard a guess that Erin only listens to Taylor's debut, and I can definitely understand that little piece of her is truly special. There are some incredible early songs. I could also play something from *Fearless* or *Red* that doesn't sound pop that she might be okay with, but I've never been one to push my opinion or listening habits onto anyone, and when I listen to my friend's music playlists, I truly enjoy stepping into someone's shoes and loving what they love. I know that making the move to pure pop definitely didn't suit everyone. But I am not one of those people.

1989 era
2014 – 2017.

"I was born in the year, *1989*!"

Content warning: this chapter makes brief reference to eating disorders.

The day 1989 came out, 27 October, 2014, I was in Sydney early for an eventful morning of Sculpture by the Sea at Bondi Beach (an art festival famous with locals and Australians alike and is exactly what the name describes). On the journey home, my mum and our friends, the Sohn's, were going to drop me at campus, and I could walk into class as normal; it was beautifully planned. We were in the car when Mum and Susan suddenly realised they could take a shortcut through the Cross City Tunnel and go straight down the highway, travelling the opposite way I needed to go. So, at a random set of traffic lights, they decided I had to get out of the van. I made an embarrassing fuss, unnecessarily angry with my mother as the van drove away, and I was left in the city I had only just started to navigate alone. I was scared, stressed and panicked. The thing was, my mum knew I'd be fine; otherwise she wouldn't have left me. I kept my eyes on Centrepoint Tower as I walked into the CBD and got the train to Redfern.

    I was in a foul mood until I realised Taylor's album was being released at 3 pm. I bought the physical album instore after class and listened to it for the first time on my computer (I was a diehard iTunes girlie) on my two-hour journey home from university. When I got back in a jovial mood, my mum was upset because I had treated her badly, and she was confused at my mood change. But that was how my release day panned out: lost and alone in a big city (very 1989-coded), and I'm sure my mum has forgiven me by now. There was so much hype because fans knew from its single, "Shake It Off," that it would be a massive step away from Red and the country melancholy well-established in her songwriting. She was entering her, shall we say, for the sake of notable Australian call-backs, Kylie Minogue electric-pop era.

    A fun comparative aside here: Kylie was 20 when she

released her second studio album, *Enjoy Yourself*, in October of 1989. I think a lot about the women who came before Taylor in the music industry from all across the world, traversing different genres and rising to the top of their game. You know their names. I think about my mum, who grew up with Kylie as her musical idol, as Taylor is mine, who passed down her pop tendencies and raised a fangirl daughter, singing songs together in the car or listening with quiet patience while her daughter attempts a 'country twang,' insufferable at the best of times. LeAnn Rimes was Taylor's first concert when she was eight, Kylie was mine, age six, and further proof there is an enduring legacy in whose music hits your ears first. It is about teaching the young girls, your little cousins, the girls who followed you around at friends' Christmases and birthday parties who were a few years younger than you, and your daughters (whenever they come around) that there is joy, light and goodness in powerful women who share their voices with the world and stay at the top for decades. How many New Year's Eve parties have you had where Kylie or Whitney or Britney or The Spice Girls have played, and people dance? For us, it's almost every year.

The week before the album release, on October 20, Rebecca, another friend and I were given audience tickets to see Taylor play her new single on *The X Factor* grand final, which I had watched religiously for a few years. I had a suspicion she would make an appearance, as most pop stars would be obliged to do with a selection of international press before a release, so I contacted a friend who knew a friend, and we were in the television studio. We were so lucky to be in such a small space to watch her perform, so it didn't matter that we heard only one song. I would have to wait another year to see the 1989 World Tour in **SYDNEY** and this performance would fill the void until then. Such is the life of a Swiftie down under.

This album marks a notable jump in Taylor's production and songwriting style, and if a shift in genres needed a catalyst, let it be this: a move from the home of country music to the most electric city of them all. Taylor moved to New York from Nashville in March 2014, and as with everything in her life, created the soundtrack to new feelings. Interviewed on *Good Morning America* during album release week, she said,

> I wanted to start the album with this song because New York has been an important landscape and location for the story of my life in the last couple of years…I dreamt about moving to New York. I obsessed about moving to New York and then I did it…The inspiration that I found in that city is kind of hard to describe and hard to compare to any other force of inspiration I've ever experienced in my life… I approached moving there with such wide-eyed optimism and sort of saw it as a place of endless potential and possibilities…You can kind of hear that reflected in this music and this first song especially.

Having never been to New York City, I cannot comment on how the first track revives memories of a whirlwind trip, but in 2021, in lockdown, when I couldn't see my friends, I lived with my parents on a small block while they built a brand-new house. We shared that space with a family we knew and loved with two small children. Their daughter used to wake me up on weekends by jumping on my bed, but I didn't care because we would turn on the speakers and sing "Welcome to New York" together, running through my house. Now, three years later, on a recent holiday to visit the same family, my parents FaceTimed me when she was singing "Paper Rings" from *Lover*. I find often, it is the littlest people who bring the biggest joys, and these songs will forever remind me of her.

  Nathan Chapman was a producer for a lot of Taylor's early career, and before I introduce you to her new production team, it is important to understand the changes that were happening from all sides with Taylor's music and creation. Chapman chatted to *Inside Blackbird* saying the end of their creative relationship was "healthy for everybody" and added, "I worked on the first, second and third album, I did half of the fourth album and had one track on the fifth album. There was a lot of growth, a lot of evolution for her, and for me...there was a lot of time where we were really in sync, and then inevitably, someone's going to grow away from where the other person is growing, and that's a good thing, that's what you want out of creativity."

If you have listened to a hottest hits countdown on the radio since 1998, the chances are you've heard a Max Martin-penned pop song. The Swedish powerhouse producer/songwriter has written or co-written the second-most number-one singles on the Billboard 100 (US) chart, behind only Paul McCartney with 32 and with 27, he is tied with John Lennon. The Swedish songwriter rose to prominence with an impressive collection of singles he was involved with. He wrote and co-produced Britney's "Baby One More Time" (1998). It was originally offered to the Backstreet Boys and TLC, but they passed. He contributed to album production and co-wrote and co-produced multitudes of songs by the Backstreet Boys, most notably "I Want It That Way" (1999) and co-wrote N-SYNC's "It's Gonna Be Me" (2000). Many artists owe their charting/commercial success to the talents of Max Martin: Kelly Clarkson, P!nk, Usher, Avril Lavigne, Jessie J, Katy Perry, Christina Aguilera, Ariana Grande, Coldplay, The Veronicas, Ellie Goulding, Demi Lovato, Adele, Selena Gomez, Ed Sheeran, Lady Gaga, Justin Bieber and more. It is no surprise Taylor was interested in working with him for her first official pop album.

Max Martin worked previously with Taylor on Red, co-writing the characteristic 'pop party tracks', "We Are Never Ever Getting Back Together," which received the Billboard Hot 100 #1 and "I Knew You Were Trouble," which peaked at #2 and also "22." For 1989, he co-wrote and co-produced ten of the 13 songs, of which "Shake It Off," "Blank Space," and "Bad Blood" were all Billboard Hot 100 #1 songs. He later worked with Swift on reputation, co-writing and co-producing eight out of fifteen tracks, and co-wrote a song called "Message in a Bottle," one of the vault tracks on Red (Taylor's Version). 1989 is the first album she worked on with Bleachers frontman and music producer Jack Antonoff. The pair met because he was engaged at the time to Taylor's close friend and star of New York-based comedy GIRLS, Lena Dunham.

At the 2015 Grammy Awards, Taylor was nominated four times, all for "Shake It Off" in the categories of Record of the Year, Song of the Year, and Best Pop Solo Performance, but she didn't win. The lead single for 1989 is an anthem for ignoring haters and moving forward with your life. The next year, at the 2016 Grammys, Taylor won Album of the Year for the second time and Best Pop Vocal Album, while also winning the Album of the Year Awards with iHeart Radio and the American Music Awards.

On May 22, 2024, 1989 (Taylor's Version) was named number eighteen in Apple Music's definitive list of 100 Best Albums of all time. It is described as "an instance in which an artist defies expectations and thrives...as the album's title reminds us, she wasn't even born until the decade was ending. But just as she played with the traditions and conventions of country music on her early albums, Swift uses the nostalgia of 1989 not to look back but to move ahead." The original album cover is a front profile. The image is cropped just under Taylor's eyes. She's wearing a blue and white sweater with seagulls on it (which I happen to own), and the deluxe album is framed like a Polaroid photograph, the image's blurry and grainy quality imitating the popular technology of the 1970s and 80s. '1989' is written in black marker over the image. In 1989 (Taylor's Version), the seagulls have moved from the sweater to the background, where Taylor's face isn't cropped; she's facing side on but staring straight ahead, smiling into the distance.

When 1989 came out in October 2014, Taylor's life and mine paralleled in terms of the paths that we have taken with our girlfriends. It is an era that I refer to as 'the rise of the girl squad.' My first year at Sydney University in the same year was filled with temporary friends, names that haven't stuck and people I lost contact with. The start of my second year was different; I transferred degrees from Arts to Media and Communications, the degree I had chosen for myself three years earlier at the start of year 11. The ATAR (Australian Tertiary Admissions Ranking) was initially unachievable, but an internal course transfer meant that I found out I was accepted whilst on a summer holiday to Queensland, and time stood still. I made the decision to be a journalist and study the mechanics of storytelling when I was about 16, in my final years of high school. I found the course I wanted, and there was only one place I wanted to go.

My Girl Squad

They will tell you that they don't remember specifics, but the days I first glanced at three particular women in my life; Annalise, Bridie and Mary, I remember like it was yesterday, even though next year it will be a decade ago. Annalise isn't an original Sydneysider; she comes from Leeton in rural New South Wales, and at the time we met, she lived on campus. Pretty soon, I was spending the breaks between classes watching *Riverdale* on her bed in the Queen Mary Building, and we weren't far off being attached at the hip. We still are. Annalise and Bridie were in a Radio Production tutorial that I wasn't originally enrolled in, but because of my tight timetable schedule, I showed up on that first week in 2015, the tutor pencilled in my name at the bottom of the roll, and that was that. I was obsessed with this intelligent, funny, and stunning new friend immediately, and though she had other friends in the class, we worked on assignments together, bonded over our video journalism skills and whined about boys in the class that made us do the bulk of the workload. We lived together during the pandemic and through thick and thin, across career highlights and disappointments. I would die for that woman.

Whenever I'm alone, I will try to have conversations (it must be a Leo thing) with the strangers next to me, be that in concert queues or university classes, it doesn't matter. In lectures, we were encouraged to "turn to the person closest to you" whenever we had to provoke discussion, and for 2015's first semester, that person was Bridie. It didn't take long for me to say (she always sat in the row below or above me in the lecture theatre), "Hey, you can sit next to me if you like" and she stayed there for almost three years. She is clever, kind, generous and beautiful and hails from Balmain, a Sydney suburb I had only heard about in passing but somewhere I came to know well because of her. When we had to go to a late birthday dinner, she offered for me to stay in the bedroom she shared with two sisters instead of trekking it two hours back home on the train. I have been obsessed with all of her family ever since. I don't know who or where I would be now if I had not met her.

I remember being in awe of Mary's brain in the tutorials we had together week after week for three years. She argued her point eloquently in our Australian Media Studies classes, and she knew all the answers. I love everything about her, not just her amazing intellect; she is selfless and gorgeous, funny and always appreciative of her friends. She spent her high school years in Singapore, moving back to Sydney to study at a university. She played touch football with Bridie, and she introduced me to her friends Alex and Elijah. This was a huge deal for me, not having made close male friends in high school. I have her to thank for those two as well. When she got married last year, I was really upset because I couldn't come home.

She made sure to talk to me before and after her big day, and I really needed that love and support at a time when I should have been loving and supporting her. As a present, I bought her a Polaroid camera so I could contribute in the smallest way. Sharing Polaroids was very 1989-coded because it was an era filled with creating and documenting memories. Mary and I had the most natural transition from strangers to friends, anticipated seeing each other everywhere on campus, and she continues to make me a better person.

It was common practice that we four would occupy adjacent seats for a Media Globalisation class for a semester every

Wednesday morning. If New York was Taylor's new playground, Newtown was mine. There were countless parties (we had five twenty-first birthdays in a 40-day period), happy hour drinks after classes, movie visits, bookstore wanderings, takeaway dinners, brunch dates in cafés, and would you believe, there is actually a video game bar on King Street called 1989. Every late-night, lonely trip home was counteracted with an offer to stay at someone's house. Instead of moving out and being endlessly in debt, I had the best of both worlds: going into the busy city to see my friends and studying at the university that I loved before going home to the ocean and my family.

These friends hold my sanity in the palm of their hands. It would be a mistake not to include them in this book; their support for me needs to be celebrated. They are my biggest cheerleaders, and I am theirs. Bridie attended the 1989 and Eras Sydney shows, but Annalise and Mary haven't seen Taylor live, and even though they're not the biggest fans, they still sing her songs, and they let me be me. I saw a future for us early, and out of the events that have defined my post-high school life, these strong women have been there for a lot of them. I lived with Annalise for nearly two years and stayed on Mary's and Bridie's floors more times than I can remember. We have made it through my break-ups, breakdowns and almost-weekly overseas FaceTimes, Annalise signed my name in the guest register at Mary's wedding because I couldn't make it back to Australia. There have been endless lockdown movie nights and walks around Sydney; I can't wait to do life with them for a really long time. If there are any teenage girls reading this who are freaking out about not having solid friendships, remember this: I struggled with gossipy girls and pretend friends for most of high school, and it took a few years, but I finally believed my mum when she said, "You'll find your people soon, don't worry." And you should listen to her too: your people are coming.

Remarkably, at almost the same time as me finding the people I had desperately searched (and prayed) for in high school,

Taylor was surrounding herself with women whose friendships flourished off and on-camera and away from the spotlight. These friends grounded Taylor in her fame, celebrating her at the cost of being with in the media circus. Alongside this stratospheric jump into pop with her new sound, there was also an intense fixation on the people she hung out with between 2014-2016, and there was a media circus making a big deal out of and accusing Taylor's celebrity friendships of being fake. In the "Bad Blood" music video released on 15 May 2015 at the Billboard Music Awards, the women featured are brilliant and attractive celebrities seen frequently with Taylor at restaurant outings and on stage with her at concerts. They were given the name by the media as Taylor's 'Girls Squad.' It included Lena Dunham, Serayah, Ellie Goulding, Martha Hunt, Cara Delevingne, Zendaya, Lily Aldridge, Karlie Kloss, Jessica Alba, Mariska Hartigay, Ellen Pompeo and Cindy Crawford. These music video cameos aren't exhaustive or current; they have been interchanged over the years with other famous faces now, people like Este, Danielle and Alana Haim, Sophie Turner, Ed Sheeran, Blake Lively and Ryan Reynolds.

Writing for The Huffington Post in October 2016, Kelseigh Ingram said that Taylor "presents a very unhealthy and unrealistic example of female friendship; a group that consists entirely of tall, thin, conventionally pretty Western white women with only a few women of colour to serve as tokens." From nasty analysis of her "fake" Fourth of July parties in Rhode Island to public feuds with people like Katy Perry, some sections of the media chose to constantly pit women in music against each other.

The public scrutiny of a rotating roster of men (that began in the Red era), which is just a euphemism for slut-shaming, peaked in the 1989 era. This happened most of the time in media interviews, where journalists pushed for answers about song inspirations. Taylor wasn't giving them any. On The Morning Show in 2014, Journalist Liza Fromer introduced her like this, "Seven Grammys, 30,000,000 albums and counting, and more break-up stories than she would probably like. That's Taylor Swift."

It was a snarky tabloid observation masqueraded as a well-placed compliment. Some in the media were counting exactly how many boys Taylor had been seen with. Reflecting on 1989's third single, released on February 9, 2015, "Style," Fromer asks, "Is this autobiographical?" and Taylor's response is,

> The song is actually about kind of like those relationships that are never really done, you know? You always kind of have that person, that one person, who you feel might interrupt your wedding and be like, 'Don't do it cause we're not over yet.' I think everybody does have that one person, who kind of floats in and out of their life, and the narrative is never truly over.

Fromer asks, "Do you have that person?" and Taylor replies, "Like I said, everybody has that person, who they kind of float in and out of your life, and I was comparing that to trends in fashion and things you see in pop culture that never really go out of style." That should have been the final poke but after this, Fromer asks one more question. "Does your person also sing?" Taylor's response is intelligent and clear. She understands, with hindsight and maturity, that naming names (like she did with Ellen in the *Fearless* era) can and would get her into trouble. There were too many eyes on her now.

> Uhm...one of the things about writing music, the only way that I can actually be vulnerable with this many people is to never name names. So that's like the one thing I have, where I want these songs to go out into the world and become whatever my fans want them to be. I want them to picture their ex-boyfriend, not mine. And I know there's gonna be a media guessing game whenever I put out music, but that does not mean that I have to confirm or help them with it.

Fromer's final comment, "The name's a little provocative, but I understand what you're saying," is annoying. Taylor dated One Direction member Harry Styles for a few months at the beginning of 2013, and the similarity between the song title and his surname was where the interviewer was trying to steer the conversation. Taylor wasn't budging.

When the allegations about the toxic work environment behind the scenes on the *Ellen DeGeneres Show* came out, and after watching years of Taylor interviews, I wasn't shocked. Ellen felt like one of those school bullies who got cheap laughs from watching the small kids run away in fear. It's like movie scenes where they're pinning them to the locker, making it impossible to escape. On YouTube, an easy search will find you a video which is just called 'ellen making taylor uncomfortable for five minutes straight.' Taylor appeared on *The Ellen Show* a total of 11 times in as many years, her first appearance being in 2008 to promote *Fearless* and her last in 2019 to promote *Lover*. During this time, there are two interviews with Taylor that are particularly cringe-worthy. In October 2011, Ellen started the interview well. "Congratulations on winning *Billboard* Woman of the Year. You're the youngest female to ever receive that award...You just keep topping yourself, everything you do is just bigger and bigger." It quickly switches back to Ellen's favourite subject, Taylor's dating life. They talk about her new perfume, 'Wonderstruck', and Ellen asks, "Does your boyfriend like the way it smells?" Taylor responds, "I don't have one, I keep telling you that." "Just trying". "I for real, don't have a boyfriend, I sit by myself and watch *Law and Order*. I don't have like even kind of a boyfriend. I don't have someone that I'm texting that's a guy, that might someday be my boyfriend, there's nothing going on right now." And Ellen's chosen answer was, "That's pathetic, but you're busy."

In October 2013, Ellen again attempted to get some answers. "You were here with your boyfriend Zac Efron last time." "We actually never dated..." "Yes, you did." "When y'all were here, obviously late nights y'all are spending together, y'all wrote that song for me, and you sang it." Taylor continued to rebuke Ellen, "I haven't talked to him in a while because we didn't date." "Why do you deny it." "Because we didn't." "Aww okay." Then, Ellen proceeded to hand Taylor a bell, and said, "You ring it, and we'll show pictures...ring it on three different guys, we'll narrow it down." "I don't know if I'm gonna do this, this is the one shred of dignity that I have."

In the midst of the terrible game, you can hear Taylor say, "Do you know how badly this makes me feel?" and, "This makes me feel so bad about myself; every time I come up here, you put a different dude up on the screen, and it makes me really question what I stand for as a human being, there's never been two guys on the screen two visits in a row, it's sad." And Ellen laughed at her. "You'll have to come back just so you go, 'Yeah, he's still there." Taylor was clearly very uncomfortable, and I don't know why Ellen believed that slut-shaming (call it what it is) a 23-year-old on national television was okay. This interview is referenced years later when Taylor spoke with Zane Lowe on Apple Music after the release of *Lover* on October 30, 2019. She spoke about how,

> People were making slideshows of my dating life and putting people in there that I'd sat next to at a party once and deciding that my songwriting was like, a trick rather than a skill and a craft. It's a way to take a woman who's doing her job, and succeeding at doing her job and making things, it's a way to figure out how to completely minimise that skill. By taking something that everyone, in their darkest, darkest moments loves to do which is to slut-shame.

Seeing other news headlines about other female artists, she said, "It sends me into a real sad place because I don't want that to keep happening, and I don't think people understand how easy it is to infer that someone, who is a female artist, or a female in our industry is somehow doing something wrong by wanting love, wanting money, wanting success, women aren't allowing to want those things the way that men are allowed to want them."

In a video from the 2015 Grammys red carpet, a female *Entertainment Tonight* journalist says to Taylor, "Can we just get a pan down of this dress? I just wanted to show the legs, as I was telling you ahead of time, you're gonna be walking home with more than just a trophy tonight, I think lots of men…" From the look on her face, it is obvious that Taylor is thinking about how to respond to this question, and she says, "I'm not gonna walk home with any men tonight, I'm gonna to go hang out with my friends and then I go home to cats." The accompanying male reporter says, "No men allowed," and Taylor replies, "Men get me in trouble." The female reporter says, "Trouble with a capital T" (whatever that means). These encounters do nothing for the news cycle but are damaging to the wider discourse about women's places in society, and nearly nine years later, I know that this kind of interview would not hold up.

Tavi Gevinson, a journalist and close friend of Taylor's, wrote about 1989 for ELLE's 'June Women in Music Issue' in May/June 2015. She writes, "I was first struck by how much more agency she had over her songwriting…and by how it felt to get permission from a girl wielding a guitar to shamelessly express one's emotions, despite how often doing so can get you called "crazy" (that sexist euphemism for 'feminine')." In the interview Taylor describes the songwriting process in the last moments of 1989,

> "Shake It Off" and "Clean" were the last two things we wrote for the record, so it shows you where I ended up mentally. "Clean" I wrote as I was walking out of Liberty in London. Someone I used to date – it hit me that I'd been in the same city as him for two weeks and I hadn't thought about it. When it did hit me, it was like, *Oh, I hope he's doing well*. And

nothing else. And you know how it is when you're going through heartbreak. A heartbroken person is unlike any other person. Their time moves at a completely different pace than ours. It's this mental, physical, emotional ache and feeling so conflicted. Nothing distracts you from it.

You replace these old habits with new habits, like texting your friends in a group chat all day and planning fun dinner parties and going out on adventures with your girlfriends, and then all of a sudden one day you're in London and you realize you've been in the same place as your ex for two weeks and you're fine. And you hope he's fine. The first thought that came to my mind was, *I'm finally clean*. I'd been in this media hailstorm of people having a very misconstrued perception of who I was. There were really insensitive jokes being made at awards shows by hosts; there were snarky headlines in the press – 'Taylor Goes Through a Break-up: Well, That Was Swift!' – focusing on all the wrong things.

Another quote from the ELLE interview has a transcendent quality where Taylor says, "With 1989, I feel like we gave the entire metaphorical house I built a complete renovation, and it made me love the house even more – but still keeping the foundation of what I've always been." This predates what will become the *Lover* House by nearly five years. The house itself features in her 2019 "Lover" music video, appears prominently in The Eras Tour and there was also an empty hallway featured in a teaser trailer for *The Tortured Poets Department* album release, that fans decode could be all a part of the same building. It is incredible how much these quotes from nearly a decade ago hold up. Gevinson wrote, "She's twenty-five now, and with her newfound perspective on romance's expiration date, she's also gained appreciation for the joy of a fling's impermanence, recovering from heartbreak, and reinventing oneself." Something, at 35, she still does.

There was another very obvious (but never spoken about at the time) demon in the room. Taylor was suffering from an eating disorder, and the daily tabloids and paparazzi pictures very quickly became toxic. She didn't address this publicly until her *Miss Americana* documentary because it was a very private health issue that wasn't fit for the media circus. In the documentary, she says,

> I've learned over the years it's not good for me to see pictures of myself every day 'cause I have a tendency, and it's only happened a few times and I'm not in any way proud of it, but I tend to get triggered by something, whether it's a picture of me where I feel like I looked like my tummy was too big or someone said that I looked pregnant or something and that'll just trigger me to just starve a little bit, just stop eating.
>
> I thought that I was just, like supposed to feel like I was gonna pass out at the end of a show or in the middle of it. I thought that was how it was and now I realise, no, if you eat food, have energy, get stronger, you can do all these shows and not feel it. Which is a really good revelation. Because I am a lot happier with who I am.
>
> I don't care so much if somebody points out if I have gained weight. It's just something that makes my life better, the fact that I am a size six instead of a size double zero, I mean that wasn't how my body was supposed to be, I just didn't really understand that at the time, I really don't think I knew it. I would have defended it to anyone who said, 'I'm concerned about you.' I was like 'What are you talking about? Of course, I eat. It's perfectly normal, I just exercise a lot.' And I did exercise a lot, but I wasn't eating. I don't think you know you're doing that when you're doing it gradually.

> There's always some standard of beauty that you're not meeting. Because if you're thin enough, then you don't have that ass that everybody wants. But if you have enough weight on you to have an ass, then your stomach isn't flat enough. It's all just fucking impossible. You don't ever say to yourself, 'Look, I've got an eating disorder,' but you know you're making a list of everything you put in your mouth that day, and you know that's probably not right, but then again, there's so many diet blogs that tell you that that's what you should do.
>
> This [shows a photo to the camera] would cause me to go into a real shame, like hate spiral. And, like, I caught myself yesterday starting to do it, and I was like, nope, we do not do that anymore because it's better to think you look fat than to look sick. We do not do that anymore, and we're changing the channel in our brain, and we're not doing that anymore because that didn't end us up in a good place.

I have always understood that the public persona of a celebrity is very rarely who they are in real life. My favourite artists, like Ed Sheeran, Taylor and Selena Gomez, have always addressed important mental health conversations and shared with the media about just how dehumanising the process of being in the public eye and suffering trauma or heartbreak really is. By creating art that reflects their state of being, they continue the important relationship with their fans, who will support them no matter what. "All You Had to Do Was Stay," "How You Get the Girl," and "I Wish You Would" are songs I will never tire of. But the standout on this album is "Out of The Woods." Production-wise, up until this point I had never heard of anything like it before from Taylor. The beginning of the song will always give me goosebumps, as do the vocal echoes and the backing track. The lyrics talk about lovers being built to fall apart but falling back together. As difficult as the question is of my favourite song of

Taylor's, is, similarly, choosing a favourite live performance is just as hard. When Taylor performed "Out of the Woods" as the opening number at the Grammy Awards in February 2016, with a cropped bob, blunt fringe and head-to-books sparkly bodysuit, I knew this would be difficult to top. She didn't need the sparkly guitar anymore; she *was* the sparkly guitar. I was absolutely in awe of her. That night, she won her second Album of the Year. I got my friend's mum to make me a copy of the pink skirt she wore on the red carpet, and I wore it to a wedding. Taylor was very inactive in 2015 and 2016, owing to what happened with the Kanye debacle, and along with slut-shaming, dealing with an eating disorder and media scrutiny over friends (and by extension her dating life) and the stress of the public feud with Kanye West and Kim Kardashian and subsequent internet backlash, she needed a break. She deserved that break, and the reset button was very much pushed. Before that, however, coinciding with her album release, she did some incredibly special and heart-warming things that are still talked about a decade later.

The Rise of Tay-lurking, the beginning of the Secret Sessions, and Swiftmas.
I am sure that the Swifties reading this know it all too well, but for those unaware, for the album releases of 1989, *reputation* and *Lover*, Taylor created the "secret sessions." The concept arose when Taylor decided to mark its release with something she'd never done, changing (once again) the way she engaged with fans. She invited hundreds of fans in small groups to each of her houses and shared the album with them weeks before its scheduled release, and it was a very intimate setting. She explained the conception of it in her *Graham Norton* appearance on October 14, 2014, where he appeared baffled that she would be so vulnerable as to engage with fans in this way, but she explains it as her way of giving back.

> Basically, I got this idea before I finished the album, and I wanted to call it the 1989 secret sessions. I was most proud

of this album, more than anything I've done before and so I wanted to give fans a chance to hear it before it came out, like a month before it came out and I'd never done this before. I wanted it to be all fans who had never met me before, I've been to seven shows, I've never met you, I camped out on the street, I never saw you. I wanted it to be these people who had been so dedicated, but I'd never gotten to thank them in person. Actually, I found them on the internet. Which is I would go online; I would look at their Instagram pages or their Tumblr or their Twitter or whatever and just kind of watch them for months and months. Just sort of cyber-stalk them and then I invited them over and they came.

This began the sub-phenomenon of what fans call Tay-lurking, where Taylor stalks fans on the internet, something I'm sure not many celebrities do. She still does it to this day, liking posts and videos on social media almost to assure us that she is also just hanging out with her phone, but clearly wanting to validate our efforts as fans. Then came the rewards that extended past just her music. Writing for *Off Chance* in an article titled "Making The Case For Parasocial Relationships: Taylor's Version," journalist Kelsey Barnes unpicks the intricacies of Taylor's unique intimacy with fans.

What set 1989 apart from previous albums was the extent to which Swift navigated and redefined what it means to have an artist-to-fan relationship. She didn't just use Twitter to tell fans to buy it, she saved their photos of the album and posted them. She didn't just do a meet and greet, she lurked fans online for a year and hand-selected them to listen to the album early with her. She curated bespoke Swiftmas gifts to send to fans, attended a fan's bridal shower, and responded often to posts on Tumblr from fans asking her what lipstick shade she was wearing to her favourite cookie recipe.

I posted on reddit looking for fans that had attended the 1989 secret sessions and got a response from Gabby D'Alessandro from the United States, who attended the New York City date on October 3, 2014. Sarah Chapelle from the very iconic Taylor Swift Style Tumblr blog attended the same one. Gabby had been a Swiftie since the first album, around 2007, and she recalled the moment Taylor Nation called her.

"On October 1, I remember I was in college, and it was my dog's birthday, so I was on FaceTime with my mom to see him – and I got a phone call from a random number, and I typically don't answer it, but it was a Tennessee area code, and at the time I was aware that the Secret Sessions were going on so I answered and they said they wanted to invite me to a Taylor Swift event, they gave me the details and told me it was confidential. But I did tell my roommate at the time and my mom because I was only twenty."

"The whole event ran for eight to nine hours, they [Taylor Nation] told us to meet at a hotel, so I went downtown, and they checked us in, we had to sign NDAs, and we left our belongings there because we were not allowed to bring anything with us. I was allowed to have my wallet but that was it. Then they put us on a bus and brought us to Taylor's apartment, where she had snacks and drinks and made cookies for everyone. Both her parents were there and her dad of course, had guitar picks with him so he gave us some. I ended up bonding with a group of people around my age, because we were probably the oldest ones there (I still chat with them every so often) and Taylor came down, did some mingling with us and then she played the album for us, and it was truly amazing."

"I remember her starting off with saying that she was so excited for this group because of the first song, "Welcome To New York". She played the whole album and she saved "Shake It Off" for last since it had already been out as a single, and then we had a dance party to it. Then she started taking pictures with everyone, and me and the group of friends I made decided to wait until the end. Everyone rushed to get to her but we knew we would get a chance so we just hung out! And when I finally met her, she knew exactly who I was, she said she found me from the Swiftstakes entry I did! And I was just amazed. I looked at her like an older sister (I still do) and being a few years younger than her, I felt like when she was putting albums out it was lining up with my life, age, and things I was experiencing!"

"We got the Polaroid picture, key chain and then she gave us some new album merch, two t-shirts and a tote bag, and I still have them. After they bussed us back to the hotel to get our things, and I went home and honestly my life has never been the same. I sometimes have to check myself and when I got nosebleed seats to the Eras Tour, I have to remind myself that I was literally invited to her house, I cannot be upset!!"

Gabby had an interesting way of receiving her secret sessions entry; she said, "When Taylor announced 1989 on a live stream, she opened a 'Swift-stakes' competition to win tickets for the upcoming tour and meet-and-greets. This involved writing a short essay for Taylor Nation, and then I was chosen as a successful entry." She had no idea that this would form the secret sessions, at the time, no one did, they didn't exist yet.

After the secret sessions, in December, there was another surprise in-store. Known as 'Swiftmas' this was a unique, one-off moment for Taylor where she partnered with UPS to deliver Christmas presents to her fans. There is a YouTube video posted on her account on December 31, 2014, that is nearly six minutes long and is introduced with text not unlike the beginning of an episode of Law and Order (it's an inside joke; she's obsessed with Law and Order: Special Victims Unit, to the extent that her second cat is called Detective Olivia Benson.) The video's text says,

> 2014 was the year of many wonderful things for Taylor and her fans. The RED Tour played its last show in Asia, the 1989 era began and a new gift giving symbol became widely known. Shortly after the massively successful release of 1989, fans on social media began to experience another phenomenon. After something that became known as Tay-lurking, whereupon every detail of a fan's likes, job, whereabouts was studied intently…A single Santa emoji would appear on their socials. From one Taylor Swift. Large Fedex boxes began to appear on the doorsteps of certain fans in what became tenderly referred to as 'Swiftmas.' These are their stories.

In the goofy homemade video, Taylor is individually gift-wrapping a selection of presents on the floor of a bedroom we can assume is her own. She says, "That is a lot of the stuff I went shopping and got yesterday for presents and that's Meredith," and "It's Christmas, I'm Santa Claus, this package is for Mallory, it's actually a Hanukkah present, it's the second day so I don't want to miss the whole thing." She reprimands her cats for sleeping on blankets meant as gifts and even hand delivers one present.

> There's this wonderful girl named Steph who I've met before, but she has a tiny young son named Leighton, who she posts videos of all the time, and I've never gotten to meet him before, so I guess we're just gonna go and drive to Connecticut and bring Leighton some Christmas presents. They have no idea we're coming; they're supposed to be home because they think that there's a package being dropped off by UPS but UPS is…me.

Twitter/X account @happinessforts posted in December 2023, "Imagine getting a package from taylor swift where she handpicked every item in the package based on your interests that she had been noting over weeks, months, even YEARS like...a dream" and an account I have been following for nearly 10 years on Twitter @HannahRae1327 retweeted with "a.... Imagine... ha....haha... ha..." I had almost forgotten about Hannah, who back in 2014 was a very young fan whose picture instantly made me remember what my Instagram feed looked like in that year. In August 2014, Taylor left this lengthy comment on Hannah's Instagram post.

> Hannahhhhh...Reading this made me so sad because I love seeing you in your videos and photos being so happy and wide eyed, like the world isn't as harsh and unfair as it actually is. I hate thinking about your pretty face covered in tears, but I know why you're crying because I've been in your place. This isn't a high school thing or an age thing. It's a people thing. A life thing. It doesn't stop. It doesn't end or change. People cut other people down for entertainment, amusement, out of jealousy, because of something broken inside them, or for no reason at all. It's just what they do, and you're a target because you live your life loudly and boldly. You're bright and joyful and so many people are cynical. They won't understand you and they won't understand me. But the only way they win is if your tears turn tears turn you to stone and make you bitter like them. It's okay to ask why. It's okay to wonder how you could try so hard and still get stomped all over. Just don't let them change you or stop you from singing or dancing around to your favorite song. You're going into high school this week and this is your chance to push the reset button on how much value you give the opinions of these kids, most of whom have NO idea who they are. I'm so proud of you and protective of you because you DO. If they don't like you for being yourself,

be yourself even more. Every time someone picks on me, I'll think of you in hopes that every time someone picks on you, you'll think of me...and how we have this thread that connects us. Let them keep living in the darkness and we'll keep waking in the sunlight. Forever on your side, Taylor.

The Swiftmas video shows a longer montage of her fans receiving the presents, reading handwritten cards and an outpouring of emotion in response to one of the biggest pop stars in the world. Then, there is a short recap of the fans' responses on social media, as well as the corresponding media headlines from Buzzfeed, Billboard, The Mirror, Cosmopolitan, and MTV News. I mentioned parasocial relationships earlier, and that won't be the last time you hear me use that term, but this is a different level, dare I say, a friendship. Carefully selecting a dedicated group of fans who love and appreciate you and showing them love in return is a kind, generous, selfless and big-hearted thing to do. Especially if you are Taylor Swift.

There were numerous fan speculations that the release of 1989 (Taylor's Version) should have been a double album with the second side being only vault tracks with features from different artists. Every Swiftie I know was patiently waiting for the "Style feat. Harry Styles" that never came. I still hold out hope. My friend Lucas was a little disappointed that none of the five vault tracks featured duets like the previous three re-released albums had. Lucas said, "I think people expected more features, because she teased some of the vault track list on Instagram and each song looked like it was written by a different person, so people thought those were written by the featured artists. I thought it would also be fun for 1989 TV to have all of her musician friends [possibly Halsey, maybe Lorde, and definitely Selena] featured on a different track." The five vault tracks released with the re-recorded album on 27 October 2023 were "Slut!," "Say Don't Go," "Now That We Don't Talk," "Suburban Legends," and "Is It Over Now?"

When I think about summarising 1989, I struggle. Listening to 1989 in 2014 and 2015 was such an incredible time in my life. It was university; it was friends, joy, overseas holidays, and it was lots and lots of dancing. It is an album that should be listened to as intended, from start to finish, spinning around your lounge room, smiling and happy crying. I play this album when I'm not feeling great, and without fail, EVERY TIME "Shake It Off" comes on, there really isn't a reason to be sad anymore. Some people had Michael Jackson's *Thriller* and I had Taylor's pop masterpiece. The lyrics are filled with my favourite imaginative daydream; what if? I didn't (and still don't) need romantic love because I found my coven. Women who will plot and scheme with me, concocting and consuming alcoholic potions, cooking, baking, spending time doing nothing together and dancing through university in a big city. Those are the shiny moments that are the ingredients for 1989. After this album, music would never be the same. I fell in love with the idea of falling in love, hopeful that it wouldn't be too much longer that I would have to wait. At this point I still couldn't match the lyrics to any one relationship. I was still living in a blurry, faded, mystical dreamscape where the face of the boy who loved me was obscured because I hadn't met him yet. That was about to change.

reputation era
2017 – 2019.

There will be no explanation, there will just be *reputation*.

Content warning: this chapter makes reference to sexual assault.

The year I was last in a long-term relationship was 2017. 1989 was three years old, and this year it turns ten. Back then, I was singing boppy love songs in a different way because those lyrics finally looked like a person. Stylised in all lower-case, *reputation* was released on 10 November, and by the end of December, I would know for the first time what a break-up was. But I also found out for the first time that year what love truly was, too. Someone who looked at me and smiled, laughed when I did dumb stuff and forgave me when I was insecure or insufferable. Someone who stopped me from talking by kissing and tipping me forward in my lounge room. Someone who was the reason I ran out of petrol at 2 am, driving back from his house and who I was safe travelling home next to on late-night trains. We had a lot of adventures. Before this, the lyrics Taylor wrote were formless, floating around in the universe loaded with possibility. Now most of them had the same face, a physical body and even a phone number. Every fan will tell you which songs have a person attached to them. For me, it's like a board with pins in it, like on a detective show, and each person's mugshot who has meant something to me has multiple songs from the different eras with coloured strings tracing back the lyrics that conjure up memories.

It's a funny thing because, before 2023, I would have told people I had only truly been in love once, and I can't say that anymore. But I will say this: the year-long relationship in 2017 was the only time he had loved me in return and when there are 1,000,000 Taylor Swift songs for both versions, I know which I prefer. The person who loves you back is someone who you will care about for a really long time, maybe for the rest of your life. He is the one who set fireworks off in my brain and rendered me incapable of speech. Believe me, I was just as surprised as you are. He matched me word-for-word in conversations, and for a girl who used to get into endless trouble for interrupting people, I never tired of listening to him talk about things he was passionate about. Of all the lessons he taught me, hard ones, fun ones, serious ones, this one sticks: someone will love me. Because he did. The ones who you love alone hurt you ten times more; don't ask me why.

Between approximately June 2016 and February 2017, Taylor's public appearances were very limited. Her singular performance around this time was October 22, at the Formula 1 Grand Prix in Austin, with a setlist of 19 songs; she wouldn't perform again to crowds until February. Aside from this show, there were no media appearances or interviews, and even the paparazzi images of Taylor were scant. Taylor broke up with Scottish DJ Calvin Harris in June 2016. Twitter rages followed, fuelled by him, encouraged to a certain extent by Katy Perry and blew wide open by Kim Kardashian. Her use of a snake emoji (after her GQ article and Snapchat videos came out) started the ugly public opinion backlash of July 2016's trending hashtags, #taylorswiftisoverparty and #taylorisasnake, then media and news outlets launched a full-scale witch hunt. Writing for The Telegraph, Helena Horton reported that,

> Taylor Swift has been the target of angered social media users after Calvin Harris accused her of trying to ruin his reputation and attempting to tear down her long-time rival Katy Perry in a spectacular Twitter rant. This has been inflamed by Katy Perry, who appears to have also confirmed the rumours, retweeting an old Tweet which appeared to originally be about Taylor Swift during their feud [allegedly about back up dancers switching between the two stars' tours] She retweeted her own tweet, which said 'Time. The ultimate truth teller', as the Calvin Harris drama unfolded. Hundreds of people have been commenting on Taylor Swift's Instagram profile with the snake emoji, in reference to the fact Mr Harris accused her team of releasing the

news she wrote his latest hit in order to make him look bad.

On Twitter, where the hashtags were most prominent, there is still a user (created in July 2016 with Calvin Harris' face as the profile picture) whose first three tweets accompany images and say, "#TaylorSwiftIsOverParty #DiversityinMusic Dear Taylor Swift: your perfect straight white girl act is so old.", "#TaylorSwiftIsOverParty #DiversityinMusic Taylor, your image is boring and tired. We're sick of hearing about you." And, "Remember when we heard about all of our favorite artists and not just Taylor? Me neither. #TaylorSwiftIsOverParty" The internet is a nasty place, and for Taylor, 2016 was a cruel summer, but through it, *reputation* emerged. In the *Miss Americana* documentary, she says, "I just wanted to disappear, nobody physically saw me for a year, and that was what I thought they wanted…The reason why that backlash hurt so much was because that used to be all I had. I felt really alone, I felt really bitter, I felt like a wounded animal lashing out. I figured I had to reset everything."

Before the album was even close to being announced, on February 4, 2017, there was a one-off concert called 'Super Saturday Night' hosted by AT&T and Direct TV. It was held in Houston to coincide with the Super Bowl VI being in the same city the following evening. Taylor played to a crowd of 9,000 in a purpose-built venue. After singing two songs, she addressed the crowd,

> I have to be really honest with you about something, as far as I know, I am doing one show in 2017…you're the crowd that I'm gonna to see in my daydreams. When I'm thinking about how I love being on stage, you're the ones I'm gonna see in my head. So, I was wondering, if you don't feel like dancing for yourself or screaming for yourself, you don't feel in the mood or whatever, you're stressed out, would you do it for *me* tonight? **Screams** Oh good thank you I was hoping you would say that…and I got a good vibe

from you for the first couple of songs, you can always tell, and from the looks of you, I think we're gonna have a good night, Houston Texas!

December 9, 2016, was the release date for a soundtrack duet release for the film *Fifty Shades Darker*, written by Taylor, Sam Dew and Jack Antonoff, and this concert would be the first live performance of "I Don't Wanna Live Forever." The studio version features Zayn Malik of One Direction fame, but he doesn't make an appearance here. The song debuted at #6 on the US *Billboard* 100, later peaking at #2, reached #3 on the Australian ARIA charts, and received a Grammy nomination for Best Song Written for Visual Media. It won Best Collaboration at the MTV Video Music Awards and the Millennial Awards and an iHeartRadio Titanium Award for 1,000,000,000 plays. In the European charts, the song debuted at #1 in Spain and Sweden, becoming Swift's first #1 single in both countries, while becoming Zayn's first #1 in Spain and his second in Sweden.

With her silence being felt by fans and non-fans alike, in an historic before and after moment on August 18, every one of Taylor's social media pages went blank (all posts from almost back to 2012 and earlier were deleted, so naturally, the fandom went into absolute panic mode). When all of her posted pictures disappeared, every Swiftie knew, and soon everyone else would find out that this era and album would be heralded by yet another tonal shift, moving through pop with different stories and sounds. On August 22, a series of three ominous videos of a large-scale slithery reptile appeared, and the music video and lead single, "Look What You Made Me Do," dropped two days later into the middle of my university lecture on August 24. It was a definitive "Do you remember where you were when Taylor did THIS moment?" I remember sitting behind one friend who was watching the music video on silent, as I was, and a friend behind me watched my screen. When the lecture ended, every Swiftie around me erupted into unintelligible squeals.

Junkee, an Australian pop culture media company, reported

that the "Look What You Made Me Do" music video made reference to and took a swipe at the armed robbery that happened to Kim Kardashian while in Paris for Fashion Week in 2016. Matilda Dixon-Smith, writes in a notably casual tone (even more so, I think, being an Australian publication) and says, "I think the evidence speaks for itself, gang." The more I watch the video, the more I try to piece together motifs that fuel the speculation that was being thrown around in 2017, but I don't think it was a deliberate dig. There was definitely residual aggressive media energy floating around.

> If Tay *is indeed* taking shots at Kim over the robbery, well, that is pretty fucked up. Kardashian-West described the robbery as a harrowing and traumatising experience. To take aim at that, in public, just because a woman and her husband revealed you to be a liar (you lied, girl, just own it) is pretty goddamn cheap and petty. Sit down, Tay. Just...sit down and chill out.

In an unprecedented play, on November 10, *reputation* was released with next to no appearances, press (interviews, magazine or otherwise) or information given by Taylor. For the first time in her career, she took a step back and let the music do the talking. In November, she made her only three *reputation*-era television appearances, the first on 9 November, an ABC special world premiere performance of "New Year's Day" filmed during her Rhode Island *reputation* secret session on 18 October. It aired during a television line-up that featured the milestone 300th episode of "Grey's Anatomy." Teenage Taylor would be shaking. She was the *Saturday Night Live* musical guest on 11 November, and her friend, comedic actress Tiffany Haddish, was host and performed "...Ready for It?" and "Call It What You Want." On November 13, 2017, there was a surprise performance on the *Tonight Show with Jimmy Fallon*, where she sang "New Year's Day" again. For any other artist, not doing any marketing would be very unideal, but with five albums behind her and loyal fans that wouldn't put up with the tabloid poison unravelling, we didn't need more information; we were there in the snake pit with her. The first week sales figures for *reputation* are a testimony to this loyalty. The album sold 1,000,000 copies worldwide, and in the USA, almost 700,000 copies after one day and 2,000,000 after four days. *Billboard* reported that after opening at number one on the *Billboard* 200, where it stayed for four weeks, its pure sales (physical copies, not including streaming) numbers of 1,216,000 were more than any other albums on the chart that week combined. I bought the two lyric magazine albums, pages filled with a gorgeous photoshoot where Taylor's hair is longer and curly (a statement fans know; if the hair changes, the album does too). I was hyped for new music. The album cover is greyscale, imitating a newspaper. She is staring down the camera lens with greased back hair, with headlines and articles that replicate her name over and over, covering half her face on the right-hand side. This could be read on a deeper level as a reflection of her bad tabloid press over the last year and there is a chain necklace wrapped tightly around her neck, almost uncomfortably so, but she is far from being silenced.

As previously mentioned, there are rumours that had the Kanye/Kim Kardashian drama not escalated, Taylor was preparing a different album (possibly titled *Karma*, somewhat sonically similar to *Midnights*) as her sixth. The space between 1989 and *reputation* is the largest gap that Taylor has ever left between album releases; just over 1,000 days, or three years and two weeks. 1989 would prove to be a tough album to follow, having won Album of the Year for the second time and shifting the songwriting sound entirely into pop from her country roots. Speaking in May 2019, on *Ellen*, she said,

> I had an album out called *reputation*, and with that album, I just basically wanted to make music and not explain it. As a songwriter, I enjoy communicating about what I've made. I really do like that part of the process, but with my career, I want to do what feels right at the time. So, at that time,

I coined this phrase, 'There will be no explanation, there will just be reputation' because I AM dramatic. That's a very dramatic thing, but it rhymed, it was catchy and so I stuck with it.

There were magazine cover shoots for *Harper's Bazaar* and *British Vogue* (December 2017/January 2018), but instead of interviews, *Harper's Bazaar* interviewed icon of the 1960s, Pattie Boyd. *British Vogue* published a poem that Taylor wrote (which in 2024 should be a nice reminder that the woman has indeed always been a tortured poet). The poem was also featured in the special edition lyric magazines of the album. It speaks to the art of healing; that letting go is the panacea, and once you let things go, the more you can hold on. She reminds us to hold on to even the small things that bring joy to life.

Finding Taylor in London, 2017 & 2024.
The music video for "End Game" was filmed in Miami, Tokyo and London, and her adventures with Ed Sheeran and Future (featured artists on the track) play out in that order. Released as the third single on *reputation* on November 14, 2017, and the video on January 12, 2018, the song won two awards at the 2019 BMI Awards and also won Pop Award at the 2019 BMI London Awards, honouring songwriters and producers. The video starts as a typical evening for most twenty-somethings with dancing and karaoke, getting ready and pre-drinks before karaoke and city wandering, pub crawling and the inevitable end-of-the-night feed at a kebab stop. It reminds me of Hilary Duff's video for "Wake Up" from her *Most Wanted* album in 2005. The London scenes, any Swiftie knows, are not hard to locate and visit easily; we are detectives, after all. So this year, in early April, I found myself in Kentish Town, one Saturday evening while having not left the house all day, feeling hungry and very stuck. I did a quick Google and then I was on the Overground. I lived close by and naturally hate wasted opportunities for a niche nerdy adventure, a little less chaotic than the video.

As it happens, I reversed the order of fun for my Swiftie pilgrimage, with the first stop being the 'Kentish Delight' Turkish kebab shop. Taylor frequented this shop when she used to live around here. On the windows and walls inside are posters, photos and selfies presumably taken in late 2017, when filming the music video was taking place because she is wearing the same blue fluffy coat in the sequences outside the shop. The facts are that Taylor lived in London, close by in Highgate, with Joe Alwyn for quite a few years through her Kanyegate drama, and I would posit this is where she found the kebab shop and then, knowing of its goodness, returned to film the music video. When I walked in, it was empty. The manager/owner, Ahmed, was there and very friendly, and he noticed me taking the photos outside. "You know about Taylor Swift? She will be here in June." "Yes, I know, I'm going to the concerts," I told him. Then he dropped a bombshell, and he showed me a section of a text message (no contact details, names or dates were shown or passed on) from a caterer letting him know about a Taylor Swift itinerary with some big orders that he was to get ready for in June and August. There would be a request for 90 kebabs, twice a day, for the June and August dates that she performs at Wembley this year. This is why you should be nice and friendly to *everyone*; they share things with you if you're open and polite and then magic will happen. I asked him how often and how many people come in every day with the same reason as me, and he said, "Every day, maybe 40-50 people come from all over the world; today there were Spanish, Italians and Americans, and yesterday there were people from China, South Korea and Malaysia here." I ordered 'the Taylor kebab' – a delicious chicken doner kebab, and since there was no one in the shop, I sat and ate mine inside. I said goodbye, thanked my new friend, and walked next door.

    The Bull and Gate is a classic London pub, unassuming and bigger on the inside, and I realised I'd walked past here a few times without noticing. Alongside Kentish Delight, it was also used in the filming of "End Game." There was an Arsenal football game downstairs. I ordered a beer, and the bar staff kindly answered my insane questions, "Has anyone worked here for more than six years?" They said yes, but he's not here at the moment, so I made a mental note to return. The staff directed me upstairs. I sat on a red chaise lounge looking at the place where the few seconds at the end of the music video were filmed (the layout, bar, shelves and chandelier are the same). The bar downstairs was also featured in the video, which was quite cool, and the fact I could walk home when it was still light outside at 8 pm at the beginning of April was a lovely addition. I'll be coming back here in the summer for sure.

A few months later, I came back in and chatted with the manager, Ed Morrissey. He said that, sadly, no one was still working there who had been around when Taylor popped in to film "End Game" (seven years prior), but he personally had been a bartender for her and her family at a private party for her brother's birthday at the Windmill in Mayfair, in March 2019. He recalled a funny story about her paying for the tab, and he almost overcharged her, but "she was super lovely, and at the time I didn't really realise who she was...she obviously booked under a different name." It's a coincidence that he now works at the pub where she shot her music video. He also informed me of the pub's history as a well-known music venue. "Before the Forum next door changed from a country music venue into a popular venue for all genres, this was *the* venue for up-and-coming bands to come and play. Names like Coldplay, Blur, Oasis, and Nirvana." The pub was a major player on the 1980s indie music scene, unsigned bands desired to play here and be scouted and signed, as was the case with one of England's most famous bands. Coldplay played a gig here on April 1, 1999, and were signed to Fierce Panda Records that night. To be eating and visiting in a place like that, just around the corner, was really cool.

In May 2018, I graduated from university and flew out a few days later to visit Europe and the UK. I listened to *reputation* on buses, in my cousin's back garden and in airport lounges, convinced that the break-up I'd gone through and the heartbreak and pain that followed me would subside. It took a few years, not a few countries, but it did, and this album will be forever intertwined with that timeline. On that trip, I made friends that I still talk to and came to the realisation that the boy I had loved and I just weren't meant to be together. I had linked up short trips with friends, saw family, revisited cities, and created new memories with the brilliant summer as a backdrop. I visited France for nearly two weeks in June and made it down to Barcelona before returning to London to see Taylor's *reputation* Stadium Tour in Wembley Stadium (the first time I had ever been there) on June 28. Accompanied by my university darling Maggie, we screamed our lungs out. I danced through the blisters on my rough, sparkly sneakers that were now stained the same colour as Taylor's fourth album. It was surreal. A few weeks later, I embarked on a two-week solo trip up and down the British Isles from London to Inverness and back, backpacking alone where I never felt unsafe except for once. In Glasgow, I booked a two-day tour of the Scottish Highlands, Inverness and Loch Ness. There were 20 people on my tour and I befriended a young German girl called Leonie, and we're still in contact. On the way back down, we visited Cairngorms National Park.

I have only ever told my mum this story and maybe two or three others. Our tour guide was a male, probably aged in his 60s. He wore a kilt, looked the part, was very knowledgeable and was as funny as you imagine 60-year-old men think they are. He was a "character." Because he wasn't boring, a few of us wanted a group photo with him. I stood next to him and smiled, and the next thing I knew, his hand was on my bottom. It was a pretty firm hold, probably not a "squeeze," but none of that actually matters except for his hand being on my "ass" as Taylor would call it, in her sexual assault trial. My whole body went rigid; I couldn't move or talk as the phone went click. In my photos, I'm wearing nothing extravagant, a black Lorde tour t-shirt and denim shorts. I shouldn't have to tell you that… "Maybe it was what I was wearing?" echoed in my head. I am absolutely obsessed with the natural beauty of Scotland and in all the photos that Leonie took before our group one, I'm smiling, posing like a goofball in an insanely perfect part of the world. Had the photos been taken the other way around, I'd look a bit more like a deer before being hit by a car. We got back on the bus and stopped a few more times including a stop at the museum that was used for the set of Outlander. I didn't speak to the guide again and went into shock.

Leonie was 19, and I was 22, so for the next few hours that we were in his company, I made sure she was nowhere near him. Call it women protecting women, which is what we have to do even when we're trying to have a nice holiday. I remember my reflections that night: "you can't do that, you can't touch me. I'm going to sue the company." I deleted the group photo, and the rest of the photos are of me having a great time. This was the first time I felt the fury at males deciding they are entitled to do what they liked to any woman at any time. Firstly, there was the grabbing of my ass, absolutely not normal behaviour for a complete stranger, and then the question arose: how many more women had he done this to? Two weeks earlier, Taylor had sung a song with me in the stadium with a title strangely relevant for this scenario, "This is Why We Can't Have Nice Things." Why am I telling you this?

From August 7 to August 14, 2017, a year before my holiday, Taylor Swift spent time in a Denver, Colorado, district court room. These events were five years in the making. On the Denver stop of the *Red* Tour on June 2, 2013, Taylor attended a pre-show meet and greet organised by local commercial radio station KYGO. David Mueller was a radio DJ who posed for a photo with Taylor and his then-girlfriend. Taylor reported that Mueller's hand went under her skirt and grabbed her buttocks.

In 2017, TIME recognised her as one of the Silence Breakers who inspired women to speak out about harassment in their 'Person of the Year' issue published on December 6, 2017, where she recalled,

> In 2013, I met a DJ from a prominent country radio station in one of my pre-show meet and greets. When we were posing for the photo, he stuck his hand up my dress and grabbed onto my ass cheek. I squirmed and lurched sideways to get away from him, but he wouldn't let go. At the time, I was headlining a major arena tour, and there were a number of people in the room that saw this plus a photo of it happening. I figured that if he would be brazen enough to assault me under these risky circumstances and high stakes, imagine what he might do to a vulnerable, young artist if given the chance. It was important to report the incident to his radio station because I felt like they needed to know. The radio station conducted its own investigation and fired him. Two years later, he sued me.

Immediately following the photograph incident, Taylor reported it to her mother, tour manager, the photographer and her security team, and Mueller was escorted away from the concert. In September 2015, he sued Taylor for defamation, stating, "The contention that Mr Mueller lifted up Ms Swift's skirt and grabbed her bottom, while standing with his girlfriend, in front of Ms Swift's photographer and Ms Swift's highly trained security personnel, during a company-sponsored VIP backstage meet-and-greet, is nonsense, particularly given that Ms Swift's skirt is in place and is not being lifted by Mr Mueller's hand in the photograph." He acknowledged that Taylor had been assaulted but blamed a different employee, claiming it was a case of mistaken identity. Kim Kardashian wouldn't be the first person to call Taylor a liar. In October, Taylor filed a countersuit for battery and assault, naming Mueller as the individual and stating that she was completely aware of the person's identity. She also necessitated a jury trial, with the arrangement being that she would donate any money won from the trial to charitable organisations that protect women from sexual assault and other gendered violence. Before the trial began, Mueller was sanctioned for destroying key evidence, provided only edited audios from phone conversations, claiming the full files had been damaged, lost or thrown out. August 7 was the first day, where jurors were questioned over their objectivity and asked if they had been inappropriately groped or accused of misconduct themselves. The chosen jury was six women and two men.

August 10 was Taylor's time on the witness stand, the day after her mother Andrea gave evidence. Taylor told Eliana Dockterman, writing for TIME, "My mom was so upset after her cross-examination, she was physically too ill to come to court the day I was on the stand. I was angry." When she testified, Taylor was questioned by Mueller's attorney about how she felt about his client's job loss. "I didn't have a reaction to a strange person I didn't know losing his job…I'm not going to let you, or your client make me feel in any way that this is my fault. Here we are years later, and I'm being blamed for the unfortunate events of his life that are the product of his decisions – not mine." If you were to take away one thing from this court reporting it would be this quote. Some victims of sexual harassment are often made to feel responsible for the fallout on the part of the perpetrator, and often this mental game-playing, and emotional manipulation is enough to stop people coming forward. Taylor said,

> Even though awareness is higher than ever about workplace sexual harassment, there are still so many people who feel victimised, afraid and silenced by their abusers and circumstances. When the jury found in my favor, the man who sexually assaulted me was court-ordered to give me a symbolic one dollar. To this day he has not paid me that dollar, and I think that act of defiance is symbolic in itself… I'm told it was the most amount of times the word 'ass' has ever been said in Colorado Federal Court.

The sexual assault trial was heavily covered in the media, and this would have been extremely traumatic, regardless of the fact she's one of the most internationally renowned musicians on the planet. She told TIME,

> People have been largely very supportive of my story since the trial began in August, but before that, I spent two years reading headlines referring to it as 'The Taylor Swift Butt Grab Case' with internet trolls making a joke about what happened to me. The details were all skewed, as they often are. Most people thought I was suing him. There was an audible gasp in the courtroom when I was named as the defendant.

Taylor's *reputation* Stadium Tour was in Tampa, Florida on August 14, 2018, a week before my twenty-third birthday. Three quarters of the way through her show, she addressed the crowd while playing piano chords fans recognised as "Clean" and "New Year's Day." She visibly struggles with words, you can see tears in her eyes, and her voice breaks a few times. When she started singing "Clean," she stopped for a moment, and the fans kept singing for her.

> This exact day a year ago, I was not playing a sold-out stadium in Tampa, I was in a court room in Denver, Colorado. Honestly, I was there for a sexual assault case and this day a year ago was the day the jury sided in my favour and said that they believed me. I guess I just think about the people that weren't believed and the people that haven't been believed or the people who are afraid to speak up because they're afraid they won't be believed. I wanted to say I'm sorry to anyone who wasn't believed...because I don't know what turn my life would have taken if people didn't believe me when I said that something had happened to me. I know that we have so so so much further to go, and

> I am so grateful to you guys for being there for me for what was a really horrible part of my life...

I echo Taylor's thoughts about anyone who feels frightened about vocalising their experiences. It is absolutely terrifying. Speaking about my experience with sexual assault isn't hard for me to write about because writing is easier than talking. Every time I do either, though, the anger and fire quickly come up to the surface and it makes my fingers shake typing on the keyboard. Nobody wants to remember. I think about the little impacts; even when my trauma seems small, I know that it isn't and that maybe, just maybe, it will make someone else brave enough to speak up if something happens (and I hope it doesn't, but the state of society right now says it will) happens. Every woman has had unwanted attention given to them in different forms (a man indecently exposed himself to me in a public swimming spot on another holiday in front of my mum when I was ten). Trust me when I say I believe you. I know what happened to you was wrong and I believe you, and I know you will be immeasurably brave when and if you decide to speak out.

The album itself spends a great deal of time reclaiming lost power, rewriting narratives and presenting a new side to Taylor. There is a shift in her personal brand too, where building steadily to 2017, people were sick of the girl-clique-famous-friends aesthetic and used the phrase "annoying skinny beautiful blonde pop star" a lot. Though the language is damaging, Taylor still desperately tried to be what her fans wanted. Being almost a decade into her career now, *reputation* was an era of understanding that she wasn't making music just for her fans anymore; it was necessary to make something for herself. Fans I have come across on the internet and in person have told me that this album has some of the best music she has made so far in her career. She started to move in a way that wasn't influenced by the environment anymore. She was the influence. Between being cancelled on the internet and interrogated on the stand to then embarking on the biggest tour of her career, a lot of people definitely expected her to fall and not get up. She wasn't nominated for any Grammys for *reputation*, and initially thought this was as a debilitating failure, but having won the highest honour for her previous album and having achieved the feeling of industry acceptance, she knew her fans would follow her artmaking regardless of her accolades. Songs like "Call it What You Want" evoke a blasé attitude to love, "End Game" is a fun song, "Getaway Car" is a heartbreaker but a dance song nonetheless and "Dress" is seductive and incredibly adult in its themes, very much not PG, showing her transition into adulthood. On May 8, 2018, the opening night of the *reputation* Stadium Tour, Taylor addressed the crowd.

> So, you might be wondering why there are so many snakes everywhere, huh? Well, the reason is that a couple of years ago, someone called me a snake on social media, and it caught on, and then a lot of people were calling me a lot of things on social media, and I went through some really low times for a while because of it. I went through some times when I didn't know if I was gonna get to do this anymore. And I guess the snakes – I wanted to send a message to you guys that if someone uses name-calling to bully you on social media, and even if a lot of people jump on board with it, that doesn't have to defeat you, it can strengthen you instead.
>
> And I think that something that came out of it that was good is that I learned a really important lesson that I've been telling you from the stage for about 10 years, but I never had to learn it so harshly myself, and that lesson has to do with how much you value your reputation. And I think that the lesson is that you shouldn't care so much if you feel misunderstood by a lot of people who don't know you.

As long as you feel understood by the people who do know you, the people who will show up for you. The people who see you as a human being. So thank you for taking the time to get to know me, for sticking up for me, for seeing me as a human being. That's you, you did that for me.

Taylor teaches me lessons about myself all the time. The greatest of these is about friendships, who to keep close, who to say goodbye to and who to love the longest. You're about to learn about something that happened to one of the greatest people in my life.

Bec's Rep Room Meet and Greet, November 6, 2018.
The *reputation* tour was Taylor's first all-stadium tour, running for 53 shows, opening in the US, playing six shows in the UK before returning to the US and Canada, then travelling to Australia, New Zealand and concluding in Japan. Compared to the previous tour, it was much smaller (mainly because of the larger stadium sizes). The 1989 tour had 85 shows, but the revenue for *reputation* was a staggering $420 million USD. My friend Bec, from the *Fearless* chapter, has always been with me on the ultimate Swiftie journey. Because she lives in Canada now, through a series of excellently summarised voice notes, she recalled her surreal experience at Brisbane's Rep Room meet-and-greet with her friends Laura and Danny.

As it happens, those of us who get to meet or see Taylor in special circumstances will often shift the way we think about the corresponding music. Rebecca said to me, "I definitely love Rep more because of seeing it live. Seeing it live changed the album for me. I liked it, but seeing the tour made it make sense. It was so iconic, and it made it my favourite Taylor era, not necessarily my favourite album." Taylor's second leg of US dates for the tour ran through the summer, and Rebecca was there travelling when I was across the Atlantic, in Europe at the same time.

"Our Rep tour itinerary was kind of crazy, the first show we went to was in Pittsburgh, Pennsylvania [Taylor was born in West Reading, PA] so we had planned a ten-week American trip and Taylor announced her tour during our trip and we formed and planned our trip to make sure we were in Nashville at the same time as her concert. But we thought, 'only ONE show, we can't do that,' so we saw a gap in our schedule when we were in Chicago, and she was playing Pittsburgh on 7 August, now for most people that's not what you call close, but for us, an eight-hour drive? That's close. So we booked tickets, hired a car for two days, drove there from Chicago and then checked into a motel, went straight to the concert. The first-time we saw Rep, we had floor seats, went back to the motel and then the next morning had to drive back to Chicago to catch our flight."

"And then, we went to the Nashville show, on August 25, which was still one of the best shows, ever ever, the whole city shut down, it was amazing. People from all over the world were there, and everyone staying in our hostel was there for Taylor, and there was other Australians and it was so much fun, and all of these tickets we literally bought on the day off on StubHub because we were not prepared, and we were actually on the show for every single Rep show, because back then it didn't cost me an arm and a leg, I thought it did but compared to now, no."

As is standard procedure with our friendship, I followed Rebecca's lead with the insane organisation needed for prioritising buying Taylor tickets. When the tour went on sale, I planned a European holiday to mark the end of my university studies and I had a Swiftie friend, Maggie, living in London at the time so we decided to buy Wembley tickets together. I hadn't even bought my flights yet. The Wembley show I attended would be only her second at the iconic venue (the night before was her first) and to this day my dad still sends me Instagram Reels of her singing "Angels" with Robbie

Williams. "Yeah, Dad I was there I remember." As fate would have it, the Australian dates would make my decision as to when I was coming back home, so I landed in Sydney on October 25, and saw the same show as Rebecca at Accor Stadium on November 2. Seeing one of your best friends in a crowd full of Swifties is a beautiful feeling. Rebecca says, "I had only initially bought Sydney dates when they went on sale, but I knew I would do the whole tour. I distinctly remember we were in Utah, visiting Danny and we were together for one night in a hotel and me, Laura and Danny decided that we needed to go to a show together again, because we were all going to Sydney, but we needed another one, so we bought Brisbane tickets that night."

"Then it was the Australian Tour, Melbourne was first on October 26, so I flew by myself and thought, 'I'll figure it out' and Leah, another friend lived in Melbourne so I went with her, and we were desperately scouring Facebook Marketplace for tickets, and found good floor tickets, as always last minute, and then I flew to back to Sydney [for the show on November]. And that night there were six of us together and it was a full rain show, it was the best. And that's where we wore our outfits for the first time and we made the outfits, all six of us for Sydney, which was our team jerseys, so because there was so many of us, so we thought 'let's go as a little team' and we had snakes printed on it and we had numbers on the back and it said swifties, and they were green, and it was uni-sex. We had signs that said, 'Ready for IT?' and 'Let the GAMES BEGIN.' So that was our sports-themed costume vibe."

When I tell other friends my friend met Taylor at the Rep Room meet and greet, it doesn't feel quite real and the minute it happened, I cried because of how proud I was and the journey she'd been on. I know she would agree when I say that to gaze your eyes upwards to a singing crowd of nearly 73,000 and realise that you've been on this rollercoaster since *Fearless* is an emotional ride.

"At this point, we had all loved Taylor for so long, and we have always wanted to get invited to the Rep Room. Dead set, on the *Fearless* Tour [her first show], I thought, 'Of course I'm going to get picked with my little dress and my sign in section one hundred.' I never thought about it much, but the Rep Tour it was such a big deal, it felt really possible, people I knew in Australia were getting picked and you knew that it was a thing that happened, back in the day, it wasn't as huge. Some of our friends got picked in Sydney, some got picked in Melbourne, so we just wanted to see Taylor, but we felt we deserved this, and we wanted this forever, so we thought this is OUR TIME."

"When we booked Brisbane tickets, I said to them, if we ever are going to get Rep Room it's going to be the three of us, this is going to be the show. So we didn't get picked for Melbourne and Sydney but then we went to Brisbane, we flew in that morning, we all got ready and I don't know, we just had a feeling, and I said aloud, 'if it's going to be any show, it's going to be THIS show' and we were determined."

"This is our last show anyway, so we were dressed in our little sports outfits again, and we had our seats and they were on the aisle at the very back section of the floor, it was really close to the b-stage and we walked around, we got there early and talked to all our friends and everyone, and then when the openers came out Broods and then Charlie XCX, we did not sit down for one second. We were jumping and going crazy, just losing our minds. And then Taylor comes on, and literally the second song of her show...Danny got a tap on his shoulder and then he grabbed me, and I turned around and it was just Andrea, Taylor's mum, standing there and I just went speechless."

"That moment is seriously incomprehensible, I feel like I blacked out, it's just one of those things, I have read hundreds and thousands of everyone's story of ever getting backstage things and everyone always says the same thing, and Andrea approached me and this happened, so in my head you know how it's going to happen. But when it actually happens to you, WHAT?! You're speechless, ugh I literally can't…I remember she walked up and we were just grabbing each other and she said, 'Hey guys, oh you look familiar, have you ever met Taylor before?' And we were like, 'no no no we've been to so many shows, five shows each for Rep tour but we've never met her,' and she said, 'Oh well would you like to?' and we said 'YES! We would!' and she hands us all the little Rep room slip [they were fluoro green] and I literally fell onto the floor, collapsed crying, and second song in it was insane and we were the first people that night to be picked for rep room, I think she walked out of a back tunnel or the back of the stadium and like b-lined straight to us, and it's like a fever dream, that moment was genuinely the best moment."

"I can barely remember that show [in Brisbane], thank God I'd been to four others. I genuinely blacked out for the whole show, it was amazing. Then she came to the B-stage for that show, and we were front row for the B-stage, it was so good. It was crazy because the tickets we had weren't even that expensive as well, we bought them months and months later off Ticketek, they were just sitting there. So we watched the whole concert and then at the very end you get give the section to go to, so we went there so we go there and there was 30 of us all up, they [Taylor Nation] comes around to take your contact details and your Facebook and everything, Twitter, so they can keep a log, so you can't lie and try and meet Taylor again and make sure you can't meet Taylor again. Then we got led backstage through the tunnels and elevators, and then we entered the Rep Room."

"It was all decked out, they had the throne, and posters everywhere. We got to chill in there for honestly, quite a while, maybe a half hour to an hour, everything was a blur. Then Andrea came around and took pictures and was talking with all of us and she even came up to us and she said, 'My first ones!! Oh my god it was so funny sneaking up on you guys, you had no idea!' (the shock was literally a jump scare.) We said, 'Ah that's us!' That was really cute. They had Polaroids in there, I think that's how we got all of our pictures, so you would just take pictures with the props and with Andrea on a Polaroid that we got given and then we all got told to line up in our groups of friends and go in one-by-one to meet Taylor."

"She actually came out to the room saying 'Hi everyone! We're gonna get the little kids in first. Can't wait to meet you in there.' Because I'm pretty sure it was a Tuesday night…so we didn't leave until well after midnight, and we all lined up just waiting and then we walked in and she gives us all a hug, and I die. The first thing she said to us was, 'do you wanna pass me the Polaroids?' then she looks down at our jerseys and said, 'Oh my God, I LOVE THESE' Danny said that they were going for a stadium/sport theme and Taylor's reply was, 'The snakes I love it!' Danny mentioned that he designed them, and she said, 'Oh my god, you're a wardrobe designer.' We mentioned to her that they get pretty gross after seven shows, and she said, 'Wait 7?!' We told her we went to Nashville and then drove from Chicago and went to Pittsburgh. Danny said to her Louisville was so hot, and she said, 'It was STIFLING. I thought I was going to get heatstroke.' Then we asked her if she liked the rain show in Sydney, and we had noticed her blow her nose on stage that night, and she said, 'Yeah, I loved it. I got a cold from it.'"

"We told her this was our last show and Taylor said, 'No way, it was meant to happen then you meeting me. So, you guys deserve a photo now,' so we took a photo, and then we finally said, right at the end of the conversation, 'Oh, our names are Bec, Laura and

Danny,' (and Taylor said, 'oh my name's Taylor' – as if we didn't already know!) We told her, 'we've had the best time on this tour, this made our year, we are so excited for the next tour.' Which nobody knew wouldn't be for another five years...Taylor's parting words to the three of them would be, 'I'm so glad I got to meet you guys, get home safe'...Then we all hugged again, and I remember walking out, and we were all so chill, then we walked out and we all just started crying. It is still crazy that I can't even believe that it happened."

What emerges from these incredibly detailed and documented conversations is the normality of it all: talking about clothes, weather extremes, getting a cold and dancing in the rain (fans know Taylor loves rain shows). Taylor shows an unending level of kindness to her fans, Rebecca, Danny, and Laura who have dedicated endless amounts of money, hours listening and dissecting music, organised holidays, weekends and hours making costumes because of their love for her and her music. The true gift is her selflessness and her sharing a small moment in time to show that she is genuinely grateful. The Rep tour would be her last until The Eras Tour in 2022 (but we didn't know that at the time), so perhaps that is why it has sent shockwaves through culture; the absence of a Taylor show is felt, and fans demand her to continue her reign as queen in the musical kingdom. Bec says this about the distinction between Taylor and other artists.

"I think Taylor concerts are so different to other concerts where there is no atmosphere, energy like it is just another level. The way that everyone dresses up, to the lyrics, and to Eras, and that's been happening since Fearless that I've been dressing up for Taylor concerts, it is such a different level. Obviously, the friendship bracelets have come into it this year, too. So, I think that's the main difference; how involved everyone gets, how much time people put into it, and then when you're there, you never hear anything so loud, or where crowds know every lyric so intensely, and never had people cry so much. I think the only comparable recently is Harry Styles in terms of the dressing up creating an atmosphere like that, but – Taylor does it the best."

"I genuinely think Taylor Swift is going to go down as one of the biggest artists of all time. Like already to me, you think of this generation; it's her. You're going to think Elvis, you think The Beatles, you think Michael Jackson, Taylor Swift. That is factual. She's the one person that every single person knows, she's the definition of a household name. She's now the first billionaire to ever be one from music alone, the Spotify stats are insane that I've been seeing lately, when you even compare her to any other female artist, it's not even the same league. I think her music will play forever, and people will listen to her always."

Before Rebecca's Brisbane concert, I saw her in Sydney in the crowd on 2 November, and it was a rain show. The significance in the fandom community with rain shows is that Taylor loves them. She has made it known on social media videos that she loves rain shows. So, after watching countless videos of her singing in the rain, it was surreal to be in one in real life. The weather doesn't stop her from performing, and she enjoys it arguably more than her other shows. I attended the show with my then-eight-year-old twin cousins, Olive and Amelia, because after some ticket troubles, I was left with two tickets.

The first thing Amelia remembers about the concert was that it was a surprise. "I didn't know what we were doing really because we got picked up from school early, and you [me, Caitlin] were in the car. Mum told us we were driving to Sydney for the concert, and I didn't immediately realise we were going inside. We sang all the reputation songs all the way on the drive."

"We all had dinner and then drew 13 on our hands, then we bought t-shirts and put them on straight away. When we went inside the stadium, I thought our seats would be high up in the stands and I didn't realise we would be so close and on the floor. Before the concert started, there was a big thunderstorm, and because we were only eight at the time, it was pretty scary. There was no undercover, and so we got soaked. The security guards saw us and gave us guitar picks which was really cool, and then everyone around us was talking to us and friendly too. When the concert started, and the rain stopped, of course, we loved it. After we got home from the show, our friends gave us their VIP boxes that they didn't want, so we were able to relive the show over and over again."

"I had been so worried that the two little girls weren't going to enjoy the concert as much because their mum couldn't come with us. I couldn't have been more wrong. I remember being inside the stadium looking into their big trusting eyes saying, 'Don't worry the rain will stop very soon and then we're going to have a dance with Taylor, because she loves dancing when it's raining – so we're going to have a good time.' Olive remembers the big moment of doing something independently with her big cousin at such a young age."

"I think because I was little and used to being with my mum, I loved the fact it was just us three girls. When Taylor came out on stage, I remember the cheers all across the arena and the echoing of sound through the stands. I just remember the warm embrace of my cousin, trying to comfort me but tears were pouring down my face mostly from joy and only a little bit because I was scared of the storm. All the glitter was running down my face and the number 13 on my fist was glowing from the wristbands. When the show started, I sang till my voice was cracking. The whole concert I was full of emotions, but since that night I haven't felt like that again. I can't describe it, it was just amazing. I still carry the free guitar pick from that night in my phone, that concert was the best one by far I have been to."

For the duration of the show, my cousin Claudia (Olive and Amelia's mum), waited outside ANZ Stadium in the pouring rain just in case the girls got scared and wanted to go out. But they didn't, so she deserved Mum of the Year for her sacrifice, and the four of us will always retell this story.

If Taylor was the artist for young girls when I was Olive and Amelia's age, then Olivia Rodrigo is coming hot through the ranks for teenagers now. She won Best New Artist and Best Pop Vocal Album at the Grammys in 2022, and her career path is similar to Sabrina Carpenter's. Each had their stardom built from featuring in a Disney Channel TV series. When I first heard the raw feeling that emanated out of *Guts* (2023), I felt immediate furious validation because Olivia encourages her young audiences to not stand for the behaviour of teenage boys who have a special way of breaking hearts. It seems that male behaviour has become more complex and manipulative than when I was in high school. She, like Taylor, is an outstanding promoter of the opinion that anger is an appropriate response to being wronged, and there is now space in music and culture that allows women to be angry but not "hysterical" as the sexist tradition had previously stood.

Olivia's song "1 step forward 3 steps back" from *Sour* (2021) uses the same piano chord progression as *reputation*'s "News Years Day." Jack Antonoff and Taylor are credited as songwriters because of the interpolation (portions of an unchanged melody – often with changed lyrics) throughout Olivia's song. This is common in the music industry (think Rihanna/Michael Jackson and Madonna/ABBA). This musical referencing is a clear indicator of Taylor's influence on younger generations of female pop stars, but in a way that is taking her perfect recipe for diary-entry storytelling and repurposing it. In this way, she nurtures their rise into the spotlight. In the same way, genius recognising genius, Taylor uses interpolation from Right Said Fred's 1991 song, "I'm Too Sexy," in the chorus of "Look What You Made Me Do."

There are fan conspiracy theories galore about Taylor's musical inferences, potential release dates, easter eggs, inspirations and lyrical connections and *reputation* and *Lover* are perhaps the most well-known for these subtleties. One area that hasn't been analysed enough in depth is Taylor's relationship with her best friend, Selena Gomez (if there are any original *Wizards of Waverly Place* fans out there, hello) and *why* they haven't released a song together. I need *answers*. They have performed on stage together only twice; on the 1989 and *rep* tours, so a collaboration makes sense. Actually, at this point, I demand it. With 429 million, Selena is third behind footballers Lionel Messi and Cristiano Ronaldo for most followers on Instagram. Theirs is a long-lasting friendship. Taylor met and became comrades in (linked) arms when they were each dating a Jonas Brother in 2008. My brother bought me the *reputation* picture disc vinyl for Christmas, and that is truly one of the best presents he has given me besides, you know, being alive. At the time of writing, *reputation* is the second-to-last, if theories are correct, yet to be released of the re-recorded albums.

I have always told whoever wanted to listen maybe my only original Taylor theory: I can *hear* Selena Gomez counting in Taylor on *reputation*'s Track 7, "So It Goes…" At the very least, I know I'm not the only one hoping for a Selena Gomez feature at some point, and I would very much like it to be on *reputation (Taylor's Version)*. If I could rub a magic lamp and ask the blonde lyrical genius three questions, they all, for some reason, relate to the *reputation* album. The first would be: is Selena counting? The second would be: who is the Taylor who is spray-painting on the plane at the end of the "Look What You Made Me Do" music video, and what does she mean? And lastly: was she watching a particular 1997 disaster epic while writing "Dancing With Our Hands Tied?" Because, blondie, the bridge's lyrics are just Kate and Leo trying to escape the icy water. There are subtle references to this: the lights going out, rooms burning down and water rushing in. The dancing scene in Titanic is what Rose and Jack hold onto despite the fear that they are going to be separated. Who's tied to the boat as it's sinking? Jack is. All this talk of frozen love, lockets and dancing? That's a movie kind of love.

Another poem featured in the reputation album magazine booklets is called "Why She Disappeared." It was featured as a visual presentation every night on the screens of the reputation Stadium Tour, as a prelude to her song "Getaway Car." The last lines are, "Without your past, you could never have arrived- so wondrously and brutally, By design or some violent, exquisite happenstance… here." This sentiment is a thread we can trace through the decades of Taylor's discography. I would argue it could not be more relevant to the reputation era and the events that led to this album's creation. Not included in the short tour video is the last line, "And in the death of her reputation, she felt truly alive." Hitting the reset button happened in 1989 with her genre shift; it happened again with this album and, as usual, Taylor knew what she was doing. We all just got to watch.

Taylor's re-recordings 2019 –

"If something says in parentheses (Taylor's Version) that means I own it."

This chapter sits alongside the Kanyegate chapter as an explainer of moments in Taylor's history that are low points in her career. They are possibly the most scrutinised, high-profile news stories with her name on them and have been made into the punch lines of jokes in attempts to discredit her success or undercut her significance in pop culture. Put simply, it's about a woman being taken advantage of in a broken system. Taylor's focus on songwriting, raw and reflective in this period, showed the world that here was a woman reclaiming her power and what is rightfully hers. Many of the quotes from this chapter are directly Taylor's, posted online in desperation to help her fans (and the media) better understand what was going on. Critics of Taylor say that the endeavour of re-recording six albums was nothing more than a money grab. For Taylor, it was about exposing the greed of large corporations in the music industry, opening up a conversation about integrity, and giving artists the right to own their work.

Some definitions are helpful in understanding the importance of the debate over Taylor's music. Firstly, the distinction between musical copyrights. In US music copyright law, there are two separate copyrights: the master, which is the first recording of the music, and from this master, copies are made for sales and distribution. The owner of the master owns the copyright to all forms of it: digital, streaming and physical (CDs and vinyl sales). Reproduction of such a recording requires obtaining a licence from the master owner. For her first six albums, Taylor Swift did not own her original masters; Big Machine Records did. The second copyright belongs to the song and composition, and owning this is referred to as a publishing right. Publishers of music are the songwriters. This covers all lyrical elements and melodies, sheet music and instrumental arrangements. It is imperative to note that had Taylor *not* been credited as a songwriter on every song since her debut album, she would not have been able to re-record her musical catalogue. Beginning in 2021, Taylor has re-recorded four out of the six albums, and they are stylised with parentheses to differentiate between the old and new. In order of release, they are *Fearless (Taylor's Version)* and *Red (Taylor's Version)* came in 2021, followed by *Speak Now (Taylor's Version)* and *1989 (Taylor's Version)* in 2023. The last two, *reputation (Taylor's Version)* and her debut, *Taylor Swift (Taylor's Version)*, are yet to be announced. For the fans, the bad situation that Taylor found herself in was softened by some welcome news:

1. The knowledge that Taylor will eventually fully own her back catalogue, and Scooter Braun, at some point in the future will stop profiting off her music. As one person, it is often hard to feel like your individual actions will make a difference, but as a Swiftie, I understand that the accumulative streams of Taylor's back catalogue put money in the pockets of the wrong people. What the fandom has done, and I do, in the case of the two albums still left to become Taylor's Versions, is to listen to both of these albums in different ways that aren't the streaming services. I bought Taylor's debut on iTunes Music around the same time as I did for the original *Fearless* in 2008. Because there was only one original purchase of the album made for *reputation* in 2017 when I bought the CD, I can listen to those songs off Spotify without contributing to streaming sales. I know a lot of people who do this.

2. The vault tracks. The promise of new music was the incentive to swap from her original albums to the revitalised ones and a chance to listen to music I had listened to sixteen years ago the way the artist intended, by owning both the songwriting and masters' copyrights. When *Fearless (Taylor's Version)* came out, I, alongside many other fans, started a playlist for all

the new music, where the previously unreleased songs have additional parentheses (From the Vault) but shortened to just 'vault tracks.' This is our reward for allowing Taylor to re-record her music, hearing brand-new songs written at the same time as the older album but not making the final album cut. In this book, the vault tracks are discussed at the end of each album chapter. But after *Lover*, there is no mention of them because those albums are all under the Republic Records label, where a condition in her contract allowed her to own her future master's recordings *and* to re-record her old work.

In November 2018, Taylor ended her contract with Big Machine Records. She signed with them at 15 years old in 2005 and had been with them for 13 years. BMR was a new label when Taylor was signed, and in the years since, they have also represented country artists like Tim McGraw, Reba McIntire, Rascal Flatts, Sheryl Crow, Lady Antebellum, Florida Georgia Line, Sugarland and Martina McBride. Upon leaving, she was immediately signed with New York-based Republic Records and left behind the master recordings of her first six albums. Republic Records was founded in 1995 as an independent label acquired by Universal Music Group (UMG) in 2000. At present, other artists signed to Republic are Drake, Ariana Grande, Pearl Jam, Post Malone, The Weeknd, Nicki Minaj, The Jonas Brothers, Lorde, Florence + the Machine, Glass Animals, Noah Kahan, John Legend and more. On June 30, 2019, *The Wall Street Journal* broke the story of Big Machine Label Group's sale and full acquisition to Ithaca Holdings, LLC., a media company led by SB Projects Scooter Braun for $300 million USD. Braun has been a manager to celebrities for 25 years for performers like Demi Lovato, Ariana Grande, Justin Bieber, Kanye West and Tori Kelly. Braun's comments in the article were,

> I reached out to him [Scott Borchetta] when I saw an opportunity and, after many conversations, realised our visions were aligned. He's built a brilliant company full of iconic songs and artists. Who wouldn't want to be a part of that? By joining together, we will create more opportunities for artists than ever before by giving them the support and tools to go after whatever dreams they wish to pursue.

Scott Borchetta also weighed in. "Our artist-first spirit and combined roster of talent, executives, and assets is now a global force to be reckoned with. This is a very special day and the beginning of what is sure to be a fantastic partnership and historic run." Taylor, having left behind her master recordings to these men, posted a lengthy social media post, responding to the sale news on the same day.

> For years, I asked pleaded for a chance to own my work. Instead, I was given an opportunity to sign back up to Big Machine Records and 'earn' one album back at a time, one for every new one I turned in. I walked away because I knew once I signed that contract, Scott Borchetta would sell the label, thereby selling me and my future. I had to make the excruciating choice to leave behind my past. Music I wrote on my bedroom floor and videos I dreamed up and paid for from the money I earned playing in bars, then clubs, then arenas, then stadiums.
>
> Some fun facts about today's news: I learned about Scooter Braun's purchase of my masters as it was announced to the world. All I could think about was the incessant, manipulative bullying I've received at his hands for years.
>
> Like when Kim Kardashian orchestrated an illegally recorded snippet of a phone call to be leaked and then Scooter got his two clients together to bully me online

about it. Or when his client, Kanye West, organised a revenge porn music video which strips my body naked. Now Scooter has stripped me of my life's work, that I wasn't given an opportunity to buy. Essentially, my musical legacy is about to lie in the hands of someone who tried to dismantle it.

This is my worst-case scenario. This is what happens when you sign a deal at fifteen to someone for whom the term 'loyalty' is clearly just a contractual concept. And when that man says, 'Music has value,' he means its value is beholden to men who had no part in creating it.

When I left my masters in Scott's hands, I made peace with the fact that eventually he would sell them. Never in my worst nightmares did I imagine the buyer would be Scooter.

Any time Scott Borchetta has heard the words 'Scooter Braun' escape my lips, it was when I was either crying or trying not to. He knew what he was doing; they both did. Controlling a woman who didn't want to be associated with them. In perpetuity. That means forever.

Thankfully, I am now signed to a label that believes I should own anything I create. Thankfully, I left my past in Scott's hands and not my future. And hopefully, young artists or kids with musical dreams will read this and learn about how to better protect themselves in a negotiation. You deserve to own the art you make. I will always be proud of my past work. But for a healthier option, Lover will be out August 23. Sad and grossed out, Taylor

Justin Bieber weighed into this conversation on the same day, with Scooter Braun being his manager since 2008 and Raymond Braun

Media Group having him as their sole signed artist. He posted an Instagram post in response to Taylor's the same day (November 30) attached to a picture of them together almost a decade earlier. He does address the online bullying Taylor mentioned, "I would like to apologise for posting that hurtful instagram post, at the time i thought it was funny but looking back it was distasteful and insensitive," but circles back to questioning Taylor's motives. She is trying to help the public understand what is going on. Bieber writes,

> for you to take it to social media and get people to hate on scooter isn't fair. What were you trying to accomplish by posting that blog? seems to me like it was to get sympathy u also knew that in posting that your fans would go and bully scooter. Anyway, One thing i know is both scooter and i love you. I feel like the only way to resolve conflict is through communication. So banter back and fourth online i dont believe solves anything.

Scott Borchetta responded later in a blog post on Big Machine Label Group's website (again, on the same day, so this would have been a busy day for journalists). It is longer than Taylor's response and Justin's combined, but this section contradicts Taylor's feelings and stance her in terms of the news breaking.

> Out of courtesy, I personally texted Taylor at 9:06pm, Saturday, June 29th to inform her prior to the story breaking on the morning of Sunday, June 30th so she could hear it directly from me. I guess it might somehow be possible that her dad Scott, 13 Management lawyer Jay Schaudies (who represented Scott Swift on the shareholder calls) or 13 Management executive and Big Machine LLC shareholder Frank Bell (who was on the shareholder calls) didn't say anything to Taylor over the prior 5 days. I guess it's possible

that she might not have seen my text. But, I truly doubt that she "woke up to the news when everyone else did"...Taylor had every chance in the world to own not just her master recordings, but every video, photograph, everything associated to her career. She chose to leave. Scooter was never anything but positive about Taylor.

This is a lot to take in. The truth is, we will never know fully who exactly was lying or telling parts of the truth or their version of the truth. For the artist, the core of this issue and public argument is the sale and ownership of the masters. Added to the Instagram bullying, the two clients mentioned in the message came from a post of a FaceTime call that Justin Bieber screenshotted with Kanye and Scooter on August 2, 2016, with the caption: "Taylor swift what up." This is around the same time as the #taylorswiftisoverparty. The image is still up on his page, but the caption has been removed. Taylor highlighted this, circled Braun in the screengrab, and wrote, "This is Scooter Braun, bullying me on social media when I was at my lowest point. He's about to own all the music I've ever made.

It was alleged that Kelly Clarkson gave Taylor the idea to record her albums again with a tweet on July 13, 2019, that said, "@taylorswift13 just a thought, U should go in & re-record all the songs that U don't own the masters on exactly how U did them but put brand new art & some kind of incentive so fans will no longer buy the old versions. I'd buy all of the new versions just to prove a point." To this day, the tweet has 2.7,000 comments, 29,000 retweets, 153 likes and 2.7,000 saves. It is rumoured that Kelly gets flowers every time an album with (Taylor's Version) gets released.

In her November 2019 *Rolling Stone* interview with Brian Hiatt, Taylor reflects on the year's events of the sale, particularly her relationship with Scott Borchetta.

When you have a business relationship with someone for 15 years, there are going to be a lot of ups and a lot of downs. But I truly, legitimately thought he looked at me as the daughter he never had. And so even though we had a lot of really bad times and creative differences, I was going to hang my hat on the good stuff. I wanted to be friends with him. I thought I knew what betrayal felt like, but this stuff that happened with him was a redefinition of betrayal for me, just because it felt like it was family. To go from feeling like you're being looked at as a daughter to this grotesque feeling of 'Oh, I was actually his prized calf that he was fattening up to sell to the slaughterhouse that would pay the most.'

On Twitter, on 14 November 2019, five months after the news of the sale broke, Taylor faced another hurdle: the use and performance of her own music. Her post is a public plea for help from her fans. She is saying, "I don't know what else to do," and her message reads like this:

Guys – It's been announced recently that the American Music Awards will be honoring me with the artist of the Decade Award at this year's ceremony. I've been planning to perform a medley of my hits throughout the decade on the show. Scott Borchetta and Scooter Braun have now said that I'm not allowed to perform my old songs on television because they claim that would be re-recording my music before I'm allowed to next year.

Additionally – and this isn't the way I had planned on telling you this news – Netflix has created a documentary about my life for the past few years. Scott and Scooter have declined the use of my older music or performance footage for this project, even though there is no mention of either of them or Big Machine Records anywhere in the film.

Scott Borchetta told my team that they'll allow me to use my music only if I do these things: If I agree to not re-record copycat versions of my songs next year (which is something I'm both legally allowed to do and looking forward to) and also told my team that I need to stop talking about him and Scooter Braun.

I feel very strongly that sharing what is happening to me could change the awareness level for other artists and potentially help them avoid a similar fate. The message being sent to me is very clear. Basically, be a good little girl and shut up. Or you'll be punished. This is WRONG. Neither of these men had a hand in the writing of those songs. They did nothing to create the relationship I have with my fans. So this is where I'm asking for your help.

Please let Scott Borchetta and Scooter Braun know how you feel about this. Scooter also manages several artists who I really believe care about other artists and their work. Please ask them for help with this – I'm hoping that maybe they can talk some sense into the men who are exercising tyrannical control over someone who just wants to play the music she wrote. I'm especially asking for help from The Carlyle Group, who put up money for the sale of my music to these two men.

I just want to be able to perform MY OWN music. That's it. I've tried to work this out privately through my team but have not been able to resolve anything. Right now my performance at the AMA's, the Netflix documentary and any other recorded events I am planning to play until November of 2020 are a question mark. I love you guys and

I thought you should know what's been going on.

Big Machine Records ended up allowing Taylor to perform her songs at the AMAs, but in her acceptance speech for Artist of the Decade, there wasn't mention of the ownership situation unfolding; instead, she just thanked her fans. "All that matters to me is the memories that I have had with you, the fans over the years. We've had fun, incredible, exhilarating, extraordinary time together and may it continue. Thank you for being the reason why I am on this stage, from the very first day of my career until now, I love you with all of my heart." However, her speech accepting the award for Woman of the Decade at *Billboard*'s Women in Music event a month later on December 12 (the day before she turned thirty) was a different story. Her speech was long, but it was the first time she spoke in person about the master's dispute.

> Lately there's been a new shift that has affected me personally and that I feel is a potentially harmful force in our industry, and as your resident loud person, I feel the need to bring it up. And that is the unregulated world of private equity coming in and buying up our music as if it is real estate. As if it's an app or a shoe line. This just happened to me without my approval, consultation, or consent.
>
> After I was denied the chance to purchase my music outright, my entire catalog was sold to Scooter Braun's Ithaca Holdings in a deal that I'm told was funded by the Soros Family, 23 Capital, and the Carlyle Group. Yet to this day none of these investors have ever bothered to contact me or my team directly. To perform their due diligence on their investment. On their investment in me. To ask how I might feel about the new owner of my art. The music I wrote. The videos I created. Photos of me, my handwriting, my album designs. And of course, Scooter never contacted

me or my team to discuss it prior to the sale or even when it was announced.

I'm fairly certain he knew exactly how I would feel about it though. And let me just say that the definition of the toxic male privilege in our industry is people saying, 'But he's always been nice to me,' when I'm raising valid concerns about artists and their rights to own their music. And of course he's nice to you. If you're in this room, you have something he needs.

The fact is that private equity is what enabled this man to think, according to his own social media post, that he could buy me. But I'm obviously not going willingly. Yet the most amazing thing was to discover that it would be the women in our industry who would have my back and show me the most vocal support at one of the most difficult times, and I will never, ever forget it. Like, ever.

As we saw in earlier chapters, growing up in the media spotlight did not stop Taylor from using online social platforms. Instead, she found safe spaces to be with her fans, building her community and being a member of it at the same time. After her history with Myspace came Tumblr, where she told Jason Lipshutz, in the *Billboard Women in Music* cover issue released just prior to the speech above, "Tumblr is the last place on the internet where I feel like I can still make a joke because it feels small, like a neighborhood rather than an entire continent. We can kid around – they literally drag me. It's fun. That's a real comfort zone for me." Lipshutz calls her an ambassador, increasing public awareness about the realities of record deals. Taylor says,

> We have a long way to go. I think that we're working off of an antiquated contractual system. We're galloping toward a

> new industry but not thinking about recalibrating financial structures and compensation rates, taking care of producers and writers...I spent 10 years of my life trying rigorously to purchase my masters outright and was then denied that opportunity, and I just don't want that to happen to another artist if I can help it...Thankfully, there's power in writing your music. Every week, we get a dozen synch requests to use "Shake It Off" in some advertisement or "Blank Space" in some movie trailer, and we say no to every single one of them. And the reason I'm re-recording my music next year is because I do want my music to live on. I do want it to be in movies, I do want it to be in commercials. But I only want that if I own it.

A month later, with the release of the documentary, *Miss Americana*, the director of the film, Lana Wilson, spoke to *Variety* for their cover story and explained the lack of mention of the master's feud.

> What's not in the film is any mention of her other most famous nemeses — Scooter Braun and Scott Borchetta of Big Machine Records, with whom she's scrapped publicly for several months. "The Big Machine stuff happened pretty late in our process...we weren't that far from picture lock. But there's also not much to say that isn't publicly known. I feel like Taylor's put the story out there in her own words already, and it's been widely covered. I was interested in telling the story that hadn't been told before, that would be surprising and emotionally powerful to audiences, whether they were music industry people or not.

Talking on *Late Night With Seth Myers*, on November 14, 2021, when Taylor was promoting the second of her re-recordings, *Red (Taylor's Version)*, she gives us insight into the reasoning behind them.

I do feel the need to explain what I'm doing, because it's not normal. Basically, I've always wanted to own my own music, since I started making my music, and you probably don't know but most of your favourite artists do not own their work. The music industry is *shrugs*, you know? There was something that happened years ago, where I made it very clear that I wanted to be able to buy my music, that opportunity was not given to me, and it was sold to somebody else and so I figured, I was the one who made this music first, I can just make it again. So that's what we're doing. So, if something says, in parentheses (Taylor's Version) that means I own it, which is exciting.

It's also interesting to go back and re-live this nostalgia with fans who are the reason why I get to do this, this time around I get to do things that I know they wish I would have done the first time. Because I'm always listening and I'm always lurking, and I'm always listening to their opinions and their theories, and they will let me know which songs should have been singles, they let me know which songs did not get videos and should have gotten videos. I'm listening and I'm making the videos and I'm doing the things.

Seth responds with, "It's quite a clever loophole, Taylor." Reflecting on her statement and how old she was in 2021 (32, about to turn 33) I think it's important to note how young Taylor was in 2005 signing this record deal. She was 15, almost 16, and it was all she'd ever wanted; she worked hard for almost four years writing songs, playing covers, honing her craft, and this was her big break. She was naïve and didn't know what she was getting herself into, but maturity and trust often go together. We don't know the difference. Older, wiser individuals learn that not everyone is out to represent your best interests. In the midst of fights over ownership and the coronavirus pandemic in April 2020, before Taylor was allowed to re-record her work, Big Machine Records released *Live from Clear Channel Stripped 2008*, a live album of songs from Taylor's EP *Beautiful Eyes* and first two albums. It features eight of her songs, including hit singles, "Fearless," "Love Story," "Picture to Burn," and "Teardrops on My Guitar." Taylor posted on Instagram Stories on April 23,

> Hey guys – I want to thank my fans for making me aware that my former record label is putting out an "album" of live performances of mine tonight. This recording is from a 2008 radio show performance I did when I was 18. Big Machine has listed the date as a 2017 release but they're actually releasing it tonight at midnight. I'm always honest with you guys about this stuff so I just wanted to tell you that this release is not approved by me.
>
> It looks to me like Scooter Braun and his financial backers, 23 Capital, Alex Soros and the Soros family and The Carlyle Group have seen the latest balance sheets and realised that paying $330 MILLION for my music wasn't exactly a wise choice and they need money. In my opinion...Just another case of shameless greed in the time of Coronavirus. So tasteless, but very transparent.

According to Alpha Data, a music analytics firm, the album sold in total 33 units and 6,000 views on YouTube. The Taylor Swift Effect took a new form in protest, and it worked, which proves that her millions of fans understand the gravity of the situation.

As with anything in Taylor's life, if it evokes big feelings, she puts them into songs. The ambiguity in some of her lyrics is her secret power, like a superhero putting a mask back on. In her eighth album *folklore*, there are two songs where the lyrics are essential metaphors for the re-recording saga. Track 5, "my tears ricochet," makes reference to a funeral and the metaphorical death is the separation between her and the music that she created. In

Track 12, "Mad Woman," the lyrics echo Taylor's pain, seen through her social media posts, of being constantly gaslit and called a liar by powerful, wealthy men. Here, we see Taylor standing up to them, using the imagery of a scorpion. There's a sting in her tail and she's letting those men and the world know she's fighting back. The term "mad woman" can be interpreted two way: mentally ill or angry. In this song, there is no room for interpretation. She is angry and no amount of bullying will force her to back down (or become ill) as she makes her way back from a painful period with new determination.

These songs are layered with meaning, and in the Brian Hiatt interview prior to releasing *folklore*, Taylor speaks about her love of the HBO series *Game of Thrones* and her disappointment in the ending of the series, particularly with the character of Daenerys Targaryen, who endured a controversial and unwarranted fall from grace at the series' conclusion. Hailed as the Mother of the Dragons, it is easy to find references and associations with Taylor's lyrics referencing dragons and flames. In the *folklore: the long pond sessions* documentary, she talks with co-creator Aaron Dessner. Taylor's comments are pointed without naming names. It is easy to discern that she is talking about Scooter Braun.

> The first time I heard that piano thing you had written, I just felt like it's got these sort of ominous strings underneath it and I was like, oh this is a song about female rage. It has to be like, I have to figure out how to make this about female rage. And then I was thinking the most rage-provoking thing about being a female is the gaslighting, that happens when for centuries we've been just expected to absorb male behaviour silently, silent absorption of whatever any guy decides to do. And oftentimes, in our enlightened state and our emboldened state, we know respond to bad male behaviour or somebody just doing something that was absolutely out of line. That response is treated like the offense itself. There's been situations with recently,

> somebody who's very guilty of this in my life, and it's a person who makes me, or tries to make me feel like I'm the offender by having any kind of defence to his offences. 'Oh I have no right to respond, or I'm crazy, I have no right to respond, or I'm angry, I have no right to respond or I'm out of line.' So you providing me with that musical bed for me to make that point that I've been trying so hard to figure out, how do I say why this feels so bad.

On November 16, 2020, just a few weeks before she released *evermore*, Taylor posted these words in image screenshots to Twitter/X, commenting: "Been getting a lot of questions about the recent sale of my old masters. I hope this clears things up."

> I wanted to check in and update you guys. As you know, for the past year I've been actively trying to regain ownership of my master recordings. With that goal in mind, my team attempted to enter into negotiations with Scooter Braun. Scooter's team wanted me to sign an ironclad NDA stating I would never say another word about Scooter Braun unless it was positive, before we could even look at the financial records of BMLG (which is always the first step in a purchase of this nature).
>
> So, would have to sign a document that would silence me forever before I could even have a chance to bid on my own work. My legal team said that this is absolutely NOT normal, and they've never seen an NDA like this presented unless it was to silence an assault accuser by paying them off. He would never even quote my team a price. These master recordings were not for sale to me.
>
> A few weeks ago my team received a letter from a private equity company called Shamrock Holdings, letting us know

that they had bought 100% of my music, videos, and album art from Scooter Braun. This was the second time my music had been sold without my knowledge. The letter told me that they wanted to reach out before the sale to let me know, but that Scooter Braun had required that they make no contact with me or my team, or the deal would be off.

As soon as we started communication with Shamrock, I learned that under their terms Scooter Braun will continue to profit off my old musical catalog for many years. I was hopeful and open to the possibility of a partnership with Shamrock, but Scooter's participation is a non-starter for me.

I have recently begun re-recording my older music and it has already proven to be both exciting and creatively fulfilling. I have plenty of surprises in store. I want to thank you guys for supporting me through this ongoing saga, and I can't wait for you to hear what I've been dreaming up.

I love you guys and I'm just gonna keep cruising, as they say.
Taylor

PS: For transparency and clarification, I have included the letter of response I sent on October 28, 2020, to the private equity group who purchased my music.

The last paragraph of the letter, is this,

> I feel the need to be very transparent with you. I will be going forward with my original re-recording schedule and will be embarking on that effort soon. I know this will diminish the value of my old masters, but I hope you will understand that this is my only way of regaining the sense of pride I once had when hearing songs from my first six

albums and also allowing my fans to listen to those albums without feelings of guilt for benefiting Scooter. Sincerely. Taylor Swift

From a fan's perspective, these pieces of the puzzle are really important. The last sentence outlines what I said at the beginning of this chapter, that fans will find ways to listen to Taylor's music the way she would want to: understanding the injustices she faces in the industry is key to supporting her. With the premiere of her *Miss Americana* documentary, she participated in a Q&A at the Toronto International Film Festival alongside the CEO, Cameron Bailey. He described her process of re-recording as "an act of reclamation and creative empowerment."

There is no question that with the re-recordings comes an inevitable change in Taylor's vocal tones and the *sound* of the music. She is nearly ten years older, and her range and skill have improved. These are most obvious in *Fearless* and *Speak Now*, and the yet to be released *Taylor Swift (Taylor's Version)* because she was 16 when that album was released and possibly even 15 recording some of those songs. When talking to *People Magazine* about *Fearless (Taylor's Version)*, she said, "We really did go in and try to create a 'the same but better' version...We kept all the same parts that I initially dreamed up for these songs, but if there was any way that we could improve upon the sonic quality, we did."

I will be emotional when her long-awaited debut is re-released (rumoured to be the last of the six to come out after *reputation*) because those teenage vocals are unmatched in their uniqueness. With four re-recorded albums, there has only been one notable lyric change between re-released songs and their original counterparts. It is Track 10 from *Speak Now (Taylor's Version)* "Better Than Revenge." Fans speculated if she would change these lyrics before its release due to their sexist nature because of the insinuation that sexual exploits are something to be shamed and ridiculed for out of spite. The lyric change is simple but necessary, unfortunately I can't have direct lyrics in this book for legal reasons but it comes in the pre-chorus. The original 2012 lyrics reference to a woman being better known for her sexual exploits. In "Better Than Revenge (Taylor's Version)" the lyrics have been changed to reflect a strong woman who is "holding the matches," and in control.

Taylor has had her fair share of slut shaming, and with hindsight, she made a wise decision not to be a voice in the damaging conversation. She knows that pitting women against each other was once seen as entertainment, and in the 13 years since *Speak Now* was originally released, she gained a new understanding of just how damaging these kinds of brush-it-off-it-was-a-joke punch lines are. Taylor told Robin Roberts on *Good Morning America* on August 22, 2019, the day before *Lover*'s release, that she was legally allowed to record albums one through to five starting in November 2020. She said, "I'm very excited about it because I think that artists deserve to own their work. I feel very passionately about that." This does not include *reputation* because its release in 2017 means that there was a time restriction of five years past the original release of the album to recording the music again, so *reputation* could be legally re-recorded in 2022.

Every Swiftie knows that at the beginning of this master's ownership journey, Taylor was hurting. I say 'was' because she has moved past that pain in a way that brings her joy, releasing never-before-heard songs from the vault and re-experiencing album releases with her fans. I shudder to think that if things had been different, with no need to record old music again, we would not have received "All Too Well (10 Minute Version) (Taylor's Version) (From the Vault)." She's pleaded with us to support her, and we do, and gifted us with promised little surprises: new music videos and new songs. There are always good nuggets of gold to keep a hold of when you are knee-deep in mud or something smellier. These gold nuggets are undoubtedly the vault tracks, and throughout this book I have paired them with the album chapters they belong with. It has been a wonderful experience hearing the songs that almost made the first album cut come out into the open for the first time.

When the re-recorded albums starting with *Fearless (Taylor's Version)* were released, this also meant that after a few years of ownership disputes, Taylor's music could be licensed again for use in television and film. On IMDb, she has over 250 film soundtrack/television credits, but some of the special releases have come from shows that resonate with deeper meaning to her wider Swiftie fandom community. On December 2, 2020, Taylor tweeted, "Okay, so while my new re-records are NOT done, my friend @VancityReynolds asked me if he could use a snippet of one for a LOLsome commercial he wrote so...here's a sneak peak of Love Story! Working hard to get the music to you soon!!" It was filmed for Match.com by the Canadian production company Maximum Effort, whose business profile tagline says, "Maximum Effort makes movies, TV series, content, ads, and cocktails for the personal amusement of Hollywood Star Ryan Reynolds. We occasionally release them to the general public." We would have to wait until a few months later for "Love Story (Taylor's Version)" on February 12, 2021 – in time for Valentine's Day, and *Fearless (Taylor's Version)* on April 9, 2021. Over a year before *1989 (Taylor's Version)* was released, Track 8, "Bad Blood (Taylor's Version)," was used in the animation film *DC League of Super-Pets*, in addition to "Message In A Bottle (Taylor's Version) (From The Vault)" a vault track only released a year prior. This early licensing and permissions definitely had to do with her friendship with Dwayne 'The Rock' Johnson, the lead voice role in the film, having met him in 2011. In the past, he had worked as the voice of 'The Man' in "The Man" music video in 2019.

The Amazon Prime Video Series *The Summer I Turned Pretty* used five Taylor Swift songs in season one and nine in season two. The writer of the book series, Jenny Han, is also executive producer and writer of her YA novel trilogy adapted to the screen, and in a July 2023 episode of the podcast *Podcrushed*, she speaks about Taylor's influence on her writing and how she managed to feature "This Love (Taylor's Version)" from *1989 (Taylor's Version)* a full year before the album's release.

> As I was writing the first book, I was listening to *Fearless* [*The Summer I Turned Pretty* was published in May 2009, and *Fearless* was released in November 2008], and I almost dedicated the second book in the series to her when I needed to get into an emotional heightened place, I could just listen to her music. My readers are really big fans of hers, so I just thought it was the biggest gift I could give them, if I could get it.

In the podcast, Jenny Han says that she played Taylor Swift's music in the Amazon pitch meeting for the adaptation of her series because she "wanted to imprint it [Taylor's music] into their minds," and she wrote Taylor a personal letter. Two songs from *Speak Now (Taylor's Version)*, "Back To December (Taylor's Version)" and "Last Kiss (Taylor's Version)" were featured in the second series trailer and episodes only a week after the album's re-release, which was very special to both Swifties and fans of the show. *reputation (Taylor's Version)* does not have a release date as of this book's publication but Track 5, "Delicate (Taylor's Version)" was also used in season two, episode six of *The Summer I Turned Pretty* in August 2023. Han spoke to the *Los Angeles Times* about getting rights to the song. "It was a secret, even within Amazon," he said. "It was such a gift to be able to get it, and I am so appreciative and respectful of the show's relationship with Taylor Swift." Writing for *Vulture* in August 2023, Bella Arnold's article, "The Taylor Swiftification of *The Summer I Turned Pretty*," shows The Taylor Swift Effect on literature and YA television. Arnold writes,

> What sets *The Summer I Turned Pretty* apart from the other Swiftian TV soundtracks is how the writers use her songs to move the plot forward, as if Swift herself is a character on the show. Her presence as a pseudo-cast member is so apparent that almost every press interview prompted the show's stars to share their favorite Swift songs, determine

which songs best-fit couples on the show, or make a general attempt to connect the singer to the show.

The idea of Taylor as a character in the show is meta because it makes the characters relatable, and Arnold also writes, "Without Swift, *The Summer I Turned Pretty* could have been nothing new, but the pairing between Han's love story and Swift's fearless language turned the show into an enchanted affair that has captivated the hearts of girls all over the world."

The Amazon Prime Video Series *Wilderness*, released in 2023, features another *reputation (Taylor's Version)* unreleased track, "Look What You Made Me Do (Taylor's Version)" in the trailer released in July 2023, alongside the tagline, 'Look What He Made Her Do.' Continuing this treat for Swifties and cinephiles alike with other unreleased music, fans have been spoilt for teasers of what is to come in trailers and scenes of shows. This is an example of Taylor's generosity with her music, and, in some cases, she could not wait to share her reclaimed music with the world. When *Speak Now (Taylor's Version)* was released in July 2023, it felt special because all the tracks from that album were written solely by her. She said in the album booklet, "I always looked at this album as my album, and the lump in my throat expands to a quivering voice as I say this. Thanks to you, dear reader, it finally will be. I consider this music to be, along with your faith in me, the best thing that's ever been mine."

Let's move into a speculative and fun space that all Swifties inhabit: conspiracy-land. On May 25, 2020, two months before she would release *folklore*, Taylor posted a tweet that read, "VERY STOKED about this cover of lwymmd on @KillingEve by Jack leopards & the dolphin club!!" Episode seven of the third season of Killing Eve, features an unknown band covering Taylor's lead single from *reputation*, "Look What You Made Me Do." What follows is a case built by the internet, and I agree wholeheartedly with the Sherlock Holmes-like investigation that this was a deliberate play to allow the song to feature on television without handing any royalties to Big Machine Records amid the ongoing legal battle over copyright and masters ownership. Because Taylor holds the publishing copyright of the song, she can approve a licence when the song is covered by another band. This is where fans begin their excavation process. Much like the scheming we know Taylor is capable of, it was executed with medical precision. Spurred on by Taylor's Twitter mention, internet sleuths discovered that the band in question, Jack Leopards & The Dolphin Club, had no previous music on streaming sites and minimal social media presence, which was suspicious. Could the band have been intentionally created?

What is not hidden or obscured in any way is quite an obvious connection to Taylor Swift. Her brother Austin's Tumblr bio states the following. "AUSTIN KINGSLEY SWIFT/ACTOR/FILM PRODUCER/LEAD SINGER OF JACK LEOPARDS & THE DOLPHIN CLUB." A Twitter/X account @TSwiftNZ posted on the same day as Taylor's tweet in 2020, states that back in 2013, Austin Swift changed his Twitter username to "The Dolphin Club" and the image for it the single is a picture of a blonde boy, with his face blocked out wearing a t-shirt that says, "Dolphin Club."

The account only has three posts, all re-blogs of accounts sharing information about the new single; one is from @TSwiftNZ with a black and white image of Taylor, Austin and Jack Antonoff. Also discovered was that the cover image of the single with the young child is, in fact, Austin himself. Austin Swift. Nowadays, Austin is responsible for the synchronisation and distribution of Taylor's music, as well as being an actor himself. In February 2020, *The Daily Mail* reported that Taylor Swift "begged" her close friend Phoebe Waller-Bridge (at the time, lead writer on *Killing Eve*) to let her brother record a song for the soundtrack. It seems this was the song.

On the song credits, Jack Antonoff is credited as a producer on the track, as is Nils Sjöberg, which was a pseudonym previously used by Taylor as a songwriter for Calvin Harris' 2016 dance anthem, "This is What You Came For" featuring Rihanna. At the time of

Taylor's tweet, there were quite a few Tumblr posts discussing the fan theories that were 'liked' by Taylor herself that discuss fans, who are "connecting the dots." Currently, in Taylor's official merchandise store, a tote and bumbag, mug and notebook with the "Jack Leopard & The Dolphin Club" logo on the front are available to purchase in the reputation album section of Taylor's online store. We know she is smart; perhaps she fabricated an elaborate hoax of a band made purely for the usage of a song on a television show. It may be that she's given the calculated middle finger approach to the limiting of her own access to the material she created. A Tumblr account called @epiphany-in-exile had perhaps the most profound word to say on the matter of ownership and could put the conspiracy to bed once and for all. It says, "Here's the thing though...It's not a FAKE or NONEXISTENT band. It's an underCOVER band." There you have it folks, case closed.

After being signed to Republic Records, Taylor's music release schedule became manic, fitting in four re-releases in between four new albums in five years. Does the woman ever sleep? There are two exceptions to Taylor's timeline of album releases, a new album every two years. One is the almost three years between 1989 and reputation, and the second is the tiny space of eight months between the release of Lover and folklore. It is reasonable to conclude that the rhyme and reason behind this close space is to make sure there was an abundance of music licensed under Republic Records for fans to listen to while she was going through this painful change over. What do fans do while waiting for new Taylor music? Listen to older albums. She didn't want us to do that, so we had to have more music. While we were waiting for the re-recorded albums, we got folklore and evermore, and in between those dates, with military precision, between the re-recorded albums, we have Midnights and The Tortured Poets Department. My predictions for reputation (Taylor's Version) and Taylor Swift (Taylor's Version) I speculate, could be the beginning and the middle of 2025 (rounding out the numerology patter of having two albums released in 2021, two in 2023, and two in 2025). When that chapter of her life is over, I have no doubt she will conclude it with something special.

With her decision to re-record her music, others have followed in her footsteps. Republic Records exists as part of Universal Music Group (UMG), and when Olivia Rodrigo signed with Geffen Records, also part UMG, she also made owning her master's a condition of her contract and sighted Taylor's public battle as inspiration. She is not the only one. In 2022, Zara Larsson bought back her recording catalogue and created her own label, and in 2023, Dua Lipa also acquired her publishing rights from her old label. Writing for *The Guardian* in January 2024, Eamonn Forde calls this setting by example "Taylor-made." He says, "It is a power-play template for younger acts who are now rising up – especially female pop stars, historically among the most exploited figures in music – alert to the fact that owning their recordings and songwriting is everything."

> This recalibration of the rules of engagement between artists and labels is also a result of the democratisation of information about the byzantine world of music contract law. At the turn of the 2000s, music industry information was highly esoteric and typically confined to the pages of trade publications such as *Billboard*, *Music Week* and *Music & Copyright*…Today, industry issues are debated in mainstream media outlets and artists can use social media to air grievances or call out heinous deal terms.

Breakout British performer Raye split from her label, Polydor Records, after reports that they had been withholding her debut album, *My 21st Century Blues*, released independently in 2023. She won six out of her seven nominations at the BRIT Awards in March 2024 and broke the record for most awards to an artist in one night. In Forde's article, he discusses the historical injustices of artists being against their labels and that "artists today are more industry-literate and aware of the pitfalls and bear traps of the past, simply because they have to be." He refers to music legends like George Michael, Prince, Radiohead and U2. Both George Michael and Prince were forced to take legal action over being exploited. In Bono's memoir *Surrender* in 2022, he writes that the band's manager, Paul McGuinness, negotiated "with Island Records for U2 to take a lower advance and lower royalties [because] it meant that at the end of a period of time, we'd get back our rights and regain ownership of our recordings." I have no doubt that Taylor would have known about these events and has done her part to create what Forde called a "roadmap to the future" in terms of taking care of her work.

Like Kanyegate, the re-recordings are a recurring topic of conversation that sparks healthy debate and results in a new level of understanding about the complexities of the recording industry. It was a deliberate move on the part of Taylor and her team to make the music industry more transparent in terms of ownership, and what better way to do that than for one of the biggest artists on the planet to say, "Hey, what I have to do to make my music finally mine again…" We're ready for *reputation (Taylor's Version)* and *Taylor Swift (Taylor's Version)* when you are, Tay. Now, it is time to introduce you to Taylor's Republic Records era.

Lover era
2019 – 2020.

Heralding a return to romance.

A pink and white snake slithering along a rainbow brick road is how the "ME! (feat. Brendan Urie of Panic! At The Disco)" music video begins. Taylor's first single released after *reputation*. The snake prepares to strike and then turns into a flutter of pastel butterflies. Gone is the snake (an icon of accusations and eras past), and what better way to herald in a new, slightly less angry era than an animal renowned for personal metamorphosis. Think back to the crimson and browns 'fall' colour palette, the seasonal metaphors and intensity of emotions *Red* symbolised, and what some fans term as "sad girl autumn," to now, three albums later – the butterfly motif and every powder pink, baby blue and related pastel shade on the colour spectrum emerged from the Swiftian chrysalis. Her seventh album was hinted at when, on April 13, Taylor posted a single close-up photo of a bejewelled heart shape with the caption "4.26."

On her socials a countdown then appeared that advertised the date again on a background of pink fluffy clouds. On the Thursday beforehand, April 18, a suspect mural in the shape of a butterfly painted by Kelsey Montague appeared in the Gulch neighbourhood of Nashville. When fans began putting the puzzle pieces together that something might be happening, they flocked to the mural on the morning of April 26 and so did Taylor. She told the crowd, "You guys are amazing for figuring this out because no one knew we were coming, no one knew this was a part of the campaign and what we're doing." As it turns out, we absolutely did. The mural, removed later in 2019 for preservation, had 13 love hearts (she likes 13, remember?) and seven stars (seventh album), along with cats and a colour scheme matching the Instagram posts. We had a new single and music video.

When "ME!" came out, I said to my housemate, Chelsea, "I probably shouldn't be dancing around like this." I was walking around on crutches, and my right leg was in a moon boot because of a broken ankle. There would be a long road of recovery ahead, and my favourite singer shouting catchy hooks at me throughout. "Taylor would be proud of you," she replied. Taylor's duets are few and far between, so to have Brendan Urie from Panic! The Disco feature on a lead single meant Taylor was preparing us for a renewed sense of vibrancy in her songwriting. Co-produced by New Zealander Joel Little (who she had not worked with before), the single wasn't initially received well. Writing for The Independent, Alexandra Pollard wrote, "Taylor Swift has been so busy dropping hints, she's forgotten to write a good song," and The Ringer's Rob Harvilla wrote, "This song isn't terribly good, but it will likely bulldoze its way into your head regardless. You know the drill." And my personal favourite, in Spencer Kornhaber's article for The Atlantic titled "ME!' Is Everything Wrong With Pop," he wrote the song "has almost none of the elements that once made her interesting, but it does have a dolphin screech for a chorus."

In the same vein as "Shake It Off," this bubble-gum pop and synth track began life as a slow, acoustic piano ballad, and as long as it makes people dance (me and my broken ankle included), that is job done. The lyrics make it a priority to embrace your individuality and though a Barbiecore marching band can irritate some, Taylor knows that being yourself is the best brand. I dare you not to smile, or you may at least involuntarily tap your toes listening to it.

The album title and release date were all announced via an Instagram Live video on June 13, which would mean something different for me than other fans. It would also stand alone from previous records. Why? *Lover*'s birthday is the same as my own, August 23. As time zones would have it, it wouldn't be mine until 3 pm in Sydney, so I would spend the day with my father, have lunch with him and my best friend, visit a family member's house where I excused myself and ran to the bathroom to listen to the first four songs. Then, it was a stop at the music store on the way home to buy the CD and diary book. It was the soundtrack to me getting ready to have dinner. I still think about the time we were sitting in the Newtown dessert bar when "Cruel Summer" came over the speakers, and I turned to my friend Meg, who recognised the sheer insanity on my face and replied with, "Yes, Caitlin, we know it's Taylor Swift…" I laughed trying to remember the lyrics I'd heard earlier in the day. Happy twenty-fourth to me. May 1 was the first performance of the *Lover* era in Las Vegas for the *Billboard Music Awards*. It was a memorable entry back into public life with Taylor hovering above the audience in a Mary Poppins-esque umbrella chair with Brendan Urie. In the *Miss Americana* documentary, she described filming the music video as "It's not gonna be a small one…there's a parade down below and whatever makes you, you… you know, emo kids, theatre, dance sequences, *La La Land*, dancers, cats, gay pride, people with country western boots, I start riding a unicorn…everything that makes me, me. If you were to split open my imagination, what would come out of it?"

Lover would continue Taylor's impassioned past-time of filling her releases with an abundance of easter eggs (named because of their hidden nature, alluding to the search for clues in unexpected places and sending fans on a "hunt"), teasing fans with surprises hidden in music videos, clothes, and outfits. From her very first album she has left 'secret messages' in one form or another. For her first four albums, she used random capitalised letters in the song lyrics that spelled out phrases; additional information about who the song was about. At the back of this book, you will find the full list of secret lyric messages.

I would struggle to fit this information into a deluxe coffee table book detailing just the easter eggs for every announcement she's ever made from the beginning of her career. Taylor plays endless games with her fans. Sometimes, these messages appeared as callbacks too; the snake in the "ME!" music video moves in synchronisation with the snake that appeared after Taylor's socials went dark, just before *reputation* was released. She has sprinkled breadcrumbs across music videos and left secrets hidden in cryptic magazine answers to the point where now, in 2024, just about anything is perceived as suspect.

To this day, her hunger for leaving hints has not subsided. *Entertainment Weekly*'s cover story on May 9, 2019, was her most cluey interview to date. If you know an erudite Swiftie, inquiring about the words, "There were five holes in the fence," is sure to bring a smile to their face. At the beginning of 2019, Taylor's Instagram grid was slowly changing colour, becoming more and more pastel with brighter colours changing from the greyscale of the *reputation* era. The photos included palm trees, glittery jewellery, and a picture of Taylor staring at us through holes in a fence posted in February began to send fans into a tailspin.

All of these were indeed easter eggs alluding to the colour scheme of the album, but as to the significance of the fence holes, no such connections were made. On August 18, she posted the same photo she had posted in February of her looking through fence holes. It had the caption, "Okay, NOW there are five holes in the fence" which, to fans, alluded to the countdown; there were five days until her album release. This fuelled discussion and speculation that, in time, would prove certain fan theories untrue and has become an active verb known as 'clowning'. When fans are proved wrong after presenting a strong line of conspiracy, they look very much like a silly clown. *Entertainment Weekly*'s Alex Suskind wrote:

> THE PALM TREES ARRIVED IN FEBRUARY, seven in all, set against a pastel blue backdrop with superimposed stars. It appeared that a new Taylor Swift era was upon us — that the old happy-go-lucky Taylor was not, in fact, dead. Or did it? It *was* only an Instagram photo, just one more picture in an infinite content scroll. But it also came from a pop star known for prodigious hint-dropping, whose fans turn every piece of info into an online archaeological dig...As expected, the summery post sent Swifties sifting through each detail with a fine-tooth comb. What did the trees

symbolise? An overdue vacation? A recently purchased beach house? A secret palm-frond collection? Or maybe, as many surmised, it was new music.

For the most part, the fan theories were correct, just not in the way they would have thought.

> I posted that [the photo of the palm trees] the day that I finished the seventh album...I couldn't expect [my fans] to know that. I figured they'd figure it out later, but a lot of their theories were actually correct. Those Easter eggs were just trying to establish that tone, which I foreshadowed ages ago in a Spotify vertical video for 'Delicate' by painting my nails those [pastel] colors.

On *The Graham Norton Show* on May 24, Taylor mentioned that she hadn't done any kind of interviews for nearly three years. A statistic from that televised appearance mentioned (a voiceover that later featured in her documentary) that, "You've done something only the Beatles have done – an album at number one (in the UK) for six weeks, for four consecutive albums." *Lover* would make it five later in October, and this year, because of The Eras Tour dates ending February, the week beginning March 4, 2024, *Lover* re-entered the Australian ARIA charts again, where she held the entire top five, five years after release.

Taylor Swift Style is a website and Tumblr blog run by Sarah Chapelle since October 2011. Her speciality is fashion analysis, and has pain-stakingly detailed every (yes, I mean every) single outfit Taylor has worn down to bags, shoes and jewellery. This fashion analysis includes dissecting the easter eggs that her eagle eye picks up in Taylor's sartorial choices. I have pre-ordered her book, coming out in October of this year, and I am excited to read it, and to see inside of someone else's brain that follows Taylor on an extremely elevated level.

On *Ellen*, on May 15, 2019, Taylor gave us another definition. "When we say easter eggs, we're not only talking about like easter eggs that you would go on an easter egg hunt for on Easter, it's kind of like a clue, like a foreshadowing kind of thing, I like to plant easter eggs in a video like that would be a lyric from unreleased music, or a hint or a wink to what's coming in the future...And it's been really fun to expand the musical experience past just listening to a song. I also want people to be watching the music video, and what's that thing in the background? And what's that song playing underneath there? And is there a reason she said that in French?" There was, indeed. At the beginning of the "ME!" music video, she is having a heated conversation with Brendan Urie in French where he says, "Calme-toi, s'il te plait" twice, translating to "You Need to Calm Down." This phrase was announced as the title of her second single and music video on June 13 on Instagram Live. Fans correctly guessed the name of the new album, as well as figuring out that showing The Chicks on a wall painting was important (they featured on Track 12, "Soon You'll Get Better"). The tuxedo dance scenes would become a reference to the penultimate single, "The Man," released on 27 January 2020. An ELLE *Magazine* personal essay piece, "30 Things I Learned Before Turning 30" published 6 March, ends with the thirtieth lesson; "I've come to a realisation that I need to be able to forgive myself for making the wrong choice, trusting the wrong person, or figuratively falling on my face in front of everyone. Step into the daylight and let it go." They are the last words in the self-penned article, *and* they are also the last lyrics from the last song, Track 18, "Daylight" on the album released more than five months later. They were there in plain sight for all to see. *Lover* was the reason I tried my hand at my own easter eggs as a homage to this. Here's a trivia question for you: what colour is the book you're holding? Is it golden? Like daylight?

It was a deliberate choice to print this book with a golden, buttery, yellow cover. There is a lot of yellow in the *Lover* era with her fashion and outfit choices and I couldn't have been happier.

I classify myself (for the most part) as an extrovert with a bright, confident, loud, sunshiney disposition, so gold is definitely a me colour. I called home when we chose the cover and said, "Mum, look, it's yellow," and she said, "Of course it is." She has since told me two stories about my obsession with yellow, both from when I was three years old. We went to a clothing store where I had chosen yellow overalls, but my mum had also bought me red tracksuit pants. "I like these a lot," I said to the lady at the checkout. "BUT NOT THESE," I added, pointing angrily to the track pants. Around the same time, my mum was involved in looking after toddlers at our church's Sunday school, and I was apparently quite a menace because she said I pushed a little girl off a chair and made her cry because the chair she was sitting on was...yellow. "Don't forget, your dad had a bright yellow 1969 Volkswagen Beetle when you were little, too." Love, being a colour that is promising and optimistic, is something that I hold onto, so when I saw the cover of the album Lover, it was apparent to me why and how it was shot.

Photographer Valheria Roche, then a 24-year-old Colombian artist/filmmaker based in Atlanta, did the work. The cover is a cotton candy wonder dream, a backdrop of pink clouds, with a lemon gold colour strip down the right-side of the image. Taylor's hair is dipped blue; she looks down and has a love heart lined with pink glitter around her eye. The mid-shot of Taylor is the same angle as the 1989 cover. It's my favourite album artwork. Valheria's images are everywhere in this era: inside the diary/album booklet, on the front, back, and inside CD and vinyl designs and promotional art for streaming platforms, billboards, performances, and award shows. On her Substack on Lover's fourth anniversary in 2023, Valheria wrote,

> The Swiftiverse welcomed me with so much love. I've never known a group of people so dedicated to the work and well-being of one human being and, though it was overwhelming and new at first, I have made friends and community in

people that still reach out to tell me how this art impacted and moved them. I only ever dreamed of filling the world with color and this project allowed my work to reach the farthest corners of the planet...Every artist deserves to thrive and this project has allowed me to do that over the years, bringing me connections and other projects that are very important to me. I have gone through phases where my anxiety got the best of me and I wanted to distance myself from pink and pastel clouds to "prove" I was more than the girl that photographed Taylor Swift. But honestly, I realise how silly that is, now, because I see how much these pictures still mean to people and I am honored to have had even an ounce of impact or influence in the world, so why is it such a bad thing if it's wrapped up in cotton candy colors? It's not. And I don't feel the need to prove myself to anyone anymore.

After *reputation*'s two magazine booklets came with additional poems and photography, Taylor once again designed her releases for her fans. The *Lover* album booklets have four versions (I own versions two and four), each with 30 pages of photocopies of her handwritten diaries from the past twenty years of her life. She wrote obsessively; the earliest entries start from 2003 and we are given almost 60 pages worth of words from Taylor's brain. She scribbles out other artists' song lyrics ("Big Star" by Kenny Chesney) and shares details about giving her crew bonuses whilst on tour, going on Australian beach holidays and writing songs on planes ("Nothin' New" which is now a *Red (Taylor's Version)* vault track), meeting her cats for the first time, performing with a chest infection, the 2009 VMAs, and talks about unreleased songs from her debut era. One of my favourite entries is in version book 1, where she writes about attending a red carpet event for the first time. Little did she know she would co-chair the very same one eight years later.

> May 11, 2008. Hey...This past week has been amazing and CRAZY! I've been in New York City doing all kinds of fashion stuff. I got invited to this event called 'The Met Gala!' which is THE party of the year, put on by Vogue. Each designer picks a celebrity to wear one of their new dresses from their new line, and I was picked by Badgley Mischka, this AMAZING team of designers. I've loved their dresses for so long, and was SO excited when I got word that I was picked by them. The red carpet for the gala was held on the stone steps up to the Metropolitan Museum of Art.

One page sticks out for me, the last page of version book two. It is very short compared to all other entries. Away from the tabloid trauma, Twitter wars and internet trolls at the end of the 1989 era, there is just this 26-year-old writing in her journal. "August, 29, 2016. Nashville. This summer is the apocalypse." It just makes me sad, and I feel the same sadness when reading that as a 16-year-old Taylor wrote about diets and counting calories, "Over the holidays I didn't watch what I ate." She is selective but also vulnerable in this artistic practice, creating a timeline that the fans already know about but from a perspective they don't: hers. There are collages of other never-before-seen photographs that are different for every booklet, giving fans a choice and the incentive to collect the different ones.

 I asked every person I interviewed for this book the question of their holy trinity (what their three favourite albums are, unranked), with *Fearless* and *1989*, *Lover* rounding out mine. I love every song. In 2019, the euphoria that came with the release date being my birthday, combined with the return to romance in the songs, was magic. *reputation* is incredible but there is a calmness in going back to doing what she does best organically rather than in response to something that's happened. There is no such need in this album, meaning there is more joy.

 In a *Vogue* cover story from August 8, 2019, by Abby Aguirre, Taylor says, "There are so many ways in which this album feels like a new beginning...This album is really a love letter to love, in all of its maddening, passionate, exciting, enchanting, horrific, tragic, wonderful glory." Aguirre adds, with reference to the easter eggs, "Pop music has become so layered and meta, but the Taylor Swift Universe stands apart. Apprehending it is like grasping quantum physics." Track 3, "Lover", the title track of this album, feels like an updated "Love Story." It is a song for first dances and couples who move into their first homes together, learning on a deeper level who their person is and who they are. I think of my friends Bridie and Alex when I listen to this one, and on Spotify Storylines, Taylor says this,

> I chose this song as the title track because it's such a perfect example of what I was trying to do with this album. I wanted to make music that in a lot of ways feels timeless and is really confessional. I wrote this one alone. Jack Antonoff helped produce this song and we wanted to make music that could've been played on a wedding reception stage in 1970.

In the music video, she swims around in a fishbowl. This is metaphoric; she's making a comment on what it's like to be constantly scrutinised. "Very oftentimes I remark that my life is like a fishbowl, and that like, if I were to fall in love, somebody's choosing to jump into the fishbowl with me and live in that world just with me. In life, we accumulate scars, hurt, moments of learning, disappointment and struggle. If someone's going to take your hand, they will take it, scars and all." These sound like marriage vows, and I truly believe Taylor wrote them as such. Tracks 2, 8 and 9, "Cruel Summer," "Paper Rings," and "Cornelia Street" all bounce around in my head as songs filled with sparkle. The latter, "Cornelia Street," is a brilliant summary of a love lost where the love lingers in locations you once frequented. I can't go back to the Blue Mountains near Sydney and the special scenic lookout without thinking of anything except the times I was there and I kissed the boy who loved me. That love is gone now, but I acknowledge it, remembering the rush of joy whilst one of those little emotional scars loosened. *Lover* was a brilliant post-break-up soundtrack for me. I fell straight back into fluttering feelings of first love and danced with my friends on my birthday.

It is a truth universally acknowledged that Taylor Swift is just as good at writing break-up songs that wreak havoc with your mental state as she is at writing bops that are easily sung on the dance floors at weddings. Perhaps if you know *Lover* well, you know which two songs I am talking about. Robert Breault, an American opera singer, is credited with saying, "So often the end of a love affair is death by a thousand cuts, so often its survival is life by a thousand stitches." Track 10, "Death By A Thousand Cuts," is not a Track 5 by any measure production-wise because of the upbeat tempo, but its lyrics contradict this. Taylor called it a "sad bop." The concept of microaggressions accumulated over time to bring about destruction is not new either. *Lingchi*, translated loosely from the original Chinese 凌遲, means the lingering death, a form of torture used in China and some parts of Korea and Vietnam from 900AD up until perhaps the early 1900s. Over an extended period of time, a knife was used to strategically remove portions of the body reserved for crimes that were particularly heinous, such as treason. Resulting in the slow and eventual death of the victim; it has also come to be known as the death by a thousand cuts. After the practice was outlawed, the concept has seeped into popular culture, giving meaning to an event, usually a romantic one gone wrong, that leaves one with a drawn-out dull pain that remains long after the initial impact. You can hear the beats and the moments of painful impact in the bridge. When I sing that part of the song, which you should go and play immediately after reading this paragraph, I tend to list them on my fingers.

During her May 2019 interview with Ellen DeGeneres, Taylor mentioned that she had recently watched *Someone Great*, a film released on Netflix on April 19, 2019. It was directed by Jennifer Kaytin Robinson and tells the story of a couple who ended their relationship after nine years. Taylor was interviewed on album release day on the *Elvis Duran Show*, where she talked about the movie at length in relation to the song.

> It's a movie about how she has to end this relationship that she didn't want to end because she's still in love with the person, but they just grew apart, and he's not a jerk. It's just sad because it's just realistic, time passed, and now they're different people, and that is the most devastating thing because it's not salacious, and it's deeply, deeply upsetting. And so I cried watching the movie, and for like about a week, I start waking up from dreams that I'm living out that scenario, that that's happening to me...I'd have lyrics in my head based on the dynamics of these characters.

On an Instagram post on the same day, Jen Robinson wrote,

> A couple of days ago, I was searching 'Someone Great' on Twitter and found something curious. There were rumors swirling around that Taylor had a song on 'Lover' called DEATH BY A THOUSAND CUTS (written with Jack Antonoff) inspired by my film. Well. Turns out, it's true. I've been listening to Taylor's music since her very first album. As she grew, I grew. Ebbing and flowing through life; a musical North Star in her catalog. In the fall of 2014 when I was a certifiable basket case wandering around LA in pajamas heartbroken over the boy I'd left behind in New York, 1989 was there like a best friend with a bottle of tequila and a bear hug. I found the most comfort in Clean, a song about rebirth after love lost. It inspired me and Someone

Great. And now, in the most surreal, what the fuck is even happening, full circle situation I find myself with a new song that will help me through heartbreak.

This is an interesting intersection of film and music and as Taylor describes, "the most meta thing that's ever happened to me," where art is created inspired by a different art form that inspires even more creation. At the NPR Tiny Desk Concert on 10 October, Taylor performed "Death By A Thousand Cuts," along with "The Man," "Lover," and fan-favourite, "All Too Well." A very small performance like this is important for an artist like Taylor, but it's an interesting choice because she says, "It's an opportunity for artists to decide a different way to showcase their music. So…I decided to take this as an opportunity to show you guys how the songs sounded when I first wrote them." This album was an interesting one production-wise. She explains in multiple appearances that all the songs on *Lover* began on one instrument first (either piano or guitar) before adding further production elements. So an acoustic show like this one strips the listening experience back to something very special and intimate, almost as if she is playing them to you on her bedroom floor. I love reading the YouTube comments on videos of Taylor. One such unedited comment from user @fixorfish on the NPR video says this,

> As a 70yo man living in Oregon, fishing and creating custom furniture, not to mention a Chiefs fan and "Deadhead" since the '60…Taylor was hardly on my radar until this year. Yeah…the Kelce connection made me pay attention to "her", but still somehow had never actually heard any more than snippets of her songs, until now. [February 2024]… after watching/LISTENING to this NPR video…my, my…I have a totally different take on this young woman. I now see the appeal, the truly evident talent and most of all…the genuineness of her personality, and the deservedness of

the accolades she has garnered.

In the last few years, there has been a shift in the perception that Taylor appeals only to teenage girls. The demographic that listens, turns up to her concerts and buys her music put this perception to sleep. I think if my pop were still alive, he would definitely be listening to her music with me. *Lover* also adds one more track to the short list of songs that are very rarely played live. Track 12 is the second feature song, with The Chicks, "Soon You'll Get Better." The song is about her mother Andrea's cancer journey. Another song I show to people who tell me that Taylor only writes about ex-boyfriends. In 2015, Taylor posted on Tumblr,

> Hey guys, I'm writing to you with an update I wish I wasn't giving you, but it's important and I'm used to sharing important events in my life with you. Usually when things happen to me, I process them and then write music about how I feel, and you hear it much later. This is something my family and I thought you should know about now... I'm saddened to tell you that my mom has been diagnosed with cancer. I'd like to keep the details of her condition and treatment plans private, but she wanted you to know... She wanted you to know why she may not be at as many shows this tour. She's got an important battle to fight. Thank you for caring about my family so much that she would want me to share this information with you. I hope and pray that you never get news like this. Love you. Taylor.

In her ELLE *Magazine* interview from March 2019, Taylor mentions that Andrea's cancer battle had returned and that her father also had the disease. "It's taught me that there are real problems, and then there's everything else. My mom's cancer is a real problem." Whilst filming the *Miss Americana* documentary, Andrea was having chemotherapy. It has been speculated that part of the reason for the shortened tour schedule that was to be Lover Fest meant Taylor could be home to spend more time with her. Speaking with Chris Willman for *Variety* in 2020, she revealed something new, "While she was going through treatment, they found a brain tumour. And the symptoms of what a person goes through when they have a brain tumour are nothing like what we've ever been through with her cancer before. So, it's just been a really hard time for us as a family."

My grandfather died from bowel cancer when my dad was 20, and two of my uncles died from a brain tumour and leukaemia. From a family member's perspective, it's a time bomb of emotions watching them get sicker and not knowing when you leave their bedside or the hospital if or when you're going to see them again. For the ones that go through it, being that ill is the scariest thing they will ever experience. I remember singing Track 12, "Soon You'll Get Better," in the car with my mum. At the time, she was helping a good friend through a breast cancer journey. She turned to me and saw tears streaming down my face as I empathised with a universal experience: family members being hurt and lost. I relate to trauma through the lyrics. Then she said, "I can't imagine how Zoe [her friend's daughter] must be feeling right now." As I write this, earlier in the year, I found out that a friend I went to university with had treatment for breast cancer, and I watched from afar in awe of her strength and resilience; it truly is an awful disease that randomly selects people. The reality is with the song's title, some people will, and some people won't get better. There is much fear and sadness in her simple melodies. There is also the denial factor where Taylor sings about pretending that what's happening isn't real and that simple acts like painting a room can make the pain go away. The bridge section plays on the guilt that family members feel balancing their own pain with being and relating to that trauma here for cancer patients. Here, Taylor poses the hard questions that we all think about when a loved one is facing possible death; our own needs, our own loss, and who to talk to once that person is no longer here.

Hours after the album's release, Taylor performed a few songs for radio station SiriusXM Town Hall. In the question-and-answer section of the performance, Taylor revealed that "Soon You'll Get Better" was the hardest song to write on the album. "That's a song I don't know if I'll ever play it live. It's just really difficult for me. It was hard to write. It's hard to sing. It's hard to listen to for me. But sometimes, music is like that. Sometimes, it's not just about stuff that was pleasant to feel." She has performed it only once, not in front of a crowd, during the pandemic in Global Citizen's 'One World: Together at Home' live-stream benefit concert on April 19, 2020.

When Emma Falls in Love. The *Lover* Secret Session, 4 August 2019.
Having not been an active online fan on sites like Twitter, Tumblr or Instagram, nor on an American one, it would not have been possible for me to attend the secret sessions Taylor hosted. But of course, I knew of their existence, and I also already 'knew' someone who had been lucky enough to be invited. I have been following @swiftiewins on Instagram since 2019 when the algorithm showed me the photo Emma Coleman has of her and Taylor. Fast forward to 2024, when I had a Zoom call with Emma, who lives in Kansas City, and I got the chance to ask her burning questions about her experience at Nashville's *Lover* secret session. The *Lover* secret sessions were held in a rental home in London on August 2, then in Nashville, and then Los Angeles on August 6.

Emma has been a long-time fan, having started listening to Taylor's debut album around 2007, where Track 7, "Tied Together With A Smile," helped her mum through a divorce. The ways Taylor selects the lucky recipients for meet-and-greets has always been mysterious to me. These secret sessions gained notoriety starting with 1989 and *reputation*, and so it was special getting the inside scoop.

What was your selection process like? I asked Emma. "I never really thought I was going to get to go the secret sessions, but I was like, if I am going to ever meet her, it's going to be this secret session or never, because I had been doing Positive Hour on Tumblr, which was basically a thing where I had people send me happy moments from their day, which was like a cup of coffee, or they had found out they were pregnant or got engaged, literally both ends of the spectrum, anything in between, and Taylor noticed it one time and she had liked 26 posts [on Tumblr] in one night, and then two days later she came back online and liked 84 posts over the course of an hour. Which was just insane, and I remember when it was the 1989 Era on Tumblr, and she would do spams of people's [photo] likes and I would think, 'Oh my gosh I can't imagine being them.' She would do 10 or 20 likes...and I had 100 in a couple of days."

Another one of Emma's Tumblr friends called her at work one day and told her she had been invited (to the Nashville secret session). The excitement was brewing, but there was also a sense of, "It's gonna be now or I'm going to make my peace that it's never happening." It wasn't until over a week later that Emma got her invite. "On 29 July, a few days before the secret session and Taylor Nation dmed me... oh my gosh it's happening. I only had five or six days to figure out what I was going to tell my job about the reason I can't come in this weekend." Being only 20 years old, Emma's mum had to travel with her because most hotels in America don't allow guests under the age of 21 to rent a room by themselves. "Luckily my mum, obviously also being a Swiftie, knew about secret sessions, and knew that this wasn't like internet people trying to kidnap me, and she was down to drop everything."

From where Emma lived in St. Louis, Missouri, to Nashville was a five-hour drive, and she said, "It was absolutely crazy, from the moment I got the secret session dm 'til I was on the bus going to her house, I was a trembling ball of anxiety, I couldn't eat. I was so excited, but also, I'm such an anxious person that I process excitement as anxiety..." Nashville's secret session was bigger than most (113 people instead of 50-60 people). Emma mentioned that someone invited to the Rhode Island secret session had leaked information and so it had been cancelled. From a safety point of view also, the Rhode Island house is her hardest to secure. So, they moved a few of the Rhode Island invitees to Nashville. Another reason for the bigger size of the group was (even though there were no plus ones), there were quite a few minors who legally needed their adults to be there because every attendee signed an NDA. There was already a sense of community present before going to Taylor's house because, "We were bumping into people that night, everyone [attending the secret session] pretty much stayed at the same hotel because that's where we were supposed to meet the buses. It was really fun, because it felt like, 'Oh this is so weird, this is my Tumblr timeline,' but we're all hanging out in person.' It was really cool."

At the beginning of the secret session and the whole reason for the event, the *Lover* album was played from start to finish, almost three weeks before the official release date. Listening to the album very early was obviously an incredible privilege. When the special listening time of the event was over Emma recalls Taylor saying, "Okay! Let's go meet people now! So, because of the number of people, I assumed this could feel slightly rushed, but there was definite move by Taylor to take time for each person," Emma recalls. "There's a lot of you, so we're gonna be here for as long as we need for everyone to get their time [with Taylor]." Emma says, "Everyone jokingly calls [the Nashville location] it the *Lover* secret session sleepover. Because we probably arrived about 3 pm at her house, I left at 2:30 am and was on the second to last bus back. The last bus didn't get back to the hotel until 5:00 am I was at her house for almost 12 hours." Almost the same amount of time as the infamous CMA Fest meet-and-greet in 2010, which ran for 14 hours.

I asked Emma how many people were in the room when she met Taylor, maybe expecting there to be more than ten. But no? "There was a videographer, a photographer and a person from

Taylor Nation. [So, a total of five, including Taylor]. Whenever they would call someone's name, everyone would cheer for them because they were so excited that they were going to get to meet Taylor…" And then finally, at almost 2 am, it was Emma's turn.

"I could kind of hear her talking to the person before me, like she said bye to them and then they called my name. Some people had a little bit more than five mins, I feel like mine was about ten minutes, but we couldn't have watches or devices, I had no concept of time but I felt like it was a long conversation…the thing I always emphasis to people when I tell them about my conversation with Taylor is that I could hear her say goodbye, and there was ten seconds before me entering the room, so there was not time for her to be fed [information like], 'this is Emma, this is what her Tumblr is, this is what you guys have interacted with on Tumblr.' But I walk in the room, I am trying to locate where she is, and she calls out 'EMMA!' I was trying to figure out where in the room she was."

"We immediately hugged, she said I love you before I could even say anything, she said 'your positivity hours on Tumblr make me so happy. I just like scroll on your blog whenever I'm sad just to make myself feel better.'" Emma replied, "I listen to your music whenever I feel sad to make myself feel better, and it was so surreal. I remember I told her about listening to "London Boy" because that song is special to me in its own way because my mum loves London. I told her about my sister and how she's a huge fan too. I showed her my anatomical heart tattoo that I got for "State of Grace" [the lyrics are "We learn to live with the pain, mosaic broken hearts"]. It was absolutely bananas, and even when she was talking about the positivity hour, she said I remember this one post about a person who said they had been struggling with homelessness and it was so specific…I was like how do you remember all of this? When people say her mind is insane, it is literally insane how good her memory is. And the one thing I also remember is, I'm doing such a good job at staying calm right now talking to Taylor and then out of the corner of my eye I saw the American Music Award, which said, 'Taylor Swift – Album of the Year.' And like holy shit, I'm talking to Taylor Swift, Emma, hold it together!"

"I had been debating what I was gonna do for my picture [fans were allowed to choose any object they saw in the room for their photo op, or tell Taylor what pose they wanted], if there's a Grammy Award there, I'll probably ask her for the Grammy, but it was the AMAs and the Moonmen (VMAs) that were there, but I was like, I'm just gonna hug her. Taylor then said, 'We have to take such a cute picture!' She was totally cool about re-doing the picture, we checked it again and then I remember as I was leaving, she was like, 'Bye Emma! I'll see you online!' And I remember she was like, 'You're taller than I thought you would be.'" Emma was baffled by this! "You had an idea in your head about how tall I would be?"

Fans will know this, but for those unaware, Taylor doesn't often do an open-mouth smile, but for Emma's photo, she did. "I told her 'I can't believe you did your open-mouthed smile' because that was such a thing. She would always close-mouth smile and only occasionally do the open-mouth smile, and Taylor's response was, 'I'm insecure about that one, so I save that for special times.'" So, for Emma, that was another rare moment; "I just got the opportunity to make Taylor Swift feel better about her insecurity. What the hell just happened? And then I left, got on the bus and just started crying. A couple of my Tumblr friends were on the bus already and it was really cool because everyone wanted to hear about everyone's conversations, and everyone was so excited when a new person would get on the bus."

Taylor hasn't done secret sessions since *Lover*. It's hard to say whether they will happen again in the future, but the main reason I wanted to tell Emma's story is to show people how much Taylor cares for her fans. There are drastic lengths to go to and so many things that could go wrong for a celebrity to say, "Hmmm, let's have 100 people over to my house," but it was obviously meticulously planned for maximum enjoyment and to emphasise just how much she knows about caring for her fans. Emma noted, "It's such quality time, genuinely. Never meet your idols could never apply to Taylor."

After we chatted on Zoom, I messaged her again, and wrote, "I can't believe I didn't ask you how you felt about "When Emma Falls in Love"." Emma responded with five or six messages detailing another great story. She calls it her "invisible string" story, and Swifties call it this because Track 11 on *folklore* has come to coin a phrase that refers to events intricately tied together by coincidence or a beautiful moment that could have only been written in the stars, playing out in the lyrics of the song Taylor wrote. The invisible string connecting the two albums is her magical happenstance chain of events between the *Speak Now* and *Lover* albums and tours. Little Emma's first *ever* concert (of any artist) was the *Speak Now* World Tour on August 13(!!) 2011, when she was 12 years old. She went with her mum and her sister (also big Swifties), and their highlight was the performance of "Enchanted," a song that tells you about the magic when you meet a person that makes your world shift on its axis.

During The Eras Tour sale, Emma wanted to try and get tickets to Nashville, in addition to her hometown, Kansas City, because the city held significance to her being the location of the secret session she attended three years earlier. *Lover*, the album was never given a world tour because of the pandemic, and so it was even more special because she had first heard the songs live when she had visited Taylor's house. On Nashville night one, May 5, 2023, at Nissan Stadium, Emma attended with two friends and Emma's now fiancé proposed to her during the final chorus of "Love Story." At that show, not long after she was proposed to, the *Speak Now (Taylor's Version)* was announced for a release date of July 7, 2023, which happens to be Kansas City, Night One, and Emma was in attendance. Surprise songs are an important and anxious moment for every show; the anticipation is high, and the expectations are even higher. On Nashville Night One, Emma got to hear "Sparks Fly" and "Teardrops on My Guitar," and on Kansas City, Night One, the release of Speak Now (Taylor's Version) meant that the surprise songs included the "I Can See You" music video, (and Taylor Lautner, who stars in the video came out on stage). Taylor also played another new vault track, "When Emma Falls in Love." Another surprise song that night was "Never Grow Up" (a special sentimental song for her family), and by some miracle, almost every surprise song for Emma was from Speak Now, circling back to her first Taylor concert. The new vault track had the same name as her, and the romance elements present in "When Emma Falls In Love" came true with a proposal. Thank you, Emma, for your new friendship and sharing your Taylor stories. You are part of the reason I still believe real-life love stories exist.

On September 9, Taylor held a special one-off concert, "City Of Lover," at the Olympia Theatre in Paris. 2,000 lucky ticket holders won their spot in the crowd through online contests or album purchases. The set list consisted of eight songs from the Lover track list ("ME!," "You Need to Calm Down," "Lover," "The Man," "The Archer," "Cornelia Street," "Death by A Thousand Cuts," and "Daylight") and eight from her other albums ("Blank Space," "I Knew You Were Trouble," "Love Story," "Delicate," "Red," "All Too Well," "Style," and "Shake It Off"). Taylor hadn't returned to Paris since performing on a boat on the Seine during the Red Era in 2013 and had not been in a concert hall since playing one show in Paris for the Speak Now World Tour on 17 March 2011 to a crowd of almost 3,600 people at Zénith de Paris. It was a unique show because of its intimate nature. The small theatre allowed her to perform similarly to the NPR Tiny Desk Concert, playing a majority of songs acoustically; the piano, the guitar and Taylor were all that there was on the stage. In contrast to The Eras Tour and its choreographed brilliance, this one-off show allowed the world to appreciate Taylor in a different way. It was her only live concert-length performance of the *Lover* era. Eight months later, on May 17, 2020, it was made available on ABC in the US and the following day on HULU and Disney+ but the recording was cut to include only the new *Lover* songs. Introducing "You Need To Calm Down" during the recorded performance, Taylor says, "So, like we've been talking about all night, this album is about all different types of love, all the different facets of love; love is so many things. Love is chaos, love is madness, love is joy. Love is, in my opinion, equality. And anyone who disagrees with that, in my opinion, needs to calm down." Stéphane Davet summarised it expertly, calling the concert "an operation in seduction."

With every new album comes the opportunity for a tour, and Lover Fest was set to become a sensation, ready to follow its hugely popular predecessor. On September 17, the tour dates for what was going to be Lover Fest were released on Taylor's official website. There were originally only 17 shows announced: ten in Europe, two in South America, five in North America, and more to be announced for the UK and internationally. The US shows (known as Lover Fest East and West) were last on the calendar, scheduled for July 25/26 and July 31/August 1, 2020, to be held at SoFi Stadium in Los Angeles, California and Gillette Stadium in Foxborough, Massachusetts. In the early days of the announcement, having only four shows in the US (five, including the tour opener in Atlanta, Capital One Jam Fest on April 5, 2020) would have enraged a lot of fans. The ticketing demand was high. This was the time Taylor's mum was very sick, and the small volume of shows was designed for Taylor to go home to be with her between tour dates. The two shows in São Paulo, Brazil on July 18 and 19, 2020, would have been her first shows played in the country, the same for her shows in Denmark, Poland and Portugal, and the Festival de Nîmes show on July 5 would have been only her second in France. The European dates included Werchter Boutique in Belgium (June 20), Berlin's The Waldbühne (June 24), Oslo's Sommertid Festival in Norway (June 26), Glastonbury Festival in Somerset (June 28), Roskilde

Festival in Denmark (July 1), Open'er Festival in Gdynia, Poland (July 3), Mad Cool Festival in Madrid (July 8), Portugal's NOS Alive Festival in Oeiras (July 9) and BST Hyde Park London (July 11). I had tickets for Lover Fest in BST Hyde Park, hoping it would coincide with my first big move to London, with my first Youth Mobility Visa approved in late February 2020, three weeks before all flights started being cancelled. The money for those tickets was used to buy our Wembley Eras Tour dates for that year, but in 2019, when I told my parents I'd be moving back home with them for four months, it turned into almost a year.

In its opening week, *Lover* debuted at number one and outsold all of the other 199 albums on the *Billboard* 200 chart combined, the first album to do so since *reputation*. All 18 tracks charted on the *Billboard* Hot 100, breaking the record for the most simultaneous chart entries for a female artist. *Lover* won Favourite Album of the Year at the People's Choice Awards, and Taylor picked up Best International Artist at the Australian ARIA Awards. At the American Music Awards on November 24, Taylor was honoured with Artist of the Decade and won six awards, becoming the most-awarded artist in AMA history with 29 total wins. She gave a special medley performance, singing "The Man," "Love Story," "I Knew You Were Trouble," "Blank Space," "Shake It Off," and "Lover." It was nominated for Best Pop Vocal Album at the 2020 Grammy Awards but lost to Billie Eilish's debut album. In the *Miss Americana* documentary, when she misses out on Grammy nominations for *reputation*, her immediate comments were, "I just have to go and make a better album." She talked to Zane Lowe with Apple Music on October 30, saying "*Lover* was a return to form. *reputation* was such an important recording for me because I couldn't stop writing, and I needed to put out that album, and I needed to not explain it, because another thing about that album is because I knew if I did an interview about it, none of it would be about music." There is a definite shift in feeling between the two albums, and Taylor acknowledges that here, that she is making music for herself again and not for the wider cultural sphere to consume.

Taylor's Brian Hiatt interview for the cover of November's *Rolling Stone* is one of my all-time favourites. For one, the photography is gorgeous. I read the interview over and over when I found it at the newsagent in Australia; it always takes a few months to make it over from America, but I was waiting for it. The colours of the photography are the colours of *Lover*; bright and bold blues, yellows and reds. And her braided hair is another favourite element of fans because she is known for different, out-of-the-ordinary styling in magazine photoshoots (Swifties will remember her *iconic* Bleachella moment, born from her *Vogue* April 2016 shoot – a choppy bob cut with bleached white hair). She briefly steps into a political sphere when her song "Miss Americana and the Heartbreak Prince" is mentioned, and Hiatt asks her, "How did you come to use high school metaphors to touch on politics with "Miss Americana & the Heartbreak Prince?""

> There are so many influences that go into that particular song. I wrote it a couple of months after midterm elections, and I wanted to take the idea of politics and pick a metaphorical place for that to exist. And so I was thinking about a traditional American high school, where there's all these kinds of social events that could make someone feel completely alienated. And I think a lot of people in our political landscape are just feeling like we need to huddle up under the bleachers and figure out a plan to make things better.

Hiatt makes reference to the song when he asks about particular lyrics, "Do you mean the illusions of what America is?" And Taylor's answer is, again, more politically charged than we are used to.

> It's about the illusions of what I thought America was before our political landscape took this turn, and that

> naivete that we used to have about it...I have that line 'I see the high-fives between the bad guys' because not only are some really racist, horrific undertones now becoming overtones in our political climate, but the people who are representing those concepts and that way of looking at the world are celebrating loudly, and it's horrific.

Swiftly moving from politics to production style, we enter the inner workings of Taylor's musical mind when she shares insights into exactly *how* she wants albums to sound, pulling specific landscapes into her sonic storytelling.

> Sometimes I'll have a strange sort of fantasy of where the songs would be played. And so for songs like "Paper Rings" or "Lover," I was imagining a wedding-reception band, but in the Seventies, so they couldn't play instruments that wouldn't have been invented yet. I have all these visuals. For *Reputation*, it was nighttime cityscape. I didn't really want any – or very minimal – traditional acoustic instruments. I imagined old warehouse buildings that had been deserted and factory spaces and all this industrial kind of imagery. So I wanted the production to have nothing wooden. There's no wood floors on that album. *Lover* is, like, completely just a barn wood floor and some ripped curtains flowing in the breeze, and fields of flowers and, you know, velvet.

The feature film remake of the 1981 Andrew Lloyd Webber musical *Cats* featured Taylor as the mischievous Bombalurina. Directed by Tom Hooper, following his success with *Les Misérables*, it was released for Christmas in 2019. It was not a great film, and I watched it with my mum on Boxing Day purely for Taylor's cameo. Part of the problem in the film is the concept of uncanny valley, which is a balance between using a mix of live-action and CGI to achieve humanistic visuals, where the closer the object is to being human, the more disconcerting it is. Seeing as *Cats* had to redo CGI before the film's release because of feedback from preview screenings, it was already headed for disaster. The film's soundtrack, "Beautiful Ghosts" written with Lloyd Webber, earned Taylor her third Golden Globe nomination. Lloyd Webber told *Variety* that the collaboration was "*the* enjoyable experience" of making the film.

Just before the world went into lockdown, Taylor premiered her documentary *Miss Americana* at the Sundance Film Festival on January 23, 2020. I will always cry when I see the ending montage of her past and present performances, walking through the crowds to the stage. It's the realisation of someone I have seen on screens for nearly 15 years, fighting and winning and still letting the fans rule her life. She will do anything for us. She speaks candidly about her life in the spotlight, and the expectations and struggles. The parts of the documentary that hit the hardest for me were discussions on sexual assault, eating disorders and conversations about anxiety. These things aren't the normal stuff of headlines with Taylor's name next to them, but they are important because she lets her fans in even further regarding what goes on behind closed doors. However, Benjamin Lee, writing for *The Guardian*, is critical of the documentary.

> Fans will surely embrace it, and Swift's brand of feminism and liberalism will definitely be of value to a younger audience, but she remains an enigmatic construct. Like so many documentaries and biopics that have been either produced or authorised by the star at the centre, we're being shown exactly what they want us to see and there's something uneasy about what that represents. Swift will remain a deservedly successful singer with a rare talent, but we may never get to know her as anything more than that.

I won't deny that we're being shown precisely what she would want us to see (as is the case with *every* celebrity-centred factual film), but what angle and value would a film about Taylor have had it not been driven by her? The end of the documentary has a quote that sums up where she is in life at the end of 2019,

> I'm trying to be as educated as possible on how to respect people, deprogram the misogyny in my own brain, toss it out, reject it and resist it. Like there is no such thing as a slut, there is no such thing as a bitch, there is no such thing as someone who's bossy, there's just a boss. We don't want to be condemned for being multi-faceted, sorry that was a real soap-box. Why did I say sorry? Sorry, was I loud? In my own house? That I bought…with the songs that I wrote about my own life?

Her tone is secure and unapologetic. In conjunction with the film, she released her single "Only The Young" directly after the film premiere. For a very long time, it was my alarm noise. I think I just liked the way she said awake in the first line as the first thing I heard in the morning. Writing for *Variety*, Chris Willman interviewed Taylor during the Sundance Film Festival in January 2020 (the film held the prestige slot on the opening night) and reflects that at this moment in time, Taylor "at 30, has reached a Zen state of cheerful realism."

> The bigger your career gets, the more you struggle with the idea that a lot of people see you the same way they see an iPhone or a Starbucks…been inundated with your name in the media, and you become a brand. That's inevitable for me, but I do think that it's really necessary to feel like I can still communicate with people. And as a songwriter, it's really important to still feel human and process things in a human way. The through line of all that is humanity, and reaching out and talking to people and having them see

things that aren't cute. There's a lot that's not cute in this documentary.

The last line here is significant. She's made it clear that she is a different person than she was ten years ago. Change is inevitable, but she is not jaded. She has adapted her public persona to be more combative because of the industry's treatment of her, rather than sitting and complying. When the pandemic brought the world to a standstill, everyone's plans went out the window, including Taylor's. She posted on socials on April 20, 2020 that all scheduled shows would not be going ahead. What I thought would be just over a year until I would see her live again, turned into five and a half.

> I'm so sad I won't be able to see you guys in concert this year, but I know this is the right decision. Please, please stay healthy and safe. I'll see you on stage as soon as I can but right now what's important is committing to this quarantine, for the sake of all of us.

> I love coming on here to tell you good news, or to share a new project with you. It's not my favorite thing in the world to have to tell you news I'm sad about. I'm so sorry, but I cannot reschedule the shows that we've postponed. Although refunds have been available since we first postponed the Lover Fest shows, many of you hung onto your tickets, and I, too hung onto the idea that we could reschedule. This is an unprecedented pandemic that has changed everyone's plans and no one knows what the touring landscape is going to look like in the near future. I'm so disappointed that I won't be able to see you in person as soon as I wanted to. I miss you terribly and can't wait 'til we can all safely be at shows together again.

Lover will always hold a special place in my heart for sharing my birthday and heralding a return to romance because it felt like (in the same vein as *reputation*) the clouds were parting, ready for the sun to come out, and everything was starting to make sense again. I saw the same boy's face (the one I had loved) through the songs, but it was a new listening experience than just imagining. The illusion of calling someone mine and them staying was, in its way, different to listening to 1989, because the ethos defined by that album was unbridled joy. I listen to *Lover*, *reputation* and 1989 now when I need to be reminded of those moments of ecstasy when time stops and you're with the person who is your whole world. Even when that someone isn't around, the songs still are. The reason for Taylor's changes in genre is to show us the full complexity of love in its melancholy, bubbly ecstasy, quiet tranquillity and fiery rage. It is a constant roller coaster of riding the highs, celebrating them and allowing yourself to grieve when it all comes crashing down.

Romantic people see romance not just for lovers; Taylor and I know this. The songs on this album are all love songs about the ones we love, for the ones we love (and have loved and lost), and the music also occupies another space: that of the different kinds of platonic love. Those I love in this way still hold just as high importance as romantic love. Platonic love, which is precious, gives the same amount of joy. I want to scream at my friends in long, healthy, beautiful relationships, saying, "DON'T YOU DARE TAKE FOR GRANTED WHAT YOU HAVE," because it's all I ever want. I have the best friends in the whole world, and I don't think my life is empty without a partner. I know that Taylor does this well when she whispers simple truths to her fans through songs, something like, "You will find that love someday, I just know it." I repeat this to myself when the over-saturation of engagements, weddings and anniversaries floods social media.

But other people being in love doesn't make me sad; I cry at weddings because of the overflow of love shared that I get to witness, and then I dance. The fear of being left alone or left behind is quickly squashed by putting these songs full of hope back on the speakers for the hundredth time. I know love exists because I see it everywhere; I just have to wait.

Even if we were robbed of Taylor's bright pastel spectacle of the European summer festival circuit, there were better things ahead. The Eras Tour was a far-off dream, and the hopeless romantics would fall to pieces with the new albums that were so soon around the corner. Waiting is what I and many Swifties do well, but there wasn't too much waiting for new music after *Lover*, as we're about to find out. This much I know: what was to come would eclipse any disappointment and make up for things that didn't end the way we thought they would. Such is love.

folklore and *evermore* eras
2020 – 2022.

The wistful storytelling of *folklore* and *evermore*.

folklore and *evermore*, Taylor's eighth and ninth albums, were released closely together. This chapter examines them in the same way Taylor has described them: as two sides of the same coin. *folklore* was the beginning of a writing collaboration between Taylor and Aaron Dessner. Dessner was a founding member of the National and of the duo Big Red Machine. Once again, she worked with close collaborator Jack Antonoff. Remember that game I played called "Where were you when?" I was sitting in my car in the dark when I found out *folklore* was being released. The concept of a "surprise drop" is not unheard of in the music industry, but in lockdown, it happened twice with Taylor. One unremarkable Friday night on July 24, 2020, I stayed in the car and checked my phone for a few minutes before going inside after driving home from work. I'd seen something appear on Instagram before I started driving, but I couldn't check anything until I arrived home. All the news came at once; there wouldn't be a build-up; it was coming out the next day. Eight friends sent me exactly the same message. "HAVE YOU HEARD…NEW ALBUM…TOMORROW…WHAT!!!" All of our little lockdown hearts were about to get a whole lot more bruised. This was her social media announcement post, preceded by a cryptic jigsaw of pieces that revealed the album cover and a little essay that told you everything you needed to know.

> Most of the things I had planned this summer didn't end up happening, but there is something I hadn't planned on that DID happen. And that thing is my 8th studio album, folklore. Surprise. Tonight, at midnight I'll be releasing my entire brand-new album of songs I've poured all of my whims, dreams, fears, and musings into…Before this year I probably would've overthought when to release this music at the 'perfect' time, but the times we're living in keep reminding

me that nothing is guaranteed. My gut is telling me that if you make something you love, you should just put it out into the world. That's the side of uncertainty I can get on board with. Love you guys so much. It started with imagery. Visuals that popped into my mind and piqued my curiosity. Stars drawn around scars. A cardigan that still bears the scent of loss twenty years later. Battleships sinking into the ocean, down, down, down. The tree swing in the woods of my childhood. Hushed tones of "let's run away" and never doing it. The sun-drenched month of August, sipped away like a bottle of wine. A mirrored disco ball hovering above a dance floor. A whiskey bottle beckoning. Hands held through plastic. A single thread that, for better or for worse, ties you to your fate. Pretty soon these images in my head grew faces or names and became characters. I found myself not only writing my own stories, but also writing about or from the perspective of people I've never met, people I've known, or those I wish I hadn't. An exiled man walking the bluffs of a land that isn't his own, wondering how it all went so terribly, terribly wrong. An embittered tormentor showing up at the funeral of his fallen object of obsession. A seventeen-year-old standing on a porch, learning to apologize. Lovestruck kids wandering up and down the evergreen High Line. My grandfather, Dean, landing at Guadalcanal in 1942. A misfit widow getting gleeful revenge on the town that cast her out. A tale that becomes folklore is one that is passed down and whispered around. Sometimes even sung about. The lines between fantasy and reality blur and the boundaries between truth and fiction become almost indiscernible. Speculation, over time, becomes fact. Myths, ghost stories, and fables. Fairytales and parables. Gossip and legend. Someone's secrets written in the sky for all to behold. In isolation my imagination has run wild and this album is the result, a collection of songs and stories that flowed like a stream of consciousness. Picking up a pen was my way of escaping into fantasy, history, and memory. I've told these stories to the best of my ability with all the love, wonder, and whimsy they deserve. Now it's up to you to pass them down.

There are a few things to unpack here. Firstly, in my final year of school, the areas of study in my favourite subject, English, were history and memory. I poured my heart into the interweaving of history's rigidity and record-keeping and memory's recollective subjective power. Secondly, when I think of fairytales, up until this point, maybe I didn't necessarily think of Taylor. She was very much writing to build a country-pop-dance anthem audience, not read us bedtime stories.

I would argue the changes from *Lover* to *folklore* and *evermore* are almost as radical as the shift from *Red* to *1989*. That's why I think both of these lockdown albums are so important. Playing acoustically is something she does at every concert, it's how she learnt to play and write songs, so going back to her and a guitar, and dedicating two albums to her old self is a beautiful thing. I have a lot of friends who wrote to me after *folklore* was released, enjoying the record because it reminded them of her "country stuff." There is no question that stripped-back Taylor is rewarding to listen to, away from the chaos of up-tempo repeated choruses. The focus falls not on the beats per minute but on the lyrical ability and the effortlessness of production. It makes us drift into another world. Laura Snapes writing *The Guardian's* first review of *folklore* says this,

> Elements of her fanbase have long wanted her to revisit the Nashville songcraft of her youth through an adult lens, but this isn't that album. Folklore is largely built around the soft cascades of piano, burbling guitar and fractured, glitchy electronica that will be familiar to fans of the National's post-2010 output – at least part of the album came about from Swift writing to Dessner's musical sketches. Swift's

most coherent record since her staunchly country days, it's nonetheless her most experimental, developing on Lover's stranger, more minimalist end.

When *folklore* was released, Dessner spoke with Sam Sodomsky at *Pitchfork Magazine* and talked about how the trio worked under complete secrecy through the pandemic, "There was no outside influence at all. In fact, nobody knew, including her label, until hours before it was launched. For someone who's been in this glaring spotlight for fifteen years, it's really liberating to have some privacy and work on her own terms. She deserves that." The trio of songwriters began with a meeting on the set of SNL in 2014, and then a text message nearly six years later, "She got in touch again at the end of April. I got a text and it said, 'Hey, it's Taylor. Would you ever be up for writing songs with me?' I said, 'Wow. Of course.' It was a product of this time. Everything we had planned got cancelled. Everything she had planned got cancelled. It was a time when the ideas in the back of your head came to the front. That's how it started." On both deluxe editions, Dessner is credited as a co-writer on nine out of the 17 *folklore* songs, 11 as a producer and on *evermore*, as a co-writer, 13 out of 17 tracks and 16 as a producer.

On its first day, *folklore* opened with over 80.6 million global Spotify streams, breaking the Guinness World Record for most opening day streams for an album by a female artist. The album also gave Taylor her first entry on the 'Alternative Albums' Billboard chart, and coming in at #1, it was the highest debut of any artist. "cardigan" was the lead single and was released with a music video the same day as the album on July 24; it has been streamed on Spotify 7,742 million plays and as of April 2024 has 1,239,107,505 and "august" follows with 1,036,952,208. It is important to mention here that when pressed, my mum told me her favourite Taylor song is "august" which potentially might have something to do with the fact it is her daughter's birthday.

In Australia, *folklore* topped the ARIA charts as her sixth #1 album (out of eight), which was more in 2010–2020 than any other artist. All 16 tracks entered the top 50 of the ARIA singles charts, breaking the all-time record for the most debuts in one week, once held by Post Malone and Ed Sheeran. *folklore* was #1 for four consecutive weeks and her longest-running Australian chart-topper since 1989, and the only 2020 album to stay there for more than two weeks. This album would win Taylor her third Album of the Year Grammy on March 14, 2021, in a very low-key pandemic-friendly ceremony. Even the album cover reflects the times, with Taylor standing alone in the woods in the centre of the grayscale photograph at a distance, taken by Beth Garrabrant.

folklore: a 'first look'

For a few years, some friends and I used to do "quick reviews" for the albums we loved. In the first week of release, we would write down a few sentences for every song and rank them. The nature of time meant that we might change favourites, so it was an important practice to do early. I did this same analysis for Harry Styles' *Fine Line*, and I remember doing it for *Red*, and *1989* but the nature of technology means that for Taylor, only *folklore* survives. If these notes don't make a lot of sense, it is because speed was key; I tried to analyse the song in almost the time that it played. I wrote fast in an exercise that writers and literary critics call stream-of-consciousness writing, where thoughts aren't heavily edited. I am so happy that I've pulled it out of the archives of my phone's Notes app, where it sat patiently, waiting to be read.

July 26, 2020, 12:49 pm

Most songs have a 10 second+ introduction which is really special, because you require patience and most songs from *Lover* begin immediately. This is a very premature ranking which doesn't mean I dislike any songs. Not at all. Such a wonderful pandemic quarantine soundtrack.

— **the 1**

This one immediately hits hard. Boppy piano echoes 'I'm doing good'. In ME! She talks about never leaving well enough alone, and the cleverness to say in again in a different tone mimics just a different (more sombre) aspect of looking backwards. The glow is fading, the reflection on the good times is there, hence why it is more upbeat but muted because it feels like a one-sided celebration of 'hey at least we tried.' I love it.

— **the last great american dynasty**

Probably the more upbeat from the album; maybe why I like it? The slow songs definitely have their time in *folklore*. A glow up from "Starlight" from *Red*, it's still like beyond ridiculous storytelling that comes full circle unlike the aforementioned. The song speaks to the criticism that women receive when they stand out and speak out. Basic moral is if you stand out, you'll be criticised. The song ends with Taylor telling us she had a marvellous time ruining everything, which proves that other people's opinions don't matter to her. Because you make the best memories doing things other people don't like.

— **my tears ricochet**

Beautiful beginning harmonies. My favourite lyrics are in this song, in the bridge where shings sings about battleships and underneath the waves. The title is really fascinating because bullets, not necessarily tears, ricochet and that's how powerful emotions are. They cause lasting effect and in this case damage. The idea of a funeral is dark but beautiful because it requires the idea of a point of no return.

— **august**

Birth month song, yes yes. You were never mine, also yes yes. More of the it-was-never-meant-to-be love storyline. *folklore* consistently has the theme of what wasn't meant to be, but it happened and it was good. We will pass those stories down. The idea of remembering the stuff that did actually happen instead of actually pushing imaginary futures. Knowing that this is pt. 2 of a teenage love triangle makes it feel sneaky and wrong but the song is still good.

— invisible string
LOVE the beginning of this. Colour imagery is nice in the song. Tells a narrative story. I would say that invisible string is a metaphor of destiny. Perfect little details. Little clues that turn into inventive questions of connection. The bridge is the best part. The different pieces of connection. Barbed wire – chains – wool – string. The meeeeeeee's are so much softer than the *Lover* counterparts. Weighing in the relationship as something that has been brewing for a long time. There's a beautiful anticipation on the journey. Here, Taylor uses unusual pairing of the words 'pretty' and 'think' (thinking can be pretty). I love that this doesn't really make sense. Thoughts aren't normally pretty. Things are pretty. But the confused adjective is really clever.

— illicit affairs
Here, Taylor gets seductive. She alludes to the colour of the face after a romantic tryst. CHEEKY girl. There are descriptions of meetings in beautiful rooms and in parking lots. The big theme of secrecy makes romance stronger by the idea that no one knows is strong here. I like the word illicit in the title, lending to its forbiddenness. And it's because of this that the thrill is strong.

— cardigan
very subtly sexy song hehe like I can see cardigan as the only item of clothing in this story. But if it's to keep the sultry tone, that is the impact of this love; fast and hard and strong and like she has said before, burns out fast. The possibilities of what would happen next are explored, but only because they won't happen. LOVE LINGERS even when it is gone. I like the idea of changing the ending – or

the idea that we think we have the power to will it. The Peter Pan references are so magical and I am here for them. Taylor said to BBC Radio 1 "This is a song that's about long-lost love, and looking back on it and how special it made you feel, all the good things it made you feel, all the pain that it made you feel." Devastating.

— **mirrorball**
one of the songs with a short intro, the highness of her tone in the choruses are rare and it's almost like she's nervous. 'shining just for you' feels like it's a cry for attention, and the song as a whole reflects the title. Because you can't help but notice a mirrorball, and that's her whole point. She wants you to notice her, and she knows that you already have. The bridge is magic. The impact of the mirror is it breaks apart easily, maybe if you're not looking at it. We try so hard for people's attention, and we get hurt when we don't get it exactly the way we want. All I do is try, and it is one of my downfalls, so thanks for this Tay.

— **betty**
another cute intro. interesting perspective. 'home room' – situates it in high school. Although I'm not the biggest fan of the lyrics because they sound petty; admitting guilt and wrong-doing, it's definitely a cute portrayal of teenage love that only realises when it's too late that mistakes have been made. Showing up to the party is a bold move with lots of risk so it takes a lot of planning and I like hearing the thought processes as to why they're going to do it. There's a lot of 'what's going to happen? – will you do this? will you do this? what will you think? And we don't know the end of the scenarios. SHE SAYS FUCK!

— **this is me trying**
trying is very one sided. If you're trying and someone is not, it gets hopeless. Shiny and rust imagery has been used before. Lyrically it's pretty sad, and sad is beautiful. Bridge is strong as in every song.

The idea of liquid confidence is brave. I do like this song because of the attempt to build bridges by baring yourself and risking a lot and wanting to be recognised.

— **peace**
long intro again. The line about wasting your honour – is just reminiscent of this constant worrying about 'am I good enough for this person?' and the idea of needing to be reassuring... maybe peace is something that is needed and is never going to come. OR peace is something that both people agree is going to be scarce and that has to be good enough. A strange concept of fighting for peace. Something that people take for granted but in the busyness is needed.

— **mad woman**
I do like this one. 'mad woman' is also a lyric in the last great american dynasty, and so this is a beautiful reflection on her character and how she perhaps gets triggered to the things she is perceived to be 'mad'. A nod to Taylor's angsty songwriting, acknowledging people don't appreciate her and deliberately try to find dirt/flaws on her. She knows how to play her characters.

— **epiphany**
war song. compares the past battles of war and covid, really clearly. There is a line about holding hands through plastic. encompasses most trauma pretty beautifully. epiphany meaning something bigger than the struggles in front of you. The piano is beautiful. The contrast of bleeding and breathing rhythmically works. It's a really simple battle but it's a bigger fight brought down to the individual level.

— **exile**
The piano is absolutely stunning and through so many songs. A glow up from "The Last Time," again from *Red*. Sadness because it's

reflecting on the 'we can't go back to what it was' which is a theme that carries through. As a theme with folklore being stories, the idea of exile is damaging but also can be freeing for new and better opportunities. It's not often we hear Taylor harmonising. And that is so darn beautiful. She sings about second, third, and hundredth chances and this prompts the idea that they have finally run out of giving chances because there's been too many. Hits real hard.

— hoax

this is a SAD SONG! The natural imagery is of burning and drought with the words 'barren,' 'ash, and 'fire'. There is something beautiful about accepting sadness when no other sadness would do. Because even though there is pain, she prefers the pain from the person she is no longer with. Maybe it's a love that is painful but she loves anyway and that is beautiful. Taylor sings of being pulled apart. The bodily injury is where this pain lives. Another scar metaphor! Scars serve as a physical indicator of pain, but there are scars people can't see. I do really like the lingering sadness.

— seven

lyrically this is really strong, maybe it's low on this list because it's a really sad song. Not that I don't like sad songs, but it's a theme that doesn't necessarily get a happy or tightly wrapped up ending. I feel like strong Forrest Gump vibes with young Jenny and Forrest and running away and childhood innocence.

There you have it, my brain in track-listed-dot-pointed form.

"the lakes" was released on August 18 as the solitary bonus track on the deluxe edition, (so it isn't included in my original review because it wasn't released at the same time). It is whimsical and takes me straight back to an exact location, a place where few tourists to the UK prioritise because of its remoteness and their tight travelling schedules. I only had one day there, but I grew up surrounded by nature, so I was drawn to its restorative power. I would go back to Windermere in a heartbeat. Wordsworth and Coleridge knew what Taylor and I know: that when nature calls, we must listen to symphonies that mend broken hearts, to days that drift by in the haze of glorious love. The poetry of letters written in *and* to the sky, dancing on the water, and guarded by trees has been studied for hundreds of years.

My London Swiftie best friend Steph grew up in the Lakes District, and at the end of April, a week after the release of *The Tortured Poets Department* and inspired by Taylor's song, she and I travelled up to her home to visit her mum for the weekend. We visited Grasmere, where William Wordsworth lived and died, and saw his houses, his family grave plot (which Taylor said that she also visited) and read stories about him walking with his sister and creating poetic verses while raising a family (who would also become writers). It's no wonder the Romantics saw the supernatural and ethereal realms in these landscapes. I adore the peace this region brings, and the way time seems to stop. We played Taylor in the car all weekend, and I enjoyed almost zero phone service. We saw wild bluebells painted through landscapes of roadsides and woods, stood on Windermere peaks and cried (like in the song's lyrics) and walked Steph's dog through the same forests, caves and mountains that the poets did. I woke up to a joyful message from home; Gabby and Guy, my long-time friends for over a decade, messaged me to say they were having a baby. It was there amongst the open skies and fields and mountains at my English friend's home, where I felt a pull back to where my family and friends were. 'It won't be long now,' I heard a voice in my head say, standing next to a different body of water – 17,000 kilometres away from Sydney. I bought a Peter Rabbit plush toy for the baby I will see at the end of the year and got on the train back to London.

folklore: the long pond studio sessions.

After *folklore's* release in July, on November 25, a documentary titled *folklore: the long pond studio sessions* was released onto Disney+. It would be Taylor's feature film directorial debut. Due to the pandemic, it was the first time the creative team could meet, perform and discuss the album together in full. It is immediately obvious that the film was made during the pandemic, with a video montage of Taylor setting up a recording studio in her house in May 2020, announcing that she'd finished the album. Filmed in upstate New York's Hudson Valley, it evokes a mystical setting, much like the Lake District's wilderness, very much setting the locational tone of the album. The Long Pond Studio, owned by Aaron Dessner, was highly sought after by other recording artists who wanted to work with him (Gracie Abrams, Noah Kahan, Maya Hawke, King Princess and Ed Sheeran) after this film was released. In the documentary, the three creators sit down and discuss each track in listing order. The success of the film lies in the intimacy of artist-on-artist conversations in an intimate fireside experience. Away from red carpets, we see three friends talking about the music that they made together while physically apart.

Jack Antonoff begins by saying, "I've never worked on an album like this." Taylor affirms the same sentiment, "Me neither," and Jack replies, "And I don't know if I ever will again." Little do either of them know, at the point of filming (what we as readers know with the delight of hindsight) that *evermore* was on its way.

Compounded with my analysis written in *folklore's* first week back in July, this documentary shows the development of ideas, confirmation of conspiracy theories, and the thematic breakdown that came from the artists themselves. It works in a way of an extended analysis, discussing each track before performing it together, clearly identifying writing partners as well. The conception of the album (and its existence in the lockdown space) is what I find interesting. Taylor says that she wrote "mirrorball" after finding out that her concerts had been cancelled. Its lyrics describe the shutting down of shows and her need to still give something to her fans (the album). There are references to the heroics of the present-day frontline health workers in "epiphany" where Taylor sings about the horror of unspeakable trauma that was stitched together with her grandfather's World War II experiences in France. Taylor steps away from her autobiographical songwriting style with this album. The work on this album, the likes of which have appeared before in *Red* with "Starlight," a song which talks about the historical romance of Ethel Kennedy and her husband Robert F. Kennedy, is a precursor to her musing about different time periods on the "the last great american dynasty."

In conversation with Jack and Aaron, Taylor mentions that she has wanted to write a song about Rebekah Harkness, (the previous owner of her Rhode Island cliffside mansion) since 2013, which is just after when *Red* and "Starlight" were released. "cardigan," "august" and "betty" are songs intertwined with opposing perspectives of a love triangle, "betty" being co-written by William Bowery whose pseudonym's identity is revealed to be Joe Alwyn. Alongside "exile" this would be only the second time she has written music with her partner at the time, writing "This Is What We Came For" with Calvin Harris in 2015 under her pseudonym Nils Sjöberg. "mad woman" delves into justifiable female rage, and "my tears ricochet" and "this is me trying" are connected on themes of loss and unrequited effort towards others. Listening to Aaron, Jack and Taylor speak so candidly about their own stories draws strings together to thread the whimsical album narrative. These are the songs that aren't about ex-lovers but instead can be the beginnings of important mental health conversations, speaking directly to addiction and substance abuse, depression, and anxiety. The lyrics give a platform where these issues can be addressed in a clear and safe way. The pandemic would continue for another year in Australia after *evermore*'s release, so once again, when Taylor reflects on the atmospheric mood of the album, she says that everybody needed a good cry. She would hold onto her reputation as a predictor of the future.

Speaking of crying, before, during and after the Covid-19 pandemic, from 2019 – 2022, a string of events happened that led me to decide to go and see a psychologist for the first time. Even though the negative events didn't happen all at the same time, the after-effects exploded all at once. I wrote letters to my best friends and my mum, apologising for hurting them and recognising that I needed to stop leaning on them and start sorting myself out. I broke my leg in April 2019, spent nearly eight weeks incapacitated and isolated workwise and couldn't really see my family. Friendship issues, self-esteem and body image were at an all-time low, and family trauma came to a head in the middle of the pandemic with the four of us – my mum, dad, brother and I – hugging each other and crying on Christmas night in my auntie's granny flat. My friends tried as hard as they could supporting me, sharing that no one's family is perfect, (I had been relatively bruised but not broken at that point). My normally very busy lifestyle ground to a painful halt and I was not hurting only physically but mentally as well. I found a psychologist in a practice in Leichhardt when I lived in Sydney in 2020, saw her for over a year and she helped me to pull apart issues that all seemed to point to the same outcome; I blame myself for the things that are out of my control and the hardest thing to learn, one that I am still persevering with is this: it isn't my responsibility to try to fix things that I didn't break. Family fractures, the untying of long-term friendship bonds and the way I saw myself versus how I know other people do affected me to the point where I began to unravel.

These albums became my anchor. I ended up singing "this is me trying" a lot in this time, particularly the line about it being hard at parties when feeling like an open wound, which manifested in me (a natural extrovert) wanting nothing more than to sit and cry in a corner of my bedroom. However, I did go out to places with my family, I just felt like I was pretending very hard to make it look like I was okay. "mirrorball" has a line that doesn't pull you out of your state; it acknowledges the space that I have existed in for so long, a place of still trying. *folklore* and *evermore* did their work putting my puzzle pieces back together to make them shine again.

If you're a fan of music, chances are you have heard of perhaps the greatest songwriting duo of all time, Lennon and McCartney. I've been a Beatles fan since probably the age of three or four when my dad used to sing "All My Loving" to me as a lullaby. One day, by chance, I heard it on the radio and found out it wasn't him who made up the song. I tell friends about the time Ringo forewarned everyone when he did a fart in the studio (the conversation features in the Peter Jackson-directed 2021 docu-series *Get Back*). Once, I spent six hours in Liverpool and went to the Cavern Club, where the Beatles performed in the early days, and I cried.

Paul McCartney is up there for me for all-time favourite artists, I sing Beatles lyrics almost as often as I do Taylor's, and I saw him perform in Sydney in December 2017 with my cousin and my dad's friends, in the same venue Taylor played her first Sydney shows (he played one of the longest sets I've ever been to). When Taylor's scheduled shows for Lover Fest, which included Somerset's famous Glastonbury Festival at Worthy Farm, were cancelled, so was the possibility of her and Paul being on a stage together. On November 18, 2019, Paul was announced as a Pyramid stage Saturday night headliner for Glastonbury and a month later, Taylor was confirmed as the Sunday night act. As we all know, neither of these performances happened, and whilst Paul returned for 2022, Taylor had to decline because of scheduling conflicts and due to her re-recording music schedule. As something that would appear in one of my fever dreams, they were featured together on the cover of *Rolling Stone*, in the "Musicians on Musicians" edition released in November of 2020. They talked with Patrick Doyle about the world of writing songs in a pandemic, having both written isolation albums *folklore* and *McCartney III* (released a month after this article was out on December 18). On missing out on playing at Glastonbury they said,

> **Swift:** It would've been so fun to play Glastonbury for the 50th anniversary together.
> **McCartney:** It would've been great, wouldn't it? And I was going to be asking you to play with me.
> **Swift:** Were you going to invite me? I was hoping that you would. I was going to ask you.
> **McCartney:** I would've done "Shake It Off."
> **Swift:** Oh, my God, that would have been amazing.

Instead of dwelling on things that didn't happen, they move quickly into the music they've both created to soundtrack a tumultuous time. Paul refers to wartime Britain with a comparison of how art is always shaped by the time it was created in.

> **McCartney:** There is a lot of parallels with the virus and lockdowns and wartime. It happened to everyone. Like, this isn't HIV, or SARS, or Avian flu, which happened to others, generally. This has happened to everyone, all around the world. That's the defining thing about this particular virus. And, you know, my parents...it happened to everyone in Britain, including the queen and Churchill. War happened. So, they were all part of this thing, and they all had to figure out a way through it. So, you figured out *folklore*. I figured out *McCartney III*.

The world-renowned multi-instrumentalist, worked with a small team in an isolated recording studio near his home where, "There were two other guys that could come in, and we'd be very careful and distanced and everything: my engineer Steve, and then my equipment guy Keith." He didn't have access to other artists so all of the sounds on the album were done alone. "Normally, I'd start with the instrument I wrote it on, either piano or guitar, and then probably add some drums and then a bit of bass till it started to sound like a record, and then just gradually layer it all up." Taylor teamed up with The National's Aaron Dessner, and she found freedom in doing something she'd never done before, not caring about how it would go commercially, and in time, she created the album that would win her a third Album of the Year Grammy. She asked him how he writes, and he replied with "All the band members live in different parts of the world. So, I make tracks. And I send them to our lead singer, Matt, and he writes the top line. I just remember thinking, 'That is really efficient.' And I kind of stored it in my brain as a future idea for a project."

> **Swift:** Yeah, and it turned out he had been writing instrumental tracks to keep from absolutely going crazy during the pandemic as well, so he sends me this file of probably 30 instrumentals, and the first one I opened ended up being a song called "cardigan," and it really happened rapid-fire like that. He'd send me a track; he'd make new tracks, add to the folder; I would write the entire top line for a song, and he wouldn't know what the song would be about, what it was going to be called, where I was going to put the chorus. I had originally thought, "Maybe I'll make an album in the next year, and put it out in January or something," but it ended up being done and we put it out in July. And I just thought there are no rules anymore, because I used to put all these parameters on myself, like, "How will this song sound in a stadium? How will this song sound on radio?" If you take away all the parameters, what do you make? And I guess the answer is *folklore*.

This *Rolling Stone* article is a relatable one; everybody was in lockdown, celebrities and artists as well. There is an air of normality here; Paul made a table in lockdown, Taylor made her friends' babies blankets, toys and she painted. Just the *act* of making something and being purposeful, kept these two, like the rest of us, busy in lockdown. I somehow managed to publish my first book, and I hope to print more of it one day. Taylor and Paul's careers parallel each other in a lot of ways; seismic fame and chaotic lives that don't seem normal but in some ways are absolutely ordinary. Playing together in a Glastonbury set would have made for some brilliant music history, and Taylor certainly leans into Paul's longevity as an artist. They bounce off each other, evident from their conversations.

A lot of the time, people asking about Taylor (including my dad) will ask me, "Does Taylor write songs that aren't about break-ups?" and with *folklore* and *evermore*'s imaginative characters, settings and mystical narratives present throughout the albums, the answer is yes. "this is me trying" is about facing the world that isn't very understanding about anxiety, trauma and depression. There are references to the books she was reading. "tolerate it" has nods to Daphne de Maurier's *Rebecca*, giving Taylor the opportunity to use "words I always wanted to use – kind of bigger, flowerier, prettier words, like 'epiphany,' in songs. I always thought, 'Well, that'll never track on pop radio,' but when I was making this record, I thought, 'What tracks? Nothing makes sense anymore. If there's chaos everywhere, why don't I just use the damn word I want to use in the song?'" "the last great american dynasty" is about a Marilyn Monroe-esque real woman called Rebecca Harkness who Taylor did a lot of personal research on (because she bought the Rhode Island house that Harkness lived in) and who the world always had an opinion on. Rebecca Harkness bears similarities to the Beatles' Eleanor Rigby. One was a real-life historical figure and Eleanor was, "Based on old ladies I knew as a kid. For some reason or other, I got great relationships with a couple of local old ladies. I was thinking the other day, I don't know how I met them, it wasn't like they were family. I'd just run into them, and I'd do their shopping."

In Paul's book, *The Lyrics* (the closest he has come to writing a biography, because the songs are his stories) published in 2021, he writes about the content of his songwriting. "There were accusations in the mid 1970s – including one from John – that I was just writing 'Silly love songs.' I suppose the idea was that I should be a bit tougher, a bit more worldly. But then I suddenly realised that's exactly what love is – it's worldly." McCartney's band after The Beatles, Wings, released "Silly Love Songs" as a single in 1976 on their album *At the Speed of Sound*. He says in his book, "The point is that most people don't tend to show their emotions unless they are in private, but deep down, people *are* emotional, and all I'm really saying in this song is, 'Love isn't silly at all.'" As two of the most successful songwriters in history, Paul and Taylor are both famous and ordinary at the same time. They just want to fill the world with silly love songs and what's wrong with that? Perhaps we should just let them. The article ends the same way as Paul's introduction to his book, telling a Beatles story.

> **McCartney:** I must tell you a story I told Mary the other day, which is just one of my favourite little sort of Beatles stories. We were in a terrible, big blizzard, going from London to Liverpool, which we always did. We'd be working in London and then drive back in the van, just the four of us with our roadie, who would be driving. And this was a blizzard. You couldn't see the road. At one point, it slid off and it went down an embankment. So, it was "Ahhh," a bunch of yelling. We ended up at the bottom. It didn't flip, luckily, but so there we are, and then it's like, "Oh, how are we going to get back up? We're in a van. It's snowing, and there's no way." We're all standing around in a little circle, and thinking, "What are we going to do?" And one of us said, "Well, something will happen." And I thought that was just the greatest. I love that, that's a philosophy.
>
> **Swift:** "Something will happen."
>
> **McCartney:** And it did. We sort of went up the bank, we thumbed a lift, we got the lorry driver to take us, and Mal, our roadie, sorted the van and everything. So that was kind

of our career. And I suppose that's like how I ended up being a musician and a songwriter: 'Something will happen.'

With the writing of this book and the expectations I had for my life in London versus what has transpired in reality, the romantic notion of "Something will happen" (in regard to both my career and love life), fills me with great anticipation. These are the hopes of famous, extraordinary people and they're mine as well. A month after this article was released, two weeks after *folklore: the long pond studio sessions* film, and a few days before *McCartney III*, Taylor released the sister record, *evermore*, announced on social media on December 10, 2020. It was her second surprise album drop in less than five months and took everyone by surprise (again). The pandemic wasn't done, and neither was she. She wrote;

> To put it plainly, we just couldn't stop writing songs. To try and put it more poetically, it feels like we were standing on the edge of the folklorian woods and had a choice: to turn and go back or to travel further into the forest of this music. We chose to wander deeper in...I've never done this before. In the past I've always treated albums as one-off eras and moved onto planning the next one after an album was released. There was something different with *folklore*. In making it, I felt less like I was departing and more like I was returning. I loved the escapism I found in these imaginary/ not imaginary tales. I loved the ways you welcomed the dreamscapes and tragedies and epic tales of love lost and found into your lives. So I just kept writing them.

On the YouTube live-stream premiere of the music video for "willow," (the first single from *evermore*) on December 11, 2020, Taylor said that if "*folklore* is spring and summer, then *evermore* is fall and winter." In the US, it was Swift's second #1 album in 2020 and eighth consecutive #1 debut, putting her behind Madonna with nine, and Barbra Streisand with 11. At the 2021 American Music Awards, *evermore* won Favourite Pop/Rock Album, as Swift's record-breaking seventh nod and fourth win in the category. She won Favourite Pop/Rock Female Artist, for a record-breaking sixth time. At the Grammy Awards on April 3, 2022, *evermore* contended for Album of the Year as Swift's fifth nomination in the category. The album *evermore* spent four consecutive weeks at #1 in Australia, tying with *folklore* as her second longest-running chart-topper, behind *1989* (11 weeks). "no body, no crime" was the second single, and featured a long-awaited collaboration with Taylor's close friends and sisters, Este, Danielle and Alana who sing together under their last name, HAIM. It played on the storytelling introduced in *folklore* and continued where the narrator sang about her missing friend and plotting to kill the murderous husband. After "exile (featuring Bon Iver)," *evermore* included a second feature with the title track, "evermore (featuring Bon Iver)" wrapping up the twin sister albums with matching songs. The album cover is the more colourful of the two lockdown albums. Taylor is facing away from the camera; all we see is a single braid down her back in the centre of the photo, and she's wearing a Stella McCartney orange and brown coat. She had also reached the point in her career where she didn't need her name or even the album name on the artwork for it to be recognised as hers.

Writing for *esquire*, Alan Light says, "More radical was her shift away from using her songs as diary entries to writing stories and sketches in the voice of characters, both fictional and real... *evermore* offers bold and striking new sounds while still coming across as a generous pandemic offering to her ride-or-die fans at a time when they may need her more than ever." Light's comments resonated with a world that needed music from their favourite artist as a remedy for all of the lost musical opportunities that stopped when the world did. The twin lockdown albums weren't distraction happy loud albums (that was *Lover's* time; existing in a magically ignorant past unaware of what was about to happen in the world), rather, they were a means of escape; they spurred us on to think about forests and stories, encouraging us to make our worlds bigger in our mind with these lyrics as a starting point. Sam Sodomsky, writing for *Pitchfork Magazine* again, called *evermore* "the quietest, most elegant music of her career." He summarises the album beautifully.

> It's the fastest follow-up in her career and her first album to not directly overhaul the sound of its predecessor: The goal isn't to recapture the glow of *folklore*'s cabin getaway but rather to extend her stay for another season...In contrast with the producers who helped amplify and smooth her songwriting for the masses, Dessner invited Swift to ramble and elaborate, to tell stories from beginning to end, to invent fictional characters with interconnected storylines. He is the friend who offers a comfortable place to spiral, leaning in and refilling their wine glasses.

There are some fantastic tracks on *evermore*. My personal favourites are the first four, "willow," "champagne problems," "gold rush" and "tis' the damn season" are filled with self-reflective melancholy callbacks to the rights and wrongs of letting go and holding onto things too tightly. The album also features two songs that are proper nouns, women's names. "dorothea" makes me cry sometimes when I am away from my family and I hear Taylor sing about seeing her loved ones on a tiny screen. Whether that be Instagram updates or FaceTime calls, in London this is how I stay connected with my friends, and when I move back home, it will be how I see the friends I have made here. The song about her grandmother, "marjorie" begins with words of wisdom passed to her granddaughter. Marjorie Finlay was Taylor's maternal grandmother and also an opera singer, so it was very special to learn that her voice actually features on the track alongside Taylor's.

Credited as co-writer for "exile" and "betty" on *folklore*, and co-producer for "betty," "my tears ricochet," "august," "this is me trying," and "illicit affairs" on *folklore* is one, William Bowery. The *folklore: the long pond studio sessions* documentary, reveals Bowery to be Taylor's then-partner Joe Alwyn. On *evermore*, they wrote "coney island," "champagne problems," and "evermore" together and also from *Midnights*, William Bowery/Joe has one writing credit on "Sweet Nothing." The extended period they spent with each other in lockdown resulted in the creation of beautiful songs, and the combined talent meant the album might be something entirely different or even non-existent had they not spent that time together. They started dating around 2017, where a huge chunk of Taylor's life was dealing with social media backlash. Joe offered her a space as a low-key celebrity who kept his life away from the cameras. A few years into the relationship, in the *Miss Americana* documentary Taylor said, "I also was falling in love with someone who had a really wonderfully normal, balanced, grounded life. And we decided together that we wanted our relationship to be private. It was happiness without anyone else's input." In the pandemic, some couples found solace in each other, like Joe and Taylor did, but it certainly wasn't the same level of comfort experienced by most people.

    Pulling apart the lyrics in Taylor's 'sad-girl-songs' is one of my obsessions. There is one story on *evermore* that I can't escape. Track 17, "it's time to go" has an important lesson to teach about romantic and platonic relationships and demonstrates to me that Taylor's songwriting continues to transcend teenage love and parties and pining after boys. One of my favourite lines in the whole album is in the second verse of this track, once again, heartbreakingly I can't include lyrics in this book but she rhymes "past" and "glass." The line, to me, helps me realise that it doesn't matter how long you feel stuck or frozen as a previous version of yourself, all it takes is time. Throughout the song she lists the different hurts and disappointments; boys that lead you on, fake friends, deserved work promotions lost to entitled colleagues, long-term relationships that run their course and broken families. I listen to this song and the same three faces materialise in my mind. A family I know who was shattered by addiction and infidelity. I knew them for decades and nothing seemed wrong. Until the brave wife and mother to my beautiful friends finally said enough is enough.

Gone in an instant was their "idyllic" family home and her husband, who hurt her so much that she couldn't bear to hold his weight any longer. In the years that have passed, her kids have grown up and moved out, but she holds them closer than before. I still think constantly of that bravery, to be able to nurse your children's hearts in a marriage breakup and to find friends that nursed hers. It's pure heartache, but through that despair I know she finds trust and joy in different relationships, with God and with people that treat her right. The words are Taylor's, but they echo what my friend has said and they are in are in the second verse leading into the chorus, where she sings about being in a toxic relationship but staying for the kids. More and more, women are being validated for leaving bad situations. I will always be proud of this friend, and I love her and her children. Taylor acknowledges this when she says that to run is the brave thing. These lyrics have a way of making me understand that bruises and scars make us who we are. We are stronger because of the battles we have fought.

In the original track listing of *evermore*, Track 7 "happiness" is one that is really important to me. I remember audibly gasping the first time I listened to it. Despite it being called "happiness," it's not about present happiness; it's a lament for past joy. Taylor tells us it's not a burden to hold onto past happiness and that happiness will return.

There's a parallel lyric in *folklore*'s "my tears ricochet." Noticeable in this song is a vocal crack or break on the word 'have' in the line she sings about not having it oneself to go with grace. When Taylor finishes this line the words brim with emotion, and the crescendo allows her to breathe and let go. It's my favourite part of the album. I asked a friend of mine Leah Brett, a professional musician, singer and recording artist about these lyrics. The crack that I can hear has a physical explanation. Vocal folds are another way of describing what some of us might call our vocal cords, housed in our larynxes. Leah says, "We all have a set of False Vocal Folds. They protect the True Vocal Folds when we go to swallow. They close over the TFV when we are nervous, angry, sick or tired. Unfortunately, they are a singer's worst nightmare, but we can use that constriction to convey more emotion; you need to know how to do it safely. In the note, Taylor has activated that constriction with a bit of cry, and her onset note sounds like a glottal stop." So, the emotional lyrics of this song have impacted the way our vocal folds let air out. The bodily effects of pain, screaming (losing your voice), cursing and crying and crying are exhalations that release tension, an important part of the healing process. I know those moments well. Crying alone in your room, the movement of your false vocal folds never sounded so beautiful.

folklore and *evermore* are the melancholic graceful twins of Taylor's albums. Their mystical quality was a quarantine tonic. It's not a coincidence that when Taylor announced The Tortured Poets Department at the 2024 Grammys, I deliberately merged my planned chapters for *folklore* and *evermore* albums to make more room for the Tortured Poets chapter in this book, still keeping to the original number of 13. Similarly, this happened on night one of the European legs of The Eras Tour in Paris where the set list was changed to include TTPD after its release. Multiple songs from the original setlist were removed to make way for seven new songs that now exist towards the end of her show.

In 2020, during the pandemic, there was pain on a small and big scale. My world felt smaller than ever, and I would cry myself to sleep because I didn't know when I would be able to see my friends again (even though they were 90 kilometres down the road). But of course, the greater planet and humanity were suffering too, and the disastrous global pandemic brought everyone to a standstill. When these things happened, my mum (who worked in hospitals and had first-hand experience working on the frontline tragedies of the Australian bushfires) would always have the strength to come home to me and say, "Find the small joys, Caitlin," and two unexpected albums in the middle of so much tumultuous uncertainty did indeed make me smile.

Midnights era 2022 – 2024.

How do you spend your *Midnights*? The sleepless lyricism of failed romances and The Eras Tour.

On August 29, 2022, at the MTV Video Music Awards, Taylor won Video of the Year with "All Too Well (10-minute version)" released on October 21. In her acceptance speech, she announced the release of her tenth album, *Midnights*. Living in London meant 13 new shiny songs dropped at 5:30 am; I listened to it once and then went back to sleep. I listened again whilst getting ready for the day and by the time I was walking to the train two hours later, there was a second release of seven more songs on the 3 am edition. "You can't do this to me, Taylor. I have to go to work," I mumbled as I got on the Tube. The album plays with the concept of 'what keeps you up at night.' Perhaps this is the closest album to stick to a lyrical theme since *Speak Now*, where every track on the album plays with an urge for her fans to act with their hearts first, without hesitation. Like *Fearless*, Taylor's introduction is perfect as a standalone read.

> It's a momentary glimmer of distraction. The tiniest notion of reminiscent thought that wanders off into wondering, the spark that lights a tinderbox of fixation, and now it is irreversible. The flame has caught. You're wide awake. Maybe it's that one urgent question you meant to ask someone years ago but didn't. Someone that slipped through the cracks in your history, and they're too far gone now anyway. All the ghost ships that have sailed and sailed away, but at this hour, they've anchored in your harbor. They sit with flags waving, bright and beautiful. And it's almost like it's real. Sometimes sleep is as evasive as happiness. Isn't it mystifying how quickly we vacillate between self-love and loathing at this hour? One moment, your life looks like a night sky of gleaming stars. The next. The fog has descended. Suddenly you're in the town you left

behind all those years ago. The trees of your youth with the phantom memory echoes of your belly laughter, and the rope indentations of your old tire swing still on the branch. All the phone numbers you still know by heart but never call anymore. The boy's devastated face as he peeled out of your driveway. The family man he is now. *What must they all think of you.*

Why can't you sleep? Maybe you lie awake in the aftershock of falling headlong into a connection that feels like some surreal cataclysmic event. Like spontaneous combustion or seeing snow falling on a tropical beach. A lavender haze crush that feels like the crash of a wave. Or was tonight the night you realised how solitary, how alone you really are, no matter how high you climb. The elevation just makes it colder.

Some midnights, you're out and you're buzzing with electric current – an adventurer in pursuit of rapturous thrill. Music blaring from speakers and the reckless intimacy of dancing with strangers. Something in this shadowy room to make you feel shiny again. On these nights, you know that there are facets of you that only glow in the dark. Why are you still up at this hour? Because you're cosplaying vengeance fantasies, where the bad bad man is hauled away in handcuffs and you get to watch it happen. You laugh into the mirror with a red wine snarl. You look positively deranged. Maybe you were trying to mastermind matters of the heart again. You've gotten lost in the labyrinth of your head, where the fear wraps its claws around the fragile throat of true love. Will you be able to save it in time? Save it from who? Well, it's obvious. From you. We lie awake in love and in fear and in turmoil and in tears. We stare at walls and drink until they speak back. We twist in our self-made cages and pray that we aren't – right this minute – about to make some fateful life-altering mistake.

This is a collection of music written in the middle of the night, a journey through terrors and sweet dreams. The floors we pace and the demons we face. For all of us who have tossed and turned and decided to keep the lanterns lit and go searching. Hoping that just maybe, when the clock strikes twelve...We'll meet ourselves.

I started my Masters degree in March 2021, unbeknownst to me, a few months before a second Australian lockdown. It was a time when my dorm room was the incredibly spacious second bedroom in Lilyfield in Sydney's Inner West in a house I shared with my best friend, Annalise, in between working at the Australian premiere production of *Hamilton*. I wouldn't change that time for the whole world. If I couldn't move to the city I had dreamed about since I was 16, I would get to live with one of the most incredible women in my life, swim in the oceans of my childhood a little bit longer, and I would write about my home. No one made it through quarantine without at least a few meltdowns, but in the midst of the chaos, sadness and global trauma, creatively, it was a chance to be still and to make space to make things. My parents built a house, my friends had babies, I wrote about my life by the beach, went back to university and published my first book. These were decisions made towards the end of 2020, a product of lockdown aspirations. I pieced together poems and essays about growing up, uni assignments and phone notes that were backdated almost five years. I had a title, and theme and hastily scribbled words that needed to be organised. When they turned into drafts, I called a very close family friend, author and editor, Jo Tuscano and said, "Hey, I think I have almost a poetry collection here, what should I do?"

After about six months of book edits, self-doubt, and the design process with my incredible friend Bobby, *Underwater Musings* was born. The printed books arrived at my door in January of 2022, at the same time as my last semester (which meant going into uni classes for the first time), and six months after that, I flew to the UK. On May 18, 2022, Taylor read the commencement speech for the New York University Class of 2022. Jason King, Chair and Associate Professor of the Clive Davis Institute of Recorded Music, Tisch School of the Arts, presented Taylor with her Doctor of Fine Arts, saying,

> You have crossed genres, demographics, age groups and borders of all kinds, to touch lives around the globe…you are a role model across the world for your unprecedented talent and accomplishment, your fierce advocacy for protection of those facing discrimination, and your commitment to speaking out forcefully, eloquently and effectively on behalf of all artists.

Perhaps my favourite quote from her speech is this, "Decide what is yours to hold, and let the rest go. Often, the good things in your life are lighter anyway, so there's more room for them." A lesson I am still learning daily. In another uncanny trick of timing, a month after Taylor's commencement speech, I submitted my final university assignments for my Masters in Creative Writing. I was jet lagged and living in an Airbnb three days after arriving in London, in June. I now consider her speech my graduation send-off since I was never able to wear the cap and gown for a second time.

Midnights is an incredible album with an even greater concept. What keeps *me* up at night is a lot of the same things as Taylor: the questions I never answered or asked, the paths I never took and the choices I made that gave me the consequences that I have to live with. This last year and a half, (even though it has been around for a longer time), I was introduced to a dating phenomenon called the "situationship."

Myisha Battle, writing for TIME on March 18, 2023, explains it this way:

> Somewhere between great love and no strings attached lies a category of relationship that needs a bit more defining. It's emotionally connected, but without commitment or future planning. The labels 'boyfriend' and 'girlfriend' don't really apply, but it's way beyond a casual hook-up. It includes going on dates, having sex, and building intimacy without a clear objective in mind.

Taylor references this hybrid connection with another person directly for the first time in Track 18, "Glitch," where she balances opposing moods and situationships, with what's in her system (meaning her blood alcohol level). She swaps the guitar-strumming tears of her adolescence for cocktails and in this growing-up phase, realises that though alcohol dulls the emotional turmoil, it never removes it completely. There is a limit on how many problems of the heart drinking can actually fix. Situationships are rarely long-term, merely distractions, where the "fun" burned-bright-fast-didn't-last kind of love makes you momentarily happy. The physical duration is outweighed by the cost of it lingering in our minds at the witching hours, between 12 and 3 am in the morning. Surely, I'm not the only one who believes this applies to at least 30 to 40 Taylor Swift songs, but most of all to *Midnights*.

We hear stories every day about how people treat each other, and it's difficult to comprehend certain types of behaviour until it happens to us. It was like a movie. It was my very first cold December; I still know what his coat and his glasses look like. We stood freezing in Soho early in the morning. We went for a walk around St. James Park, laughed at tourists taking phone box photos in Westminster and rode the Jubilee line together just once. He had a don't-you-wish-you-had-me (I did) grin; he sounded like Hugh Grant, and I fell for him because he was kind. I went to Prague for a weekend with friends and was with him the day before I left. When I returned to London, he was waiting outside the train station for me. Snow was on the ground as we held hands, walking back from the movies. To me, everything seemed to be going well. I didn't realise until it was too late that it wasn't the same for him. The feelings weren't reciprocated. It was the same month of the year that I had fallen in love for the first time, but in a different hemisphere. The metaphors of summer versus winter danced in my head, and song lyrics wouldn't stop following me home. I lost my wallet on a night out and called him eight times at 3 am, convinced he cared enough to help. I was wrong. I went home to Australia for a few weeks in March 2023, and I never saw him again. The fallout was nuclear.

The boy I see in my mind when the *Midnights* album plays still haunts my dreams and his names follow me everywhere too: a famous character in F.R.I.E.N.D.S and a guitar brand that Taylor is well-known for playing. He told me his favourite Taylor song was "Don't Blame Me" from *reputation*, and sir, I can take easter eggs from Tay, but you have nerve. In this song, Taylor sings about a situation familiar to anyone who has fallen in love: the crossing of lines, wasting time, the feeling that you're losing your mind, and then telling us that love can make us crazy. My time was certainly wasted. But was it beautiful, and did I almost lose my mind? Also, yes. Did I go too far? Yes. Should I have seen the signs? Absolutely. As with all my romantic failings, I will always blame myself, not the other person. Taylor wrote a song in *Lover* called "London Boy," and for a brief shining moment, he was mine. I'm sure I will use this somewhere in a book of poetry soon, or maybe even a song, but something I wrote in my Notes app once around this time, at 1 am, is very *Midnights*-coded. Probably one of the saddest sentences I have *ever* written is this, "I sleep on your side of my bed, but then I remember there was never a your side of my bed." My self-penned lyrics call back to security that I didn't have because if that secure feeling only exists for one person in the relationship, then it doesn't exist at all. Delusion is supremacy.

Taylor's favourite and lucky number being, 13, the date of her birthday, applies to me, and my lucky number is 23. I have another favourite number, 17, and my aunty once pointed out that one plus seven equals eight, which is the eighth month, August. In my conspiracy-filled little brain, after my first relationship took up all of 2017, I always believed that the second love of my life would appear, by pure coincidence, in 2023. To my credit, I wasn't wrong. Lucky numbers don't mean anything unless too many things happen that prove their worth. I did love a boy in 2023, it was fleeting, magical and painful, but it *was* love. I have learnt that just like I wait patiently for another album release, hopefully, I don't have to wait too long for the next boy who pays enough attention.

Taylor sings about her relationships the same way I write my personal essays. We're both obsessed with imagery, sprinkling our stories with just enough detail to be both damning and interesting, examining the twists of fate and recognising the physicality of heartbreak being a whole-body experience. And yet still, there is an overwhelming fear that stops hopeless romantics from trying again, and specifically for me, it's the fear of being told we're "too much" too often. Going on dates and seeing different people only intensifies the knowledge that a lot of my attributes, most of the ones I worked hard to treasure about myself, are the ones that make people run in the other direction. Where are the multiple-choice options for closure? Tell me the buttons to press that give the answers. Would you like to know exactly what you did wrong? Yes, please, I do. So, I won't do it again. I was a profile-writer enthusiast at university and dreamt about writing about celebrities, so when I read the impressive portfolio of London-based Canadian music journalist Kelsey Barnes and her popular culture articles, profiles, album reviews *and* multitudes about Taylor, I fell in love. She wrote a *Midnights* review for *Coup de Main*,

> The themes are exactly what to expect from Swift after writing, recording, and releasing 10 studio albums, but

what feels unique to *Midnights* is how predictable it is in the best way – but only if you've grown up alongside her. At first listen, *Midnights* sounds like the love child of 1989 and *reputation*, dripping in electro-infused synth pop and tied together with sprawling soundscapes...at its core, 'midnights' is more about reflecting rather than reinventing. It might just be the record where Swift realises that she doesn't need to constantly pull at new personality strings in order to appeal to the industry that has, at times, put her through hell. She's comfortable with her life, her love, her career, and acknowledging that sometimes she's the cause of her own demise.

My heartbreak has always sounded the same; this was just a new, updated chapter. Track 7, "Question...?" is without a doubt the song that hurts the most. I have tried to forget what that boy looks like and what we did together, but every line calls back to us. This song resonates with me because I was a good girl, he was a sad boy, we were in a big city and...we made the wrong choices. Here is where I love the strong future associations calling back to past hurts, with a parallel lyric from "All Too Well" about balancing versions of who we were before meeting important people, with how they change us when they leave. We hand over part of ourselves when we love someone enough; the tricky part is the other person reciprocating it long enough to return it to us. Rarely are we unscathed; soon, we start to section our lives into timelines defined by before and afters. I recently found a screenshot of a message sent to my friend in January 2020, "I want to fall in love, Bridie, not fall into bed with someone." When most people in my world were settling into working from home life with their partners in the same room and sharing quarantine time together, I stayed with my parents and felt like time was going backwards. Three years later, when I strangely fulfilled both of those desires that I had messaged my friend about, I found myself replacing the bricks in a wall that came down whenever I chose to care about someone deeply.

The pre-chorus, chorus and second verse of Track 1, "Lavender Haze" speaks about a love inside a bubble. The love that existed at the time between her and Joe Alwyn was very private, and safe, and they seemed to shield each other from the outside world, and this song exists as being appreciative for the protected nature of the relationship. There were a lot of marriage rumours circling around the couple, who had been dating for nearly five years, and as every celebrity knows, tabloid gossip is just that. Celebrities under inspection exist like figures in display cases to be examined. Such is popular culture. The reference to the 1950s and the lavender haze Taylor explains below. The traditional roles of people in relationships now are still very much informed by historical expectations. My brother and I both had partners for over a year, and even in that short space of time, we were both asked by strangers and friends if marriage was something we were thinking about. It's nobody's business. That early on in a relationship, it should not be expected, but for other couples, I know who have dated for longer and marriage isn't a priority, like Taylor and Joe, it is a personal choice that shouldn't be judged or even brought up in conversation. To stay in a private sphere of your own making is where the magic of the relationship is strengthened. Taylor revealed the song's inspiration in a video she posted before the album's release,

> I happened upon the phrase 'lavender haze' when I was watching *Mad Men*, I looked it up because I thought it sounded cool and it turns out that it's a common phrase used in the '50s where they would just describe being in love, like that you're in that all-encompassing love glow and i thought that was really beautiful. I guess theoretically when you're in the lavender haze, you'll do anything to stay there and not let people bring you down off the cloud. I think a lot of people have to deal with this now, not just

'public figures' because we live in the era of social media, and if the world finds out that you're in love with somebody, they're gonna weigh in on it. My relationship for six years, we've had to dodge weird rumours, tabloid stuff and we just ignore it and so this song is sort of about the act of that stuff to protect the real stuff.

Taylor and Joe co-wrote Track 12 "Sweet Nothing" together, which follows the same narrative of "Lavender Haze," a secret, simple and quiet love affair. In this song, Taylor sings about the endless speculation about her relationship at that time and the external pressure that makes her appreciate her private and normal relationship (like humming in the kitchen) with him. The final song of the standard edition – Track 13 "Mastermind," is one I love because it talks about power and controlling the narrative. It stands out to me because it sounds like the start of a level in a video game, but the gaming references do not stop there. The title is the same as a long-running BBC television quiz show (she was a specialist subject for a contestant on an episode that aired in 2019), and, having lived in the UK for quite a long period of time, I've no doubt Taylor could have watched. It is an ode to manifestation and willing events to happen. It is ironic, then, that the first verse references one of the hardest games to learn and play. There are references to fate, to the stars aligning and to countermoves, checkmate and pawns.

There are lyrical parallels with her 1989 single "Blank Space," where, once again, love is compared to a game. There is more enthusiasm in the earlier song, with the lyrics implying destiny lies in the pieces first to fall. One of the lessons taught to Swifties over and over is that nothing is accidental, and when you enter the playing field, all bets are off. There is a sense of organisation and planning evident in my favourite lyrics, where Taylor sings about planning, failing, and strategy being an important factor in the outcome. "Mastermind" perfectly summarises the fluctuation between loss and gain in this album.

So, to open the album enveloped in the lavender haze, closing it with masterminding, and extending the idea of sleepless thoughts in the middle of the night with a song about longing is a varied metaphor showing just how diverse these late streams of consciousness are. Track 15, "Bigger Than The Whole Sky," on the 3 am and *The Til Dawn* extended editions of the album is about wanting something back that was good but wasn't a part of the universe's plan. Taylor sings about having no words left after a break-up. The imagery here is of the natural world: "salt," "sea," and "sky," and her hurt is bigger than all of this. She has to say goodbye to the person that should have been. Thematically opposite to the love bubble of the first track, it reminds me of *Fearless'* Track 10, "The Way I Loved You," because there are two loves evaluated, and the lyrics prefer the love that is gone.

There is a nice time connection here in the older song's lyrics, talking about the early hours of the morning (2 am). That song has some of my favourite Taylor lyrics in it and introduced me to the "roller coaster kind of rush" feelings that I chased as a teenager and found in my situationship as a 27-year-old. Now, I am left with holes in my calendar, calls that won't be answered and the cold days that remind me of him when he put my hands in his pockets to keep them warm. The repetition in this song also echoes the going over and over of decision making, wanting the good things back and thinking about second chances and whether the paths I took would be different if I could take them again, but I can't. I told you I like her sad songs. An interesting note: both "situationship" and "Swiftie" were finalists for the Oxford Word of the Year in 2023.

Taylor had a small role as a character called Elizabeth in *Amsterdam*, a film by David O. Russell released in September 2022. In the opening half of the film, she is pushed into oncoming traffic by a hitman because she revealed that her father was murdered. Though O. Russell's films normally do well (he directed Jennifer

Lawrence's Academy Award-winning performance in *Silver Linings Playbook*), this film was sadly a box office bomb. *Midnights* was Taylor's 11 consecutive #1 album on the *Billboard* 200 in America, her fifth to sell over 1,000,000 first-week copies, and the best-selling album of 2022. She is the first artist to monopolise the top 10 of the *Billboard* Hot 100, with lead single "Anti-Hero" peaking at #1. "Lavender Haze" released October 21 and "Karma" released May 1, 2023, were the following singles. At the Grammys in February 2024, she became the only person in the award's history to win Album of the Year four times. The end-of-year performance chart for 2022 saw *Midnights* in the top ten for ten countries, #1 in Australia, #2 in New Zealand, #3 in the UK and #4 in the US. The album peaked at #1 on the weekly charts in a staggering 27 countries. Continuing her tradition from *reputation* and *Lover*, in an interview with Jimmy Fallon in October 2022, she said that the "Bejeweled" music video has "A psychotic amount of easter eggs, we have a PDF file for the easter eggs in this video because there are so many that we could not keep track." These videos are always a special experience for fans and show just how attentive Taylor is in giving us what we want, which is secrets hiding in plain sight.

    · The album cover for *Midnights* is unique in that it is the only album cover of Taylor's to include the track list on the front cover. The original and *3 am Edition* have a white background with blue and purple text, and *The Til Dawn Edition* has a navy, orange and pink gradient background with white text. Both images have Taylor looking down at a flame on a lighter; her face is blurred slightly, and the foreground (her fingers and the lighter) is entirely out of focus. The image is off-centre in the bottom right corner but takes up 75 per cent of the frame. There were four original album variants; the back covers with separate images of Taylor had numbers that joined together to make a clock.

    When receiving her award for the Songwriter-Artist of the Decade at Nashville at the Songwriter Awards in September 2022, Taylor shared a fascinating anecdote about the way her songs come about. "I have, in my mind, secretly established genre categories for lyrics I write. Three of them. They are affectionately titled quill lyrics, fountain pen lyrics, and glitter gel pen lyrics." One song for each of these categories that she mentions is "ivy" – quill lyrics, "All Too Well" – fountain pen style, and "Shake It Off" – glitter gel pens. "Writing songs is my life's work and my hobby, and my never-ending thrill." When Phoebe Bridgers presented Taylor with the Innovator Award at the iHeartRadio Music Awards, the ceremony on March 28, 2023, she said this,

> When I was little, I wanted to be a songwriter. I had lots of big feelings and I wanted to write songs about them… one day I was listening to country radio with my mum and Taylor came on. I heard a girl not much older than me, singing a song she had written about her own life, and the song was really good. As I grew up, so did Taylor and so did her songs. Taylor has always told the truth, she has written songs from exactly where she is, her music has shifted genre in the same way life does, in the same way being 16 is totally incomparable to being 18, 22, 25, 28. I'm grateful to have grown up in a world with Taylor Swift in it, or the world (Taylor's Version).

At the Grammy Awards in February 2024, and with her announcement of *The Tortured Poets Department*, the end of this era happened rapidly. Of all of her albums, I found this closure difficult to accept because the sentiment of this album is still raw, and not enough time has passed for me to be okay with everything that happened romantically. It is easy to slip and fall back into unrequited feelings. Knowing that being with that person was wrong, but doing it anyway because you desperately wanted things to be different was very *Midnights* of me and I still see his face in a lot of post-*Midnights* music. If you're a Swiftie, you know that eras don't truly end. You play old albums on repeat. You wake up one day, and it's a gorgeous summer morning with the potential to be a 1989 day. Or you could be dropping your 15-year-old cousins at high school and screaming *Fearless* on the way home because you can picture what it was like when you were their age. It might be the middle of autumn around a fire, drinking a glass of Shiraz with your girlfriends, talking about absolutely nothing; that's *Red*.

Welcome to The Eras Tour...it's been a long time coming.
Less than two weeks after the *Midnights* release, on November 1, while on *Good Morning America*, Taylor announced the initial run of US dates for what she called, "A journey through all of the musical eras of my career." The Eras Tour was imminent and, as always, would start in the USA. Thus begins a period of Swiftie history defined by a singular cataclysmic event: the great war of Ticketmaster. The reference comes from the Track 14 of *Midnights*, "The Great War," which sings of allegorical love, and let me tell you right now, it truly was a twenty-first-century digital ticketing bloodbath. #isurvivedthegreatwar was trending on social media. When the US tickets went on sale on November 15, being her first tour in just over four years, there was a system put in place to help with the ticket-buying experience in north America and with her European show dates (but not her Australian ones), the only chance you had to get tickets was to sign up for the 'verified fan program,' which would then randomly assign you an access code to be in the queue. Ticketmaster reported that there were 3.5,000,000,000 system requests (four times more than the company had ever experienced and at the end of the pre-sale day, 2,000,000 tickets were purchased, the most ever sold for an artist in a single day. The day before the general sale was scheduled, it was cancelled, and Ticketmaster wrote,

> Even when a high demand on sale goes flawlessly from a tech perspective, many fans are left empty handed. For example: based on the volume of traffic to our site, Taylor

would need to perform over 900 stadium shows (almost 20 times the number of shows she is doing) ...that's a stadium show every single night for the next two and a half years.

And...Taylor wasn't happy. She posted this response on social media a few days later.

> Well. It goes without saying that I'm extremely protective of my fans. We've been doing this for decades together, and over the years, I've brought so many elements of my career in house. I've done this specifically to improve the quality of my fans' experience by doing it myself with my team who care as much about my fans as I do. It's really difficult for me to trust an outside entity with these relationships and loyalties, and excruciating for me to just watch mistakes happen with no recourse.
>
> There are a multitude of reasons why people had such a hard time trying to get tickets and I'm trying to figure out how this situation can be improved moving forward. I'm not going to make excuses for anyone because we asked them, multiple times, if they could handle this kind of demand and we were assured they could. It's truly amazing that 2.4,000,000 people got tickets, but it really pisses me off that a lot of them feel like they went through several bear attacks to get them.
>
> And to those who didn't get tickets, all I can say is that my hope is to provide more opportunities for us to all get together and sing these songs. Thank you for wanting to be there. You have no idea how much that means.

She did indeed provide more ways for the fans to get there, adding extra dates on almost every tour stop. I saw the *reputation* Stadium

Tour at Wembley stadium in 2018, the second of two shows. This year, in June and August, there will be eight Eras shows there. For the European dates, I didn't have any success with getting a registration code, but my friend Steph, who I went with in June, did get one, and our tickets were together. For the August date, I used another friend's code because they didn't need it anymore. But I did.

The tour began on March 17, 2023, in Glendale, Arizona, with the final show scheduled for Toronto, Canada, on December 8, 2024, totalling 152 dates and five continents, a few days before Taylor turns 35. The Eras Tour had a gross income of $1.039 billion USD from 60 shows in one year. It is the first tour to pass the 1,000,000,000 mark, making it the highest-grossing of all time. This figure doesn't reflect the current European and second North American legs that will close the tour. In June 2023, when tickets went on sale in Brazil, fans received threats of violence from ticket scalpers, and consumer protection agents removed more than 30 people from the line, arresting at least ten. This led to Congress presenting a bill that would penalise scalpers with up to four years prison time and a fine of up to one hundred times the ticket's value. Nicknamed the "Taylor Swift law," the issue led to two more São Paulo dates being released and as of April 2024, it advanced from the House to the Senate.

Australia's announcement also came in June, but Taylor played those shows sooner than her European leg. Speaking to a friend, I correctly predicted the summer run of shows for Sydney and Melbourne, slotted for February 2024 between the end of the South American dates and the European ones. Australian ticket sales were impossible. Instead of the safety net of the 'verified fan' lockout, there was only a pre-sale, which began on June 23, and a general sale exactly a week later on June 30. I stayed up till 1 am on both days to try and help my friends buy tickets back home, with some being lucky and some unsuccessful, even with seven people trying on different accounts. I also know someone who found out a week before the show that a friend had a spare ticket. Such is the luck of the draw. I had a ticket to see the Sydney show as an insurance policy in case I lost my nerve over the English winter and decided to fly home. I didn't make it. It's been a wild ride from little Caitlin at the *Fearless* Tour with her mum and her high school best friend Jess, in a Sydney crowd of 20,000 to now. The huge difference between this tour and *reputation* Stadium Tour is this: Tiktok and Instagram have evolved enough to allow high-quality video content to be shared across the world. We know every night what The Eras Tour will contain, and we track what the surprise songs are in order to guess what our nights might be. My friend Lucas and I embargoed watching The Eras Tour film in cinemas and on Disney+ to have the whole physical experience. But we watched the live streams and online videos in anticipation to see what the secret songs were each night of the tour were and what the colour variations of costumes would be. The additions to the European set to include *The Tortured Poets Department* tracks, I know already and there isn't such a thing as watching out for spoilers anymore; we just know. I haven't missed an Australian tour since 2013, so watching the hometown shows online was hard, but as I have done for many years now if I missed out on something, I scoured the news.

Holly Berckelman, my friend, journalist and digital editor for *Body+Soul* magazine focuses on an-important topic in her review of the Sydney Eras Tour. She writes, "So while Swift's presence on stage was completely mind-blowing and overwhelmingly special, I knew what I was in for, and I got exactly that. What surprised me about my experience with The Eras Tour actually happened off the stage." I knew without reading further what she meant when she said, and it has become a defining statement of The Eras Tour and has defined the fandom from the very beginning: the fashion.

> For as long as I've been allowed to dress myself, there have been items that young women and little girls have been

> encouraged to stay away from: tops that are too low-cut, hems that are too short. It's a patriarchal way of thinking, thanks to years of damage done by reinforced gender roles and objectification of women...but standing outside Accor Stadium, it seemed like none of those 'rules' applied at all.

She goes on to say,

> Taylor has long been a supporter of body positivity, and as I've mentioned in previous chapters, with her over-the-top way of communicating with her fans, we expand that love of Taylor outwards to each other and the whole stadium is basically a pulsating energised ball of joy.

Every woman I know has been criticised, objectified or judged (primarily by men but sadly also by some women) about the choices we make around the clothes and outfits we wear. Other people have made it their business to decide what looks good and what doesn't. Soon enough, we start to construct a narrative for ourselves that simply isn't true. That "because we look the way that we do, and the size of our bodies; we can't be allowed to wear this, or we have to cover up this part." Holly says that it's a choice made for our "safety" because we sadly still exist in an age of danger that should have ended long ago.

> For many of Taylor Swift's fans, the other members of the audience are their family in a way, even if they're united under the parasocial relationships they have with a distant mother. The outfits at the Eras Tour are symptomatic of a wider feeling perpetuated by Swift herself – one of fun, confidence, belonging, and community. And of the 82,000 people in attendance, I bet not one person felt like they didn't belong in that crowd.

Leigh Sales, revered Australian journalist (of whom I am absolutely a fangirl) and self-confessed Swiftie, attended The Eras Tour in Melbourne in February, the weekend before Holly did. Sales attended with her lifelong friend Lisa Millar and though neither of them fitted the original high school teenage girl demographic, the point is, they once did. A lot has changed since 2006, not to mention the people who adore her. Sales comments on Taylor's versatility, knowing somehow that she has a song for everyone.

> I listened to her strumming her guitar, dressed in her floaty dress, and thought of Stevie Nicks. And then she was sitting alone at the piano, and Carole King came to mind. Later, she was in a spangly sequinned number dancing in sync with her backup crew and suddenly I was conjuring Kylie Minogue. It's a rare artist who has the courage to traverse such wide terrain, let alone master it all. You don't go to see Billy Joel and during the concert find yourself thinking of Justin Timberlake, Thom Yorke and Dave Grohl.

What I hope is highlighted enough in this book is the idea that Taylor knows how every fan feels about her, and this sentiment is shared by Sales. "Like all great songwriters, or writers in general, she phrases sentiments in a way that make you feel she is talking to you personally about your direct experience, even though once again: you're you, and she's Taylor freaking swift. You didn't get dumped by Jake Gyllenhaal, and yet somehow, it's exactly like the time you had a crush on that dufus who didn't fancy you back, or like the time that flake told you he loved you one day and had a sudden change of heart the next."

The importance we feel about relationships, not just romantic ones, is validated by Taylor in every stage of her career. You inhale when you hold the stressors and pressures of work, life, drama, family, and friends too close. You listen to Taylor, and you exhale. Sales writes, "I've never been to a concert where so many people in the audience seemed to know every lyric to every song. I've never seen so many women in one place nor so many universally cheerful, friendly people." This is what Taylor has always been about: spreading raw and uninhibited positivity through music but, along the way creating a safe space for feelings, emotions and the pinnacle of those being joy. Her final show is scheduled for December 8 in Vancouver, Canada, five days before she turns 35. In addition to her second night at Wembley, I attended a second Eras show on August 17 for night six (out of eight), six days before my birthday.

> **June 19, 2024, 12:34 am**
> I'm nervous, it's four more sleeps. Finally, it is my turn for The Eras Tour. Rebecca saw it in August 2023, and Bridie saw it in February 2024; it's now June, and it feels like a lifetime ago that I was screaming down the phone to Steph because she managed to get our tickets. My outfit came two weeks ago, and I'm insanely happy with it. I've been slowly, slowly making friendship bracelets, but Ned is coming over tomorrow to dip-dye my hair à la *Lover* and we're finishing them off and making a night of it. Taylor's set starts somewhere around 7:30 pm, but we could make it to the stadium by 12:30 pm because why not? Our early entry line opens at 3 pm Thinking about going to the concert is overwhelming, and I'll probably cry getting ready which won't be helpful, so I will hold it until we're there. I'm going to hand book postcards out in the lines and inside the stadium. See you soon, Tay.

The morning after The Eras Tour, London Night 2: June 23, 2024.
June 23, 2018, was my first Taylor Swift concert at Wembley Stadium. Yesterday, June 22, was my second. It's the morning after feeling that everyone who attends concerts will know all too well. The noises, the sheer magnitude of the crowd, the expectations, the

anticipation. It's all over. My friend Steph bought the tickets last August, and that was a time when I didn't actually think i would ever be able to go to The Eras Tour. I didn't get a pre-sale code, so if Steph had decided to take someone else, well, that's a scary thought. I left my house at 10 am, and even though it's a 600m walk from there to the Tube station, I asked Steph to come and get me because my anxiety says that if you dress like Elle Woods was a Taylor Swift fan (I've no doubt she would be) very early in the morning, with no context to the said outfit, people will look. A few years ago, that wouldn't have phased me, but repeated encounters over time have proved to me women cannot walk down the street dressed for particular occasions without being made to feel unsafe. And I wasn't wrong. A man smiled and looked me up and down as I entered West Hampstead Tube, and I quickly walked through the turnstile. That was the only bad part of my day. We got there at 10:30 am and sat down in the queue on a ramp on the side of Wembley Stadium for an hour. After that, they moved us into an orderly queue next to the ticket barriers. I handed one hundred flyers out and complemented everyone's outfits, I would hazard a guess to say 60% of them were handmade.

There's no other music fanbase that dresses the way that Swifties do for a concert. I packed food and didn't buy a single thing that day. We won't talk about how much I spent on Friday night. We entered the stadium close to 4:00; if I was playing in a football game, I'd probably be on the halfway line, but here's the thing, I sat on the floor at Wembley, and I was barrier for the back general admission section for Taylor, and both of those things I've never done that before. The last two concerts, *reputation* and *1989*, were both seated floor tickets, so this was a new level of incredible. There were little behind-the-scenes videos and photos of Taylor on the screens before the opener and old photos to share with a few people in the audience of Taylor's long history as a performer. My favourite photos of her they showed are in a ballet tutu as maybe a four-year-old and then in the recording studio with dead-straight hair at about

15 when she had just been signed. We made some friends, Emily and Tash, in the queue during the seven hours we waited, and they found us in the crowd inside. Emily had the beautiful, Speak Now purple dress on (the same as the one Taylor wore in 2012 when I hugged her).

Her openers were familiar and fun. I loved Griff when I first saw her open for Ed Sheeran in Munich, and she's since gone on to open for Coldplay and released her debut album this year. Taylor has a long history of supporting Griff (a long-time Swiftie) since the 2021 Brit Awards. Taylor spoke of her at the beginning of the night with incredible grace and kindness, "We started off getting to see an artist, who I am such a huge fan of, this girl, she is so creative on every single level, she is in complete control of everything that goes into her writing, her producing, she even makes her own outfits for the stage. I love her so much...will you please give it up, 'cause this is her hometown show, Griff was here tonight!" I only know the radio hits of Paramore, but I'm still a big fan. "This is not the kind of crowd we're used to seeing; we hope that we make some new friends tonight...are you ready to rock Wembley?" Paramore don't tour often, and due to their close relationship with Taylor, this opportunity is rare and exciting to witness. Taylor said later in the night about Hayley, "you're my longest music friend," having grown up as teenagers in the Nashville music scene together. The band is brilliant, Hayley's vocals are pure insanity, and for their last song, she hit an incredible falsetto that will make me listen to Paramore more. Not long before Taylor's set began, Taylor's dad, Scott, walked past us a few times. He waved at us, and on Friday, he gave my friends guitar picks, but we were unlucky yesterday. Soon after, there was a roar in the crowd that I couldn't initially understand, but a noisy frenzy erupted in the crowd, and I recognised a woman with a beautiful auburn ponytail. Andrea Swift, Taylor's mum, was making her way through the crowd. Cameras were flashing, and in the chaos, I managed to place a friendship bracelet in her hand. She wiped tears from her eyes, overwhelmed by the support of the crowd and today no one in the park where I am sitting now knows how close I was to Taylor's mum last night. She is one incredible lady.

The countdown on the screens started at two minutes until show time, and it was 7:20 pm The opening sound of the show is an instrumental montage of slowed-down clips that introduce the titles of each of her albums, "it's Fearless" "and they said Speak Now" "loving him was Red" "my name is Taylor, and I was born in 1989!," and "straight from The Tortured Poets Department," "meet me at Midnight," "Lover." With me and *Lover* having the history we do, this first era had me from the beginning. She emerges from a flowy material chrysalis, and having not toured her last four albums (*Lover, folklore, evermore* and *Midnights*), she sings the opening line to "Miss Americana and the Heartbreak Prince," this time once more through her microphone, "It's been a long time coming," because, well, it has. When Taylor started singing "Cruel Summer" that was the first time out of six that I cried (I counted). Emotions are high at Taylor Swift concerts, and particularly, I think this time around for me it was because it had been so long since I had seen her perform. I had listened to the live version a few times, and now I finally heard it for myself. I heard her say so many times online, "Who here knows the lyrics to this bridge? Prove it!" And I did. When you listen to that song, I dare you not to be in a good mood. With the various alternative versions of costumes available, we had the pink and orange sparkly leotard and matching bejewelled blazer.

Because I knew the concert would fly by, I tried to take each era on its own, but it was still the fastest three and a half hours of my life. I love the *Fearless* era so much. She asked the crowd, "Are you ready to go back to high school?" And truly, yes, I was. All I could think of was where I was exactly right now and where I was back in 2010, in an arena with my mum singing the same songs. The dress she wore, another alternative, was nicknamed "the noodle dress" because of its loose tassels at the bottom. It's white, and she was wearing one of my favourites. I am so glad I saw her in it. She walked up our end of the runway, maybe five metres away, and it's always surreal when artists are that close. She sang her sing-along anthems, "Fearless," "You Belong With Me," and "Love Story." Listening to these songs was the second and third time I cried.

The Red era's first two songs have been given new meaning when played live. They truly have taken on a new life of their own. Every night, someone out of the crowd is chosen to receive the black hat that Taylor wears during the song "22." I believe that this little gesture is important because she doesn't do meet and greets on this tour, so over 150 people by the tour's end will have a special piece to treasure forever, and that is part of the incredible care that she takes with fans. The girl who was given it yesterday walked past us, and on her way back, we waved at each other. The next thing that is special about the Red section is language. The lyrics in the chorus of "We Are Never Ever Getting Back Together" (the same as the title) are responded to by one of Taylor's back-up dancers, Kam, who changes the original lyrics, which are "like, ever" with a no, but specific to that language and region (local dialects, accents and colloquialism are used, especially if the country is predominantly English-speaking) and it's a crowd favourite. In Melbourne and Sydney, he said, "like, naurrr," "yeah, nah," "nah, mate," "rack off," "bugger off," "tell him he's dreaming!" (the last being from the legendary Australian film The Castle). The three London one's were, "Why don't you just bog off!" Yesterday's was, "Do one, tosser!" And tonight's was, "Up yours wanker!" There is research and care taken to include these tiny details; they are fan favourites. Next, Taylor queries the crowd, "There is one more song from the Red album that I was wanting to play if you happen to have about ten minutes to spare?" And I can now say that instead of scream-singing it alone in my car, I have sung "All Too Well (10-minute Version)" with 88,507 people at Wembley (Taylor told us the exact numbers). That was time number four, matching album number four when the tears fell down my cheeks. After Red, the Speak Now era is the shortest of all, singing only "Enchanted" after crowd favourite "Long Live" was cut to make way for new songs.

It feels like an old Taylor Swift concert because, well, that is exactly what it is supposed to be. She glides across the stage in a glittery scallop-layered off-white ballgown. And I can remember her wearing something structurally very similar in 2012. The whole point of The Eras Tour is nostalgia, if you haven't noticed already. I think the *reputation* era and the *folkmore* (*folklore/evermore*) were the fastest sets of the night for me, with four songs from *reputation* and eight from both lockdown albums just speeding by. I enjoyed the costume callbacks to the "Look What You Made Me Do" music video, where her back-up dancers wore all the eras, lining the stage, stuck in boxes. She stayed further away in the *folkmore* set and stayed in the middle for a lot of the *reputation* set. It was almost an hour into the whole show, and I was just enjoying myself, singing, and not filming or taking too many photos.

Next was 1989. I just felt as if I was at a huge party. She looked absolutely incredible in another alternate costume where the colours changed, and last night, we got the pink skater skirt, purple top and mismatched Louboutin ankle boots. 1989's setlist was similar to *Fearless*, the hit singles and nothing more, which is exactly what everyone wants. If you were a neutral fan attending this concert, this set is for you. Everyone knows every word, and we sang "Style," "Blank Space," "Shake It Off," "Wildest Dreams," and "Bad Blood" together with the woman who wrote them. I think this era, *Lover*, *Fearless* and the one to come, were the ones that were the most fun.

To no one's surprise, my favourite era of the night was the new *The Tortured Poets Department* set, and I would hazard a guess to say it could be Taylor's favourite to perform. She looks truly joyful; the songs are only months old; everyone knows them, and it is unlikely we will be graced with a full *Tortured Poets* tour, so we don't know when and if we will hear some of these songs for a while. It invokes a narrative like her other eras, and props were used heavily. An enormous bed etched with TTPD on the bedhead in "Fortnight," a lounge in the shape of lips and a moving part of the stage set that she held onto for "Who's Afraid of Little Old Me?" Tonight's (Sunday's) rendition of "I Can Do It With a Broken Heart" had Travis Kelce appear on stage with the back-up dancers, getting Taylor ready and prepared to perform. The internet was well and truly sent into a tailspin and is yet to recover. The anticipation for the surprise songs in her acoustic set was building after the end of TTPD. My friend Steph said something really important earlier in the day when we were lining up, "You don't get the surprise songs you want; you get the ones you need," and that is true. I was jealous of the Friday night mega mash-up of "Death by A Thousand Cuts" and "Hits Different" and the London references in both "The Black Dog," and then "Come Back...Be Here" together with "Maroon." But for two out of three surprise songs to be ones she had never played live, she redeemed herself. She sang both the surprise songs very close to us on the top of the stage, so it was special. In this moment of the show, she always addresses the crowd with an explanation.

"I was thinking about, you know, getting to play Wembley Stadium, and that's not remotely normal...and we get to play Wembley stadium eight times this summer, and when I'm thinking about that, you think about being grateful and being thankful for all the people who wanted this for you. And that's all of you here tonight... you wanted this to happen. But then, on the other hand, it really makes me think about how every time somebody talks shit, it just makes me work even harder, and it makes me that much tougher, so it also makes me incredibly thankful for those people. I've never played this one before, wish me luck."

And then she played "thanK you aIMee," the Kim Kardashian disstrack from *The Tortured Poets Department*. She mashed it up with *Speak Now*'s "Mean." The crowd was uproarious, including me. I have always loved when her live performances of "Mean" included noteworthy location-based lyric changes about playing at Wembley. To bear witness to a little perfect moment was just brilliant, and, big shock, I cried again. Each time I cry, it is always an indicator that those particular songs have memorable lyrics, and moments give way to a physical outpouring of emotions and sentimentality.

These two songs were a fun reminder that the people who throw shade at you truly, truly do not matter. I thought back to the girls that were awful to me in high school, and the one in particular who I trusted a lot and how she had turned against me. I had sung "Mean" in my London kitchen, far, far away from my close circle of friends and family, a few months before, and now I sang it with Taylor for the first time together since I was sixteen. A fun moment in the midst of the madness was when I glanced down at my wrist, and I was wearing a friendship bracelet with "Mean" on it. There was one other surprise on stage remaining: the piano song. In a video I recorded, Taylor says,

> "It means so much to me how much you've supported me re-recording my music...it's truly meant more to me than what I would be able to say to you. So in the process of re-recording, i was trying to reach out to artists that I was such a fan of, or in the case of one of the albums, specifically on *Speak Now*, I reached out to people who had been so influential in my music and writing, and I asked an artist who I am such a huge fan of to collaborate with me and she said yes."

Then, Hayley Williams from Paramore walked out and joined Taylor at the piano. When the European shows started, I thought: "I wonder when she will play "Castles Crumbling" because Paramore is now her opener." Never in my wildest dreams did I think I would get to see them sing it together. It's a beautiful song, and it was a special moment – two songs from *Speak Now* and one that had never been played. I was happy. Emily, next to me in her purple dress, turned around and sobbed into my shoulder, and in that single embrace, it represented how much she meant to so many people.

I had only met her a few hours beforehand, but we behaved like we had known each other for years. After Hayley left, Taylor dove under the stage, transported through a hidden tunnel to start her last era. When the "Lavender Haze" clouds came out, it was inevitable that we only had a few more songs left. Midnights and TTPD both had longer song lists; being the most recent albums, it was important to include more songs, with seven each. She has an incredible quick change in the middle of this set. Going from a glittery t-shirt dress to a leotard under the cover of her dancer's umbrellas, it is stage mastery at its finest.

On Thursday, August 15, I had the opportunity to be interviewed on BBC Radio 1 Upload with journalist Raffaella Coleman. It was a pinch me moment, because I have dreamed of working for the BBC since I was a teenager. I chatted to her about coming together as a fandom in the aftermath of the Southport knife attack on July 29, where at a Taylor Swift-themed yoga and dance class in Merseyside, two girls (aged six and seven) were killed at the scene and a third (age nine) died a day later in hospital. Nine children and two adults were treated for injuries and Taylor commented on her Instagram Stories, "The horror of yesterday's attack in Southport is washing over me continuously and I'm just completely in shock...These were just little kids at a dance class. I am at a complete loss for how to ever convey my sympathies to these families." On the radio I also I read out the poem that is included at the back of this book, titled "Taylor Swift (Caitlin's Version)." I noted on social media, "I shouldn't say words like 'mum' and 'nan' because feels." My poem also talks about being a young fan and I struggled to keep it together, thinking about the innocent lives lost, that I hadn't let my mind wander to, and also being so far away from my own family in a milestone moment. Following Taylor's lead, I also can still do things with a broken heart.

In another hard moment for the fandom, three shows scheduled for Vienna on August 8, 9, 10 were cancelled after two people were arrested on suspicion of planning attacks. A statement from the organisers said: "Due to confirmation by government officials of a planned terrorist attack at the Ernst Happel Stadium, we have no choice but to cancel the three planned shows for everyone's safety." Taylor Nation, shared this announcement and all tickets were refunded. Taylor posted online on August 21 marking the end of her Europe tour and the London shows where she said, "Let me be very clear: I am not going to speak about something publicly if I think doing so might provoke those who would want to harm the fans who come to my shows. In cases like this one, 'silence' is actually showing restraint, and waiting to express yourself at a time when it's right to. My priority was finishing our European tour safely, and it is with great relief that I can say we did that."

On August 17, I woke up early, bought paint markers up the street and decorated and drew the names of my new and old friends all over a t-shirt that matched Taylor's from the 2009 "You Belong With Me" music video. I missed the openers for my show because I was going alone, and spent time with family who were visiting from Germany in the afternoon. Initially, I thought I would be sad to not share this experience with someone but going to a Taylor Swift show by yourself is a beautiful experience because you are not alone, you are surrounded by 92,000 people who love the same thing as you. I made friends in the stands who took my photos and sent me their videos when my phone stopped working. The surprise songs were *reputation*'s "I Did Something Bad" and a mash up of TTPD's "My Boy Only Breaks Hist Favourite Toys" and *evermore*'s "coney island." I was very happy. Happy and very lucky to once again have the opportunity to be in one of my favourite places to see my favourite artist. At one point for a few seconds I stopped singing, and the chorus of so many people continued and I listened to the perfect unity of voices screaming the words. This is what it is to be a Taylor Swift fan.

Three days later on August 20, I watched the final night of the European leg from a stranger's balcony. I had planned to watch from outside with hundreds of other fans, and I wandered into the grocery store to get dinner when I bumped into some Swifties, saying they were going to watch it up from an apartment block rooftop. After I jokingly offered to pay for their snacks, they without hesitation said, "You can come and join us if you like." And so I followed and made three new friends. We bonded immediately and listened to her bring out Florence Welch from Florence + The Machine to sing their duet "Florida!!!" as a surprise addition to the TTPD setlist, we saw her bring long-time collaborator Jack Antonoff out to play a mash up of *Lover's* "Death By A Thousand Cuts" and *reputation's* "Getaway Car" alongside the much-anticipated, "So Long, London." No other solo artist in history has played eight sold-out shows of a single tour at Wembley Stadium. She told the crowd, "I've always loved playing for you here in London, but this is the best. I've never had it this good before. I've never had a crowd that's so generous." At the end of London's final show, she surprise released the music video to "I Can Do It With a Broken Heart" while fans were leaving the stadium. I have no words that will ever be good enough to describe my appreciation and love for her.

And so inevitably every Taylor Swift concert, and eventually the whole Eras Tour in December, must come to an end, as they always do with confetti and fireworks. One of my favourite looks of the tour is the "Karma" leotard and the shimmery tinsel jacket that she wears to say goodbye to her crowds. It is the epitome of fun, and I am sure I will wear it to a fancy dress party soon. Even though I wasn't given the "22" hat, I still had couple of amazing nights at one of the most iconic stadiums in the world.

I sang, I cried one last time, and I will tell my children one day about these experiences with the hope that they will share in the same joys. There's not really an end to this story, even though we've reached the final chapters of this book. I still pinch myself that these essays, historical recounts, personal anecdotes and Swiftie trivia have made their way out of my brain and onto paper. When I was 13 and listening to Taylor for the first time, I didn't know that writing would be what I wanted to do for the rest of my life, but that was around the time I was starting to figure it out.

If I could tell that teenager dancing in her bedroom singing "You Belong With Me" into her hairbrush that she would see Taylor three times, almost four (if you count listening from the rooftop) at Wembley and write a book about the same curly blonde girl with a sparkly guitar that she loved and now the world does too, I don't think she would believe me. But here we are. With The Eras Tour being such a significant cultural moment for the fandom (when it ends, it will have run for almost two years), I remember just how far I have come on this journey with her. I have been lucky enough to be in stadiums and crowds so many times and share in the joyful collective experience of her music, and now you, "Dear Reader" have joined us. We have made it to her newest album.

The Tortured Poets Department era

2024 –

Aren't we all just tortured poets?

April 17, 2024, 9:04 pm
Every Swiftie knows the last hours and days before a new album comes are special. We've said goodbye to the "newness" of words and music we've made our own for almost two years and acknowledged the space and time they existed in. The anticipation of what's coming is building. She's getting ready to strike. Every other person in the world will hear the news and read the headlines, sure, but we will hold these new songs in a special compartment in our heads and enter the waiting room preparing for a life-changing operation, where the musical scalpel is held by perhaps the greatest lyricist on the planet.

"All's fair in love and poetry, sincerely The Chairman of the Tortured Poets Department." This is the introduction Taylor gave us to her eleventh album. She now stands alone as the only person in Grammy's history to have won the Album of the Year award four times. On the same night, February 5, 2024, in her acceptance speech for her thirteenth Grammy for Best Pop Vocal Album, she announced the album.

> I know that the way that the Recording Academy voted is a direct reflection of the passion of the fans, so I want to say thank you to the fans, by telling you a secret that I've been keeping from you for the last two years, which is that my brand-new album comes out April 19, it's called *The Tortured Poets Department*, I'm gonna go post the cover right now backstage.

She was in the middle of her unprecedented world tour, just days before flying to Australia for the Asia/Oceania shows.

The woman truly does not sleep. At what time was she recording new music? But the new-album-every-two-years schedule struck again. The social media post included the album cover and an image of a few sheets of paper that were perhaps in her handwriting.

> And so I enter into evidence
> My tarnished coat of arms
> My muses, acquired like bruises
> My talismans and charms
> The tick,
>   tick,
>   tick
>   of love bombs.
> My veins of pitch black ink

It was clear from the outset that this album was going to mean something prophetic at this moment in my life. When she announced TS11, I was already writing this book, and without seeming overly dramatic, I consider myself a tortured poet. By occupation and reputation, traditional creatives, artists and poets are not those in the highest tax bracket. We gain our wealth by producing what we love in many different ways and hoping people will buy what we pour our hearts into. Trying to make a career out of writing (something that most people know pays next to nothing unless you strike the gold) was a self-sacrificing choice I made to pursue passion and joy, but there is an enormous amount of instability that comes with that decision. Choices involve contradictory elements at times. My lack of financial security comes with my decision to live where I do, in one of the most expensive parts of London, in a global cost of living crisis, in the vicinity of Hampstead Heath. And so did Taylor. I walk in the woods whenever I can (almost more than twice a week), and in place of the noise of crashing waves and the feeling of sand and saltwater, I have chosen to live where, for hundreds of years, the prolific poets, writers, artists, Romantics,

romantics and daydreamers, also called home.

The Heath forests and open meadows are medicinal, and they whisper my favourite line from *Pride and Prejudice*, one that Taylor would no doubt approve of, "What are men compared to rocks and mountains?" Naught. Samuel Taylor Coleridge and John Keats were the key figures in the English literature movement of Romanticism. They were known as 'The Lakes Poets,' and having studied them in high school, I feel a deep connection with their contributions to the broader intellectual and artistic movement. The Romantics reacted against what they saw as the decimation of the natural world due to the changes brought about by the Industrial Revolution in the late eighteenth and early twentieth century. Economic progress was anathema to writers and poets, who moved away from man-centred works into works about the beauty of nature. Similarly, in France, writers and artists moved away from neo-classic works to a more emotional and passionate style, which included literature and painting about nature.

Wordsworth says poetry begins with "the spontaneous overflow of powerful feelings." This is what *The Tortured Poets Department* evokes. The poets and Taylor have this in common with me: the ability to deeply, *deeply* feel things. For want of a better descriptor, tortured in a beautiful way. An album announcement and release when writing this manuscript? Terrifying but brilliant. A Track 5 by the name of "So Long, London," when it's unclear how much longer I will be able to stay here? Harrowing. I feel as though I am about to be ripped into little pieces and put carefully back together again like a jigsaw. As with any Taylor album (including the surprise ones), the release schedule is meticulous, and release dates are never unorganised. Clare Lampen, writing for *The Cut*, summarises just one of the latest in a string of TTPD theories brilliantly,

> Depending on whom you ask, April 19 holds cultural significance for Anglo-American relations in one of two

ways: On this day in 1775, rebel colonists finally clashed with British redcoats at Lexington and Concord, which jumpstarted the Revolutionary War – an explosive split with a perceived oppressor that ended in independence. Nearly 250 years later, on April 19, 2024, American pop star Taylor Swift will fire her own shot to be heard round the world, apparently aimed *at least one* British man who may have committed intolerable acts of his own...The timing could be a coincidence: comparing the end of one's transatlantic relationship to a transatlantic conflict that helped determine the course of modern history would be the height of melodrama, but then again, the two foundational principles of Swiftian lore *are* melodrama and cryptic references. Coincidence does not exist, but conspiracy definitely does.

The first TTPD cover has a square frame with a light border. Taylor is lying on a bed in a black lingerie set, with light coming in the window, and as in a majority of her albums, excluding maybe *reputation*, *Midnights* and *1989*, where there are only a few design elements; its brilliant simplicity echoes how the musical story is told through a shift in colours and imagery. All *The Tortured Poets Departments* photographs we've seen so far have been taken by Beth Garrabrant, Taylor's album photographer since *folklore*. There are four alternate cover variants (Taylor did the same for *Midnights*, to make the shape of a clock), and three of these were shared while on tour – all named for the bonus track exclusive to that variation. "The Manuscript" was announced the day after the album, February 6. She then revealed the second, "The Bolter," in front of the largest crowd of her career, 96,000 in Melbourne's MCG on February 16. Sydney (February 23) was given "The Albatross," and Singapore, on night one (March 3), saw the first look of "The Black Dog." Each back cover shows a lyric line from the featured bonus track. After the first four alternate covers, fans theorised that they served as the five stages of grief. Writing for *Billboard* on February 26, 2024, Hannah Dailey says,

> The stages, as first described by Dr. Elisabeth Kübler-Ross in her book *On Death and Dying*, are as follows: denial, anger, bargaining, depression and acceptance. With that in mind, Swifties believe that "The Manuscript" connects to the first stage, denial. The theory is supported by the version's tagline, as seen on its back cover: "I love you, it's ruining my life." Next up, "The Bolter" and its tagline – "You don't get to tell me about sad" – may represent anger. Thirdly, "The Albatross" – which asks, "Am I allowed to cry?" on the back cover – could symbolize bargaining.

Published before the Singapore show, Dailey's theory has now been acknowledged and confirmed (as she often does) when, on April 8, Taylor released exclusive Apple Music playlists titled to match the albums with the grief stages they. The fans had been correct in their theories. There is a fifth playlist for acceptance that says, "I can do it with a broken heart." There was a solar eclipse visible in some parts of the US on April 8, and Taylor took this opportunity to tease the first lyrics from the album, referencing moonshine and an eclipse, revealed to be from Track 16 "Clara Bow."

Fans in Los Angeles were treated to an exclusive pop-up library hosted by Spotify in the lead-up to the album launch. The LA-based content creator and fantastic conspiracy clown host of *Swiftie School* podcast, Reagan Baylee, was one of the first in line to visit The Grove, an outdoor shopping destination that played host to a specially designed square set designed and set out like a library, where LA-based fans could visit and get excited about the album. Sponsored by Spotify, it temporarily existed in the week prior to April 19. The space featured statues, books, and trinkets. For someone who wasn't in LA at this time, Reagan's video content shared a unique insider look at the physical marketing campaigns for Taylor's album. It made me feel like I'd lined up with her and got to experience it. Most, if not all, of the items on display in the library space were easter eggs, and there was a digital book that changed at 2 pm every day to reveal more lyrics. Fans were queuing and given clipboards with a checklist asking them which songs they were most looking forward to, and they got to take home an instant photo souvenir. Artists and Spotify need to do more of these exclusive album-themed events, not just Taylor, because it's a fantastic way to engage with the music. It's fun, and it is really rewarding for fans, and it is very Taylor.

The album's lead single and first music video, "Fortnight (feat. Post Malone)" were announced on April 18 and released the next day. Before the album's release, I thought this wouldn't be too much of a shouty "I Knew You Were Trouble" and "We are Never Getting Back Together" album, angry because of the heartbreak in separating from Joe Alwyn in April 2023 (they were together for nearly six years). He co-wrote songs with her, including "Sweet Nothing" on her previous album, *Midnights*. There is always the media circus after a celebrity break-up with journalists and "sources" ready to speculate on why it happened. These people are looking for interviews where one or the other artists willingly criticises the other. But if the last 18 years have taught journalists anything, it is that Taylor's answers lie in her lyrics, so no further comments from The Chairman of the Tortured Poets Department, your honour. When the album dropped, the vultures circled with the names of a string of Taylor romances. Matty Healy is getting a lot of attention, Joe Alwyn seemingly none or scathingly so, and Travis Kelce has scored himself two beautiful slow ballads. I have not gone deeper than Taylor's lyrics, searching for exactly who, when, where and the gory details. I care about the storytelling from her perspective, most of all while acknowledging that the men she dates are a part of that. On April 19, at 5 am (British Summer Time), which is midnight in New York City, Taylor posted this to her social media:

> The Tortured Poets Department. An anthology of new works that reflect events, opinions and sentiments from a fleeting and fatalistic moment in time – one that was both sensational and sorrowful in equal measure. This period of the author's life is now over; the chapter closed and boarded up. There is nothing to avenge, no scores to settle once wounds have healed. And upon further reflection, a good number of them turned out to be self-inflicted. This writer is of the firm belief that our tears become holy in the form of ink on a page. Once we have spoken our saddest story, we can be free of it. And then all that's left behind is the tortured poetry. THE TORTURED POETS DEPARTMENT is out now.

There were signs and hints, of course, and at 7 am BST, Taylor released an extension to *The Tortured Poets Department* album, "The Anthology," so for her first-ever double album release, the world kept listening to 15 more songs. Greg James, my favourite BBC Radio 1 morning host, started his set and announced, "Oh for God's sake, Taylor, ten minutes into the breakfast show and she's just released another album, there's gonna be no one listening now, there's no point."

> It's a 2 am surprise: The Tortured Poets Department is a secret DOUBLE album. I'd written so much tortured poetry in the past 2 years and wanted to share it all with you, so here's the second instalment of TTPD: The Anthology. 15 extra songs. And now the story isn't mine anymore…it's all yours.

As conspiracy theories and speculation float around the internet, it is often the simplicity of a social media reaction that will confirm truths presented by fans. I had initially connected two dots, threading *Midnights* with this new era. The last song on *Midnights* ends with Taylor singing about hearing a key turning in the door and wondering if she is going to be taken away. The first song on The Tortured Poets Department, "Fortnight," opens with lyrics about how she was supposed to be sent away, but they forgot to come and get her. These matching lyrics hint at a connection between endings and beginnings and the sending away to perhaps an asylum. A few days later, I watched a TikTok video from user @PattyPopCulture, who saw the exact connection between the albums, only this time, Taylor herself liked the post. The hallway features heavily in the short video teasers for the album, and the setting of the "Fortnight" music video appears to be an asylum. Furthermore, to add layers of meaning and meta-descriptors, "The Dead Poets Society" film starring Robin Williams was released in the year Taylor was born, 1989 (not to mention the film and album title similarities) and two actors from the film – Ethan Hawke and Josh Charles have cameos in the music video as electro-shock therapists. Lyric parallels can also be found in a "Hit's Different" lyric and the new single "Fortnight." She continues to leave easter eggs for fans, proving once again her unlimited ability to play cryptic games with us. Once again, there are some staggering statistics for Taylor's album release. Billboard reported that The Tortured Poets Department sold 1.4,000,000 units on its first day, and the first 14 tracks of the Billboard Hot 100 were all hers. TTPD's second week at #1 was the biggest second week by units (439,000) for any album since Adele's 25 in December 2015.

I have always been drawn to reviews when it comes to journalism. I started a blog in my last year of university that focused on music, book and television reviews, and I called it "Headphones, Pages, and Screen." It wasn't a sustained venture. As a youngster, I ripped the double-page spread of movies out of the newspaper, and I've read reviews of Taylor's music for as long as I can remember. Upon the release of her eleventh album, The New York Times review and its clickbait title, "On The Tortured Poets Department, Taylor Swift Could Use an Editor" was met with scathing reactions from fans. But I understand Lindsey Zoladz's opinion. She writes,

Swift has been promoting this poetry-themed album with hand-typed lyrics, sponsored library installations and even an epilogue written in verse. A palpable love of language and a fascination with the ways words lock together in rhyme certainly courses through Swift's writing. But poetry is not a marketing strategy or even an aesthetic – it's a whole way of looking at the world and its language, turning them upside down in search of new meanings and possibilities. It is also an art form in which, quite often and counter to the governing principle of Swift's current empire, less is more. Sylvia Plath once called poetry "a tyrannical discipline" because the poet must "go so far and so fast in such a small space; you've got to burn away all the peripherals." Great poets know how to condense, or at least how to edit. The sharpest moments of "The Tortured Poets Department" would be even more piercing in the absence of excess, but instead the clutter lingers, while Swift holds an unlit match.

I agree with Zoladz's comments about poetry, but we are constantly told as writers to show but don't tell, and to leave pieces for the readers to put together. Her fans have always played the game. I have a few rebuttals to this review, which I mostly agree with. Susie Goldsborough, writing for *The Times* on April 22, adds to the question of when enough is enough: "I would like to appeal directly to Ms Swift: if you write me ten shattering, soulful songs, I'll listen to them each 29 million times, I swear. And so will everyone else." First and foremost, by trade, she is a songwriter but there could be arguments made that she is also a poet, because she has written and engaged with poetry, and they are comparable mediums. I often share time with my friends listening to Taylor's music, as she has told us repeatedly, is like opening her diaries. Her early music reflects this and as her career has progressed so has her diaries become more profound and poetry. Our quick thoughts about recounting our days as such are rarely poetic but Taylor has learnt to seamlessly combine these genres and writing styles. One of my favourite musical artists like Maggie Rogers, has an ethereal quality to their lyrics that, read aloud sans backing track, would be indistinguishable from poetry. The tortured poet, as Taylor introduces to us in this album, is also a character she has created, like those we meet in *folklore* and *evermore*.

Secondly, in defence of Jack Antonoff, Taylor's partnership with him has repeatedly produced incredible albums. Taylor would not rush to break that bond. Though the music could sound repetitive outside of the fandom community, they creating new stories, each for different purposes. Similar to the longevity of Bernie Taupin and Elton John, three out of four of Taylor's Album of the Year Grammy Awards have come from this pairing of Taylor's songwriting and Jack's production genius. He works with other artists and is a touring musician himself, so it will be interesting to see his sonic footprint throughout pop as it continues.

Thirdly, I understand Taylor's need for excess. The first three of her five Republic Records albums were released within one year of each other. The need for new music was clear; she wanted to distance herself from Big Machine as quickly as possible. She has then followed the regular bi-yearly album cycle after *evermore*, with *Midnights* in 2022 and *The Tortured Poets Department* in 2024. The need to please her fans and give them what they want (new music) will never disappear. Zoladz concludes, "If there has been a common thread – an invisible string if you will – connecting the last few years of Taylor Swift's output, it has been abundance…In this imperial era of her long reign, Swift has operated under the guiding principle that more is more." Here lies the great debate of this review. More (in this case, 31 new tracks) doesn't reward quite as much as less for many people, but every Swiftie will vehemently disagree. For poetry's sake, perhaps *The Tortured Poets Department* is her version of Samuel Taylor Coleridge's *Rime of the Ancient Mariner*.

The Tortured Poets Department: a 'first look'

Repeating the process of song analysis, as in the *folklore* chapter, I have included my first thoughts on Taylor's eleventh album, compiled while listening to it the first week of release. The order you read is the order that I've attempted to rank the songs, from 1-16, but every Swiftie knows each song is brilliant; it's just a fun game to play.

April 19, 2024, 7:23 pm

It's a Friday, but not a normal one. I didn't go to an album release day or give myself the whole day to sit in the music. The eleventh album dropped at 5 am, an early morning when I did nothing but wake up and press play, and for the next two hours, I fell down a rabbit hole of extreme validation. After two listens through, at seven, I got ready to go to work at the primary school where I teach, and fifteen more songs appeared. I made it through most of them, breaking through the silence of the morning, and later, the staff room was empty when I listened to the last three songs and silently cried at the beauty of it all at 10 am. Here are my first listens and notes:

— I Can Do It With a Broken Heart

This is a fantastic "it might not be right now, but it's gonna be okay, you'll be fine, I know you will" song. The first verse immediately got me. She sings about doing a major concert tour after a messy break-up. This takes me back to "mirrorball" from *folklore*, where she describes breaking down on the floor as the crowd screams for more. I heard a great easter egg for this song: the click track that plays in Taylor's ears while she is on stage is present in the song's production. It's a matter of listening closely, or you'll miss it. The matching sounds of depressed and obsessed travel through to the ad-libs at the end, which scream faked self-assurance. Which is not necessarily truthful, but it is certainly a step in the right direction.

— **So Long, London**
First listen of this song was beautiful and jarring. My extended thoughts are in the Red chapter, but this is a brilliantly tragic story. Of leaving a city where you had paved a life and the extreme sadness that comes with moving on. I feel this song because I will inevitably have to do this myself. The ending lyrics are a melancholy inevitability, as Taylor describes trying to hang on to a relationship that is dying. She pulls him in tighter as he is drifting away. Reminds me of another track fiveeee. There is quiet resentment rife throughout this song. Wishes that we could call this city ours forever, but we can't.

— **But Daddy I Love Him**
There was hype about this song when the track list was released because of Taylor dressing up as the Little Mermaid, and this being almost a direct quote from the Disney film sets up a narrative of disapproval that weaves its way through the song, which is about being beautifully blind to other's judgements. I love the references to dancing in the summer in pretty dresses because it recalls the optimism of Fearless. I'll tell you something right now: I will not forgive her for breaking the fourth wall. That was a big shock. Taylor makes it clear she doesn't need anyone's approval to live and love the way she wants to.

— **The Tortured Poets Department**
If "Fortnight" is an eighties prom song, then the title song for this album is definitely the one that would play in the credits of a Breakfast Club/Pretty in Pink classic. There's an aura of an insanity plea through this whole album and you don't even need to look close to find it. The name-drops of Pattie Smith and Dylan Thomas are important in different ways; both are writers, both tortured but brilliant. The Charlie Puth reference is rogue but funny. I wonder in which order the lyrics and the title came from and how many poets went through the selection process.

— Who's Afraid of Little Old Me?

I hope I am right in the prediction that this song will make the Eras setlist additions, purely for the screaming that will happen with the song's title. There is fear and paranoia, pain and yearning for understanding in this very long song; it goes for nearly five and a half minutes. Almost a favourite line of the song, of which I'm not alone in deciding, is the one where she makes reference to the asylum where she was raised. Considering an asylum is a place where tortured minds (and poets, hello Oscar Wilde, Virginia Woolf and Sylvia Plath) reside, it's a confession of Taylor understanding her upbringing in the spotlight was far from normal.

— My Boy Only Breaks His Favourite Toys

The beginning and the end of the back track of this song sound like "Out of the Woods." The line where she refers to herself as a queen of the sandcastles that he destroys evokes Speak Now's vault track, "Castles Crumbling (feat. Hayley Williams)." The references to dolls and sandlots conjure up an infatuation that is immature and childlike. She likes to use castles a lot as well, used previously in both in *Speak Now* and 1989, where there is a line where she turns the bricks thrown at her into a castle, and here, sandcastles, as opposed to regular ones, allude to the 'toys' in the title.

— loml

At its core, this song deals with truths you believed wholeheartedly until they weren't true anymore. This song deals with the themes of loss and betrayal. The track sheds light on her romantic past with Alwyn and what really led to their split. Perhaps the highlight of the song was the bridge, where Swift sings about feeling betrayed by the person she loved and wishing she could forget about him. The tone of this song is a sad joy—the end of a love affair and all of its wounds that continue to bleed. I can see similarities lyrically with *Lover*'s "Death By A Thousand Cuts," with the matching lyrics that flip happiness into dark grief. She also sings about love at first sight and the agony of that being false. There is a great play on words in this song that could send fans into a tailspin with a fantastic dramatic reference here to Mr. Harry Styles. We can only make up our own stories at this point.

— The Alchemy
I have made a lot of comparisons back to past Taylor songs (most of them are lyrical callbacks), but I struggle with this one and that's why I like it. The title refers to the chemical reactions of love, and that's refreshing in an album like this, where everything could be seen about pining and loss, but there are signs of hope returning. The pace is different, too; it's a consistent waltz sway, which differentiates the romance from the heartbreak. There really aren't any questions about who this song is about. Hi Travis, we see you.

— Fortnight (feat. Post Malone)
I love that the starting lyric of this song echoes the closing line of midnights from Hits Different. The backing synth track sounds like an eighties prom song. This song will be the anthem of short-term relationships everywhere that screams to me: IT DOESN'T MATTER FOR HOW LONG WE WERE TOGETHER. It matters the emotional impact. She is very clear with this, leading into the whole TTPD narrative with this as the lead single.

— Clara Bow
At five am, when I first listened to this song, like everyone else, I thought that was the end of the album. With all of Taylor's narrative-led songs, you can group or pair these together as wiser versions of each other. I think Clara Bow sounds like "The Lucky One" from Red, which was allegedly written about Joni Mitchell. The references to Clara Bow and Stevie Nicks and herself show how women who have publicly forged their path under camera lights should be recognised for what they sacrificed, their hard work ethic, their strength of character, and the power they wield. At the same time,

they are CONSTANTLY compared to one another. Women are also expected to be emotional beings, but they are endlessly criticised for being so.

— Florida!!! (feat. Florence + the Machine)
I like the sustained theme of escapism in this song. There is a desire to run and be uprooted just for the sake of (your sanity) and start again. The idea of home as a solace is crushed and given temporary status with cheating husbands and nobody asking questions. We know what she is capable of with *evermore's* "no body, no crime," this song portrays Taylor committing crimes of the heart that we see in other songs.

— Down Bad
This is such a "I'm sad but I'm still in public" song. It's a recalling of falling hard and the time between staying on the ground and getting back up. It's a sacred and sad place to stay. It reminds me of *evermore's* "'Tis the damn season". There's a lyric parallel that comes from 1989 (there are a few of these in TTPD).

— Guilty as Sin?
We have come a long way from inferred activities in *Speak Now* with reference to the drawer of her things at his place. It's pretty clear reading these lyrics that Taylor understands that her once early teenage, now adult audiences have grown up alongside her, and their tendencies to fantasise and pine after lost loves have also evolved. She recalls the things they never did, underlying the ultimate what-if. I like the way this song could be connected to "False God" with its discussions of guilt, sin and desires.

— I Can Fix Him (No Really I Can)
There are a few fluctuating Taylor moods in this album: anger, depression, and sombre joy. They float around the stages of grief that were talked about in the album variants. This song is dripping

with delusion and denial right up until the last line. "Who's Afraid of Little Old Me, (the previous track) is a screamer, but this song is a mellowed monologue of wanting to rise to a challenge and prove people wrong. It's a common theme in her music that strong women fixate on things they want until they get hurt, and this narrative of repairing things that we didn't break in the first place is interesting. The imaginary setting of this song is an old western country saloon, where a woman sits reminiscing on her failed attempts at intertwining herself with someone who was troublesome to begin with.

— **Fresh Out the Slammer**
I have created a narrative around Getaway Car and Fresh Out The Slammer. I like to think that the lovers that stole the getaway car did their time and have written a reflection of their inCARceration. One of the best (my favourite) double meanings in these lyrics is "handcuffed to the spell I was under." Twice over, we are entrapped and under a trance that covers our eyes.

— **The Smallest Man Who Ever Lived**
This is a scathing song, and as we come towards the end of the regular album (before she had snapped and released the second set of 15 songs as the Anthology), it truly sets the negative tone, but it shifts quickly to a soft return of joy with the next track. It's the grown-up version of "The Moment I Knew" and "Dear John."

There you have the first half of The Tortured Poets Department.

I am not analysing the following fifteen songs (there are 31 tracks in total) of TTPD: The Anthology because I too, was not prepared for a double album, it being the first time she has done it. But I won't ignore them either. A fan theory online connects the tracks, "Cassandra," "Peter," and "Robin" by proper noun song titles, ordering them to form the acronym 'CPR' which then comes back to the motifs of the death of her relationships throughout the album; cameos of Dead Poets in music videos and mentions of post-mortems (the first line of "How Did It End?"), and birds that lure sailors to safe waters only to be shot down. Track 18 is named "imgonnagetyouback" and it's not often that Taylor removes punctuation and spacing in song titles. This song is about the early stages of a relationship and the question of what happens next. The title echoes the lyrics by being a double entendre, getting someone back, meaning either retribution or recovering the relationship.

Track 19 "The Albatross," has narrative connections to Romantic poet Samuel Taylor Coleridge's definitive poem *The Rime of the Ancient Mariner*. I have an annotated and highlighted copy of this text that is eight pages long, sitting in a box of archived schoolwork in my bedroom in Australia. When I saw the variation single, I was taken back to the weeks I spent when I was 16, obsessing over every word. Now, I reread those words, which take on an updated meaning. In the poem, the albatross guides sailors through troubled waters only to be wrongfully killed. Bad luck follows the guilty sailors through the rest of their journey, and they see it as an omen for their crimes. The narrative could be read as if Taylor is "The Albatross," and indeed, she dressed like one in white with black gloves for the 2024 Grammy Awards. Fans online noted that albatrosses spend the first six years of their lives without touching the ground, and she spent the same amount of time in her longest relationship.

Track 24 "thanK you aIMee" is an interesting one because, to fans, there are clear indicators about the subject of this song. It is known that Taylor puts secret messages in her lyric booklets using random capitals, but this is the first time she has done this in a song, which is significant. The letters spell KIM. This can be added to the list of Taylor's songs about bullying (*Speak Now*'s "Mean," *folklore*'s "Mad Woman," and *Lover*'s "You Need To Calm Down") but are also about Kim Kardashian with pointed references to a bronze spray-tanned statue (*reputation*'s "Look What You Made Me Do" and "This is Why We Can't Have Nice Things" also have pointed references).

Aimee could be anyone, but Taylor has a habit of making efforts to hint at identities without confirming them. This is ultimately a middle finger song, and it is easy to change names and hide the real ones in plain sight. There is a second person, more obscure, mentioned in this song. Taylor dealt with a lot of bullying at school when she was starting out. In early interviews, she talks about dreading the days at school after newspaper articles about her music came out because she was teased for it. It makes me think of past lyrics from the *Speak Now* era, where she writes about people throwing rocks at things that shine. Once again, she triumphs over bullies, whoever they are.

Track 27 "Cassandra," tells the story of the Greek goddess gifted with speaking truthful prophecies but cursed with no one ever believing them. A big fan of details and sharing her writing process, Taylor seldom includes voice memos, but when she does, listening to them is like unlocking a new level of appreciation. She did them with her 1989 release with certain tracks, and also for TTPD with the tracks "Who's Afraid of Little Old Me," "The Black Dog," and "Cassandra." Of the latter, she said, "I love this track so much…read into this what you will based on our current social and cultural climate." In Track 28, "Peter," she adds new lyrical phases and youthful disappearances to previously mentioned literary characters. I messaged some friends the next day after the album, saying, "Taylor did write about me in this album."

Track 17 on *The Tortured Poets Department* is called "The Black Dog." In south London, The Black Dog is a pub next to the beautiful Vauxhall Pleasure Gardens. The album had been out for five days when I visited the pub. It was lively but not uncomfortably so, and getting more packed as Wednesday went on. It is a proven stereotype that British pub culture dictates that the end of every workday is time to visit the local watering hole, not just Fridays, so by the time I left at 8 pm, it was still not time to go home. The BBC interviewed the event manager Lily Bottomley, who described the Swifties' reaction to the iconic name-drop as, "Amazing and overwhelmingly positive. The Black Dog is a beautiful neighbourhood pub. It's really small and really cosy so I can imagine the neighbourhood feel, the community, would appeal to her. Obviously, being as famous as she is [it's] maybe a nice break. We've had [the album] on non-stop in the pub. We've had singalongs from fans. It's been amazing." I chatted with the bar manager on shift, who said when I asked how many journalists had been in the last couple of days, "Too many, I've lost count." Josh Barrie, writing for The Evening Standard, said,

> The Black Dog in Vauxhall was, until the mighty Taylor Swift effect, a fairly average, albeit higher-end South London pub. It hasn't been a boozer for some time: drinkers will find branded lager, local IPAs and bottles of Chablis; the food menu dips into pub classics but is more a haven to burrata and wild mushroom risotto. Then the most famous pop star in the world named a song after the place and fans – sorry, "Swifties" – soon started to descend. They turned up to shoot TikTok videos in an unlikely pilgrimage. To tourists it might even be a little hard to find…it more often serves office workers and locals – and so the sudden deluge is all the more impressive. Apparently Swift didn't ever visit – pub staff say they scoured CCTV to see if they could spot her, to no avail – but her ex-boyfriend, London actor Joe Alwyn, supposedly did. The events and social media manager for the small hospitality group SC Soho, which owns the pub, pretty much confirmed his attendance to the media as interest piqued.

The pub's marketing manager, Amy Cowley, added: "This is the Taylor Swift Effect – anything she touches goes viral. We're super excited. It was a great atmosphere last night with the fans. We're not sure if she visited. She might have done – we wouldn't even know. It's a possibility, but it's great to keep her fans in suspense. We have members of the team who are big Swifties. On Friday, everyone got a swift half of our Black Dog lager and we're running that for the next week with food purchases." In a cover story interview with *The Times* in June, Joe Alwyn mentions his downtime involves going to the pub with friends. Laura Pullman, the interviewer, jokes that it probably won't be The Black Dog, and Alwyn's answer is, "I've never been to Vauxhall," so there could be more to this story, or it's simply about someone else.

    Before I walked into the pub, I took photos of the outside where they had made a board with Taylor's lyrics on it, and I was interviewed for CBS News who were hunting around looking for Swifties on their pilgrimage to the location that now had become a song. It was cold for an April afternoon, but I welcomed the extended hours of the sun. For the few hours I was there, I could almost tell who was a Swiftie: the ones standing outside and snapping pictures and not walking in, but also the ones that came for a pint and then left. I met two American Swifties, Daniela and Jacqueline, who were visiting the pub for the same purpose as me. Their trip to London was booked before the album had been announced. They'd seen the pub on TikTok and decided to visit on their last day in the city, enjoying the happenstance of it all. When the New York-based sisters showed me their days-old matching Taylor tattoos, "Love you to the moon and to Saturn," I knew I had picked the right people at the bar with whom to have a conversation. These moments are wrapped in gold. I remember when I sat, wrote and watched "The Taylor Swift Effect" in full force. The same thing happened when my new friends left; I asked a pair of siblings to mind my bag and we ended up just talking about the album. They weren't fans, so I enjoyed explaining the hype about how some people were here just because of Taylor.

    After the Australia/Singapore leg of The Eras Tour wrapped up in March, there was almost a three-month break until the first night of the European leg in Paris. On May 9, the setlist was adjusted to include TTPD after its release. Six songs were removed; "The Archer," "Long Live," "the 1," "the last great american dynasty," "tis the damn season," and "tolerate it" to make way for seven new TTPD songs: "But Daddy I Love Him," "So High School," "Who's Afraid of Little Old Me?," "Down Bad," "Fortnight," "The Smallest Man Who Ever Lived," and "I Can Do It With A Broken Heart." Previous Taylor Swift tours were around two hours in length, but The Eras Tour was a gargantuan exception. The concert was three hours and fifteen minutes long, and 45 tracks were performed at that time. In comparison, on the *reputation* Stadium Tour, Taylor performed 19 tracks. For the 1989 World Tour, she performed 18 tracks, and The Red Tour and the *Speak Now* World Tour had 17 songs each.

    I love that the album in its colossus can be summed up in its final song. Track 31 "The Manuscript," is the one that made me cry in the staff room at work on release day. The stripped piano intro is so beautiful and simple, and the bridge hurts me to the point that it's overwhelming. Looking backward is what Taylor and I have done for the majority of our teenage years and our twenties, and she has taught me that is a perfectly normal response to experiencing pain. There are direct parallels in this song to the way she wrote "Tim McGraw" her first single from her debut album. There is repetition in the first and last lyrics of that song, the same as there is with "The Manuscript." It does make me think how this is symbolic, she is still writing songs the same way she did as a teenager. In music it's called a repeat: a return to familiar sounds and a place in the song we've heard before. In poetry it is called a cyclical. For Taylor to return to the same technique she used in her very first song is a beautiful way to look all the way back. She's done it for every album, and *The Tortured Poets Department* is no exception: reflecting on the hurt, picking herself back up again, and learning from one mistake at a time. I have done it with my past relationships, too, sorting through my insecurities and searching for souls lost to old photographs.

From one tortured poet to another. Here's to another 18 years of listening to your music, Tay.

The Taylor Swift Effect.

How exactly did this Tennessee teenager become one of the most influential people on the planet?

My favourite word is "zeitgeist," I learnt it back in high school. When it came time for me to study it at university, I remembered the German translations for "time" and "spirit/ghost" and became obsessed with how only two syllables can encapsulate a whole sentence in English. Zeitgeist means "the spirit of the time/age, the cultural context we exist in, the moment." For me, it has been the twilight of the twentieth century and the first quarter of the twenty-first, filled with music, not just Taylor's. Growing up, my parents made sure that my brother and I knew how to enjoy ourselves through singing and dancing in all contexts. They weren't musicians, but they were music fans. I can tell you their favourite songs, and which ones make them swing you in their arms in the kitchen and which ones make them weep quietly over computer screens in the office (it was one time, and it was an accident, right, dad?). Whether we were taken to live music events or singing karaoke on family picnics or at home, music has always brought my family together.

At her core, Taylor creates music that reaches millions, but the "Taylor Swift Effect," as it has come to be known, transcends songwriting. I don't want people reading this last chapter to think that I think Taylor Swift is *singlehandedly* changing the ways people think about complex issues around gender equality, feminism, politics, music diversity and ownership, but she is a defining voice of the zeitgeist of the last two decades. She has an enormous platform with the ability to mobilise entire generations of people into action. When it comes to important conversations, loud voices are the ones that are heard. The following list of the Taylor Swift Effect is not exhaustive, and this phenomenon truly has its own dedicated Wikipedia page for every possible sector of culture, so I have tailored this list from my personal observations.

For some fans, the Taylor Swift Effect and her music meant a taste of the outside world. In 2023, Joe Garcia, writing for The New Yorker, stated, "Listening to Taylor Swift in Prison: Her music makes me feel that I'm still part of the world I left behind." He retraced his time incarcerated, beginning in 2009, and was sentenced to life in prison. Garcia contributed to the Prison Journalism Project, a non-profit organisation that trains incarcerated writers to be journalists and publish their stories. Taylor's albums were a respite for Garcia, the timeline being significant. Red reminded him of his sweetheart, "Everything Has Changed," called back to a time spent with his partner by his side. When "We Are Never Getting Back Together" played, he reflected on the time spent apart. "It didn't seem fair to expect her to wait for me, and I told her she deserved a partner who could be with her. But we didn't use the word 'never,' and deep down, I always hoped we'd get back together." Though initially chastised by some inmates, he did find Swiftie friends,

> When "Red" arrived, I finally found out why Lam had been clowning me in front of Hung. "Red" was the only Swift CD that Hung didn't own – because he considered it a misguided pop departure from the country greatness of "Fearless" and "Speak Now." Eventually, Lam outed himself as a Swiftie, too. For six months, the three of us would work out and debate which album was best.

He recalled being in isolation during the pandemic in 2020, unsure when life would return to normal. "I followed San Quentin's Covid-19 related death tallies on the local news. Would I die alone in this cell, suddenly and violently breathless? I made a playlist of Swift's most uplifting songs, listening for the happiness in her voice." The end of Garcia's article is reflective and repentant.

> In "Karma," Swift sings, "Ask me what I learned from all those years / Ask me what I earned from all those tears." A

few months from now, California's Board of Parole Hearings will ask me questions like that. What have I learned? What do I have to show for my twenty years of incarceration? In the months ahead, when these questions keep me up at night, I will listen to "Midnights." The woman I love says she's ready to meet me on the other side of the prison wall, on the day that I walk into the daylight. Recently, she asked me, "If you could go anywhere, do anything, that first day out, what would you want us to go do?" That question keeps me up at night, too.

For other fans, the Taylor Swift Effect means the creation of businesses and careers. Sarah Chapelle, who runs her Tumblr blog and social media pages as @taylorswiftstyle, reports meticulously on Taylor's clothing. She has catalogued jewellery, shoes, elite designer brands and accessible fashion duplicates for fans to copy, tracking Taylor's styles since 2011. Her wealth of knowledge is unprecedented. She attended the New York City 1989 secret sessions in 2014. She has almost 340,000 Instagram followers and makes a deliberate decision not to publish photographs in her fashion analysis if paparazzi have taken them. Instead, she uses artist impressions or drawings, acknowledging Taylor's privacy in a respectful way. I have much admiration for this Swiftie. Her book, *Taylor Swift Style: A Journey Through the Eras*, comes out in October.

Fan reaction videos are an important cultural element of fandom, which is how I discovered @chatsandreacts. These fans are two women from Melbourne: Bonny Barker and Emily Hunt. I found them earlier this year during the Melbourne shows in February. They've been making YouTube album reaction videos since August 2020, starting with Taylor's *Lover* album in 2020. Their style of unfiltered joy and outpouring of emotion garnered worldwide attention when they were featured in TIME *Video* the day before Taylor's most recent album was released in April. Their YouTube Channel has 253k subscribers, and most of their videos have over 1 million views.

In the TIME Video interview, Emily says that in lockdown, "We just decided that not only were we needing something to fill our time with but also that we felt that people were not understanding what Taylor Swift was doing at the time, and so we decided in that moment that we wanted to be starting a YouTube channel so we could just talk about the albums and share why we think she's so incredible." Their Patreon page for the channel is their only source of income and after beginning as "a fun little side project," Bonny says that "Patreon is the only way that we make money currently by doing this. It took almost a year…there's nothing better than being able to talk about Taylor Swift as a full-time job." "It all comes back to the power of the Swifties," Emily says, "Taylor Swift fans are such die-hard fans, and so I think it really makes them feel seen and understood when they're able to see two people who love Taylor Swift to the same level that they do."

The positivity and overwhelming joy emanating from their faces in the reaction videos is medicine. In the video, Bonny says that although the world seems more connected than ever, there is still an epidemic of loneliness that hides behind everyone's social media profiles, and if they can add to that happiness, then that is part of the magic of their job. At the last Melbourne show, February 18, they were invited into the VIP tent, where they met Sabrina Carpenter and were given personal letters from Taylor by her dad, Scott. Taylor is still, in 2024, lurking on the Internet and giving dedicated Swifties incredible rewards.

Alex Hughes worked as the Swiftogeddon DJ (a dedicated Taylor Swift-music club night) when I attended one of the Troxy events in east London on April 12 of this year. Eight other DJs work at these club nights, but she and her DJ partner, Dave Fawbert (of whom this dedicated club night is his brainchild), were responsible for playing nearly six hours of Taylor music for me and my Swiftie friend Steph (and the rest of the packed-out venue) from 8:30 pm until almost 3 am. When it came to the dancing, we clocked nearly 15,000 steps in five hours. Alex shared some of what it's like to work at the club night "for fans to come together and worship at the altar of Taylor Swift." Their summer schedule of club nights is stacked, in twenty-two separate locations across the UK and Ireland, covering particular album groupings because of Taylor's UK concerts, and they also played DJ sets in Wembley's BOXPARK on the same nights as Taylor's shows in June and August.

"The first Swiftogeddon was in the summer of 2019, in Moth Club in London. It was much smaller than the Troxy shows that we do now, but it was fantastic! I worked on the door in 2019, but then COVID-19 hit, and we did a few live-stream shows before starting up again in summer 2021. By that point, I had learned how to DJ, so I also started to do that. I did my first solo DJ show (as in the main room, not the request room) in Brighton in February 2022, and I usually do two to three shows a month, sometimes more during busy periods. The fans who attend our nights are always super kind and supportive, I have seventy friendship bracelets now – all given to me from Swiftogeddon attendees. I still work at my day job, which is as an oncology radiotherapist in the NHS."

What I noticed at the Taylor Swift club night is the raw positivity of strangers dancing together and dancing with friends. I wouldn't be surprised if there were people who attended alone and made friends just by being there. Alex says that this outpouring of joy is because of the Taylor fandom. "It genuinely feels like a community. Growing up and going out, I never had the experience of what I would call "safe" clubbing, as in non-threatening. Swiftogeddon is a room full of people who are inclusive, kind, and there with the sole purpose of sharing a lovely experience. It's extraordinary, and I'm so pleased we've managed to be a small part of that community." I agree wholeheartedly with the concept of "safe" clubbing. There is always an element of wariness and being on your guard for things to go wrong in other nightclub venues, but here, all sense of danger disappears the minute you walk into the building.

Taylor, the Role Model.
There is undoubtedly a sense of "passing the baton" when it comes to the generations of women who have been making the music I've listened to, created both now and before my time. This legacy of examining the female experience through pop music is what Taylor is possibly most known for, but she stands on the shoulders of giants. This legacy existed before her, and it will happen after her, too. Every woman in music has made me appreciate her in their own way. All of these women who have filled my ears are role models. There are home videos of me scream-singing Whitney Houston with my cousins and mum at a party, my first ever CDs were The Veronicas and Missy Higgins, Delta Goodrem and Kelly Clarkson, and of course, I grew up in a house filled with Kylie Minogue and ABBA. The way Taylor has held my hand through heartbreak and celebration at every stage of my life is something I will never be able to express enough gratitude for.

In January 2014, I met a girl at a church summer camp when we were fresh out of high school. She was a Sydney local, and I would often be in the city at university. We spent the week together, and I was so afraid of not seeing her again that I remember saying, "You're not allowed to hang out with me only once a year." A few years later, when I was twenty-three and she was twenty-two, she called me and said she was having a baby. She would be the first of my close friends to start having kids, and it's such a fun and incredible experience to be a part of. Unofficial aunty duties began when her eldest was born, and I adore her and her younger brother. For her third birthday, I bought her first pair of ballet shoes. This family was a constant source of joy when I was stuck in the city during the pandemic.

Now, that precious little girl is five, and I'm in awe of her parents and the amazing person she is becoming. She starts school next year, and I know she is going to blaze every trail, be an incredible sponge of a learner, treat everyone she meets like they're the most important person in the world and just radiate kindness, joy and energy. Her parents send me videos of her singing songs in the car and dancing to new music as if she's listened to Taylor her whole life because, well, she has. Her favourite Taylor tracks are "Look What You Made Me Do" and "Love Story" and if ever there was a perfectly opposite pairing that just magically paired together (like the personalities of her mother and myself), these would be the songs. When my cousin Greta was not yet five, the same age as my friend's daughter is now, and "Look What You Made Me Do" came out originally, I taught her the hook, "I'm sorry, the old Taylor can't come to the phone right now, why? 'cause she's dead" and we danced so much. Now I get emotional thinking about my friend's little girl, who, after not seeing me for almost a year and countless FaceTimes later, ran up to me at the Waterloo train station concourse last summer and said, "Caitlin! I don't have to see you on the phone anymore!" I nearly burst into tears. She loves her brother ferociously (and everyone else) with her whole heart, like I do mine. We are unashamedly ourselves, and I can't wait to think about anyone who tries to tell her that she's not allowed to do something.

This is where the passing of the baton happens again: building a supportive community for the children and the families, we have and will have, raising girls (and boys) to know they can be strong, creative, clever, caring, wise, and protecting them for a little while but also preparing them for a world that should not be afraid of our strength of character. After receiving the award for Woman of the Decade at the *Billboard* Women in Music event in December 2019, Taylor quotes herself from the same event five years earlier. When she accepted the award for Woman of the Year in 2014, at the end of her speech, she said, "Somewhere, right now, your future Woman of the Year is probably sitting in a piano lesson or in a girls' choir, and today, right now we need to take care of her." Cut back to 2019, the next chapter unfolds, and she continues, "I've since learned that, at that exact moment, an eleven-year-old girl in California really was taking piano lessons and really was in a girls' choir, and this year she has been named Woman of the Year at the age of seventeen, her name is Billie." Billie Eilish is a force to be reckoned with in new pop music. Her brother FINNEAS's production talents and writing skills are very special, and she is doing what the women before her have done so well – showing the next generation of teenagers and young people that they can unapologetically be themselves.

Being a role model is a huge responsibility, whether or not you exist in the public eye. Setting examples for the next set of young girls to look up to is important. Taylor proves herself time and time again as a role model for girls to see their potential; a powerful, talented, intelligent and caring woman who spends time in concerts giving her everything to fans and letting them take something away. At every concert of The Eras Tour, Taylor or her team carefully selects (online research and Taylurking is done prior to the show) a member of the audience to receive the "22" hat, the one she wears singing the song from *Red*. This tradition has created a tear-jerking moment at every show where Taylor and the fan have a brief interaction, swap a friendship bracelet and embrace before Taylor joins her line of dancers and sings directly to the audience member. A majority of these chosen few are young girls, though there are exceptions, and this interaction proves to me, again, the enormous lengths she goes to in taking care of her fans. My friend's beautiful daughter, my cousins Olive, Amelia, Lilly, Greta, and all the girls I know who are turning into brilliant young women before my eyes. I love being a part of the community that gets to take care of you.

Taylor, the Man.
Women experience sexism far too early, but if the advent of social and multimedia platforms has positively changed the way we communicate, it has given young women the confidence to voice their opinions and learn the difference between constructive criticism and blatant misogyny and enable them to stand up for themselves.

I am very grateful to have been surrounded by supportive and kind males in my immediate family. And also, because the other families that surrounded us growing up were very much male-dominant, it meant I had to keep up with the boys. But it's not about keeping up. It's about making space. Once, when I was fifteen, I went to a youth group dress-up night with the theme of superheroes. I spoke to friends about costumes, expressing interest in going as the Black Widow, mostly because I am a massive Robert Downey Jnr fan, and *Iron Man 2* (2010) was in cinemas. The costume was simple; I could wear all black, find a chunky belt and curl my hair. I remember a boy I went to school with saying to me, "Oh, you can't go as her, you don't have the body for it." I don't remember what I ended up going as and I wish I'd had the vocabulary to address that situation back then. Earlier than that, maybe a year or two before, another male friend at school sat next to me while we were waiting for science to start. He tapped me on the knee, smirked and said "How's it going, Chewbacca?" referring to the volume of hair on my legs that I had to let grow before it was easily removed. I started waxing my legs at age 11, and his comment could only mean that he thought it was about time I shaved my legs. He had no understanding of how offensive that comment was and even less of an understanding that it was none of his business. It didn't affect him at all. It affected me; the comment stuck. Why do men say such hurtful things based on gender? A lot of the time, my questions start with why. Why did you have to say that? Why is that okay? Next year, I will be 30, and I'm still flabbergasted by the audacity men have to speak about women's lives with negative trolling instead of kindness and love. Taylor introduces her song "The Man" at her NPR Tiny Desk Concert like this.

> This is a song that I had wanted to write conceptually for a very long time, because over the course of my life it has occurred to me that we have a bit of a double-standard issue in our society. It's something I've thought about, about 700

million times a day for the last ten years of my life and I was always just wondering like can I write a song about this, is there a concise and catchy way to write a song about this, what angle would I take, and so I decided the most fun thing to do would be to imagine what my life would be like and what people would say about my life, if I did all the same things, but if I was a...man.

Do not let this catchy electro-pop track behind the lyrics distract from the message it begs you to listen to. All women are tired of wondering if we would get to the places we want to go faster, if we were cisgender men. The music video, directed by Taylor, stars Taylor as a man, *spoiler* (I remember when the video came out, and it took me all of four seconds to think, "Hey...OH that's HER!") The song is a biting exploration of gender disparity. Released as Lover's fourth single on January 27, 2020, and co-written and co-produced with Joel Little, who worked on "ME!" with her, the lyrics play very unironically with the dichotomies of dating commitments vs. conquests, career accomplishments and working hard vs. power plays, twisting the turn of phrase, "You're THE MAN" from an affirmation into a daydream. Taylor asks us what it's like to be believed. Why does the line from this song affect us so much? Because it reflects Taylor's experiences of the unfairness in legal environments where victims of sexual assault claims are not taken seriously. It reflects every sexual assault victim's experience of not being taken seriously. Why are men taken at their word but not women? The workplace inequalities of focus on clothing instead of strength of character and intelligence aren't left out either, summarised in a single line. Taylor is using her platform and industry experience to lay it out very clearly. "What I was wearing, if I was rude, could all be separated from my good ideas and power moves?"

Facing criticism as a powerful, talented woman expressing her feelings and her experiences through the songs without explicitly identifying her detractors and abusers is not something specific to Taylor at all. Taylor told Tracy Smith while promoting *Lover* on *CBS Sunday Morning*, "There's a different vocabulary for men and women in the music industry. A man does something, and it's strategic; a woman does the same thing, and it's calculated. A man is allowed to react; a woman can only overreact." In an interview with Sydney's 2DAY FM, while promoting *1989*, Taylor answered a question regarding the relationship-heavy subject matter in her catalogue. "People are gonna say 'Oh...she just writes songs about her ex-boyfriends.' And I think, frankly, that's a very sexist angle to take. No one says that about Ed Sheeran. No one says that about Bruno Mars. They're all writing songs about their exes, their current girlfriends, their love life, and no one raises a red flag there." In 2024, when I still get asked whether Taylor only writes songs about her exes, I direct whoever asks to at least 15 songs, sometimes more, from each album. I shouldn't have to, but here they are: "Tied Together with a Smile," "The Best Day," "Innocent," "Starlight," "Welcome to New York," "Look What You Made Me Do," "Soon You'll Get Better," "epiphany," "no body no crime," "You're On Your Own, Kid" and "Clara Bow."

Aretha Franklin, Dolly Parton, Joni Mitchell, Stevie Nicks, Whitney Houston, Selena Quintanilla-Pérez, June Carter Cash, Madonna, Lady Gaga, Britney Spears, Shania Twain, Kylie Minogue, Beyonce, Jennifer Lopez, Janet Jackson, P!nk, Kelly Clarkson and so many more coming through the industry, have been studied for their contributions. Every one of them has had to fight the battle against sexism since the beginning of their careers. Almost as pernicious as the embedded sexism is the battles they have fought (fabricated by the press or otherwise), as the media is always looking for a victor after pitting women against each other. P!nk's hair looks like a boy's, Gaga's outfits are offensive, Britney is off the rails, Beyoncé can't sing country, Janet needs to apologise for something Justin did, Billie needs to wear more feminine clothes, the list is exhaustive and exhausting. The disparity between cases of stalkers, public shaming and female artists fearing for their lives (Selena Quintanilla-Pérez was shot and killed by the president of her fan club when she was twenty-three in 1995) is way too unbalanced in comparison to male artists in the music industry.

It also begs the question that if we are to be making progress as a gender, the pay gap – which is quite frankly both exasperating and offensive – needs to be closed. Olivia Colman, the Oscar-winning actress spoke out about the Hollywood pay gap on CNN in March 2024. Journalist Christiane Amanpour asks, "Are women considered now big box office draws?" To which Olivia replies,

> Research suggests that they have always been big box office draws...but male actors get paid more because they used to say they draw in the audiences, and actually that hasn't been true for decades. But they still like to use that as a reason to not pay women as much as their male counterparts in our industry...I'm very aware that if I was Oliver Colman, I'd be earning a fuck of a lot more than I am.

All women, regardless of industry or popularity or career level have their own version of the same story. Another thing that needs to stop is sexist jokes for the sake of easy laughs on film and television. A Netflix series, *Ginny and Georgia*, made a slut-shaming joke in 2021 aimed at Taylor, where a character says, "What do you care? You go through men faster than Taylor Swift." Taylor took to social media to call out the show's poor form. "Hey Ginny & Georgia, 2010 called, and it wants its lazy, deeply sexist joke back. How about we stop degrading hard-working women by defining this horse shit as FuNnY. Also, @netflix, after Miss Americana, this outfit doesn't look cute on you. Happy Women's History Month I guess." We've come a long way? The overturning of Roe vs. Wade in the US Supreme Court disagrees. We need to keep going.

Taylor, the Muse.

A *New York Times* article written by Joe Coscarelli on May 17, 2024, titled "How Big is Taylor Swift?" is a succinct analysis of her reach and discography. It mentions musical acts that we assign to different sections of meteoric musical success: The Beatles, Michael Jackson, Britney Spears, Elton John and Bruce Springsteen, Madonna, Drake and Beyoncé all bearing different headings to their name: hit singles, album sales, pop-stardom, tour veterans, reinvention through eras, and modern heavyweights. Taylor, as it turns out, takes pieces of each star and makes everyone pay attention. She has her own muses and inspiration, and many of them have been trailblazers in their own right. Coscarelli writes, "Besides music being personal and subjective, the nature of success (and how it is calculated) has changed drastically over time. Much of a star's grip on the zeitgeist is also intangible – a vibe in the air, their influence moving subtly but undeniably through culture." When referring to the Beatles, the chokehold on pop culture is clear but also the phenomenon of hit singles and records broken is defined. With *Midnights* in 2022, Taylor became the first artist to occupy the entire Top 10 on the Hot 100 at once, and also repeated that feat, eclipsing herself in April with the Top 14 being songs from *The Tortured Poets Department*. Coscarelli says,

> The length of Swift's career has allowed her into the Beatles' vaunted ballpark by giving her the chance to evolve her sound, grow her loyal audience and take full advantage of technological advances. Yet as wild as it is for the Beatles to have accomplished so much in so little time, Swift's longevity might be considered equally impressive in pop music, which often overvalues the new and – especially among female artists – the young.

Madonna is key in representing longevity and reinvention in pop music. Michael Jackson still holds his records for album sales;

his "solo albums have been certified 72 times platinum. Swift's 11 original albums have been certified 50 times platinum." Bruce Springsteen and Elton John are 50 years into their careers and still achieving popularity and commercial success with their long-running world tours. The dizzying trajectory of pop-music fame is what connects Taylor and Britney; they both released debut singles at 16, occupying a dominant place in the cultural conversation, but without being labelled a singer-songwriter, Britney sadly became part of a group that Coscarelli calls "pop singers that audiences can treat as disposable, with a new model always on the horizon." Standing with Beyonce and Drake in the modern era, Coscarelli says they all,

> Have maneuvered the industry transition between CDs, downloads and streaming to become defining modern superstars while also maximising those intangibles like cultural reach and celebrity domination... Beyoncé, now 23 years into a solo career after her time with the group Destiny's Child, stands with Swift when it comes to versatility and longevity, plus sustained commercial dominance...and then there is Drake, a relentless hitmaker. Like Swift, Drake has optimised his output to take advantage of the way streaming has reshaped the industry and its accolades to set new records, including 328 total entries on the Hot 100. Swift, with 232, is the only other artist with at least 200.

When it comes to touring records, Taylor's *reputation* Stadium Tour is the highest-grossing of all time by women and comes in at fourth place, under The Rolling Stones, U2 and Elton John, appearing three decades later than U2. Her legendary status is attributed to the speed at which she reached these milestones. For Taylor, being placed in the mix of musical juggernauts is one thing, but for other artists to emerge and younger contemporaries to be compared to her is another. In the *Tortured Poets Department*, Track 16 is titled "Clara Bow." She spoke to Amazon Music, saying,

I used to sit in record labels trying to get a record deal when I was a little kid. And they'd say, 'you know, you remind us of...' and then they'd name an artist, and then they'd kind of say something disparaging about her, 'but you're this, you're so much better in this way or that way.' And that's how we teach women to see themselves, as like you could be the new replacement for this woman who's done something great before you. I picked women who have done great things in the past and have been these archetypes of greatness in the entertainment industry. Clara Bow was the first 'it girl.' Stevie Nicks is an icon and an incredible example for anyone who wants to write songs and make music.

In the final lyric of the song, which refers to the future being bright and dazzling, I believe Taylor is talking about women in music who are following behind her: twenty-something females breaking into the scene and amassing millions of fans. Maisie Peters, Griff, Gretta Ray, Cate Canning, Gracie Abrams and Sabrina Carpenter come to mind. This group are all brilliant performers who grew up listening to Taylor, just like I did and most of them have, or soon will, play in stadiums like Taylor does. These artists remind me of Taylor for their presence on stage, fan interactions and songwriting skills.

Griff and Maisie Peters are UK artists and I've seen their careers skyrocket thanks to the support of fellow British acts. Maisie Peters was originally signed to Atlantic Records but left at age twenty-one to release her first album with Ed Sheeran's Gingerbread Records label. She toured with Ed Sheeran throughout 2022-23 with select dates in England, Europe, Australia, New Zealand and the US, as did Griff for dates in Germany and Switzerland. On May 27 2024, Griff announced that she would be Taylor's Eras Tour opener for the Wembley Stadium show on June 22, which is the show I attended and on August 5, Maisie announced she would be The Eras Tour opener on August 19 for the second set of London shows. Maisie is currently the youngest (22 years old) solo British female artist to claim a #1 album on the UK charts in almost a decade with *The Good Witch* in 2023. Griff was named the Rising Star at the 2021 Brit Awards and was one of the youngest winners at 20 years old. Later this year, both will open for Coldplay's *Music of the Spheres* World Tour with select dates in Europe and Asia. They have also both had successful arena headline tours across the world. They are both very vocal Swifties, and when I saw Maisie play a headline show at the Hammersmith Apollo in April 2023, she covered "Dear John" from *Speak Now*. Maisie's "Hollow" (2021) and Griff's "Astronaut" (2023) are filled with words that will come to epitomise new generations of heartbroken teenagers.

Cate Canning is a Canadian pop-country singer-songwriter who is good friends with Maisie Peters and is brilliantly navigating the UK festival circuit. I can see her playing events like Glastonbury in the future, headlining country-wide arena tours or embarking on a US tour of her own. Her song, "Ruin" (2022), is one of my favourite sad-girls-still-dance anthems, and it reminds me of "Cornelia Street". Maisie and Cate were announced as supporting acts for BST Hyde Park in July 2024.

In 2016, Gretta Ray released "Drive" while still in high school in a suburb of Melbourne, Australia. It went on to win Triple J Unearthed High, an annual musical competition that searches for undiscovered young talent. The song also won the Vanda & Young Global Songwriting Competition the same year. In her most recent album, *Positive Spin*, the song "Dear Seventeen" by title alone could be seen as influenced by "Fifteen" from *Fearless*. She introduced "Dear Seventeen" in her recent London concert (her largest headlining show outside of Australia) on May 13 at London's Lafayette with this insight, "If I could tell my seventeen-year-old self anything that would happen to her in the future, I wouldn't, because it's important to let her figure that out on her own." She also name-drops Taylor in the song, which fits perfectly into her musical journey: "And have no doubt you're still in love with Taylor."

At her sold-out Lafayette show, the crowd screamed that particular lyric, which was soon followed by a cover of "Guilty As Sin" from *The Tortured Poets Department.*

Sabrina Carpenter and Gracie Abrams are US artists who opened for different dates across the Taylor's Eras Tour. I have seen all the aforementioned young artists live except for these two. Their popularity already transcends national borders. Gracie Abrams worked with Aaron Dessner at The Long Pond Studio on her first album, *Good Riddance* (2023), after his success with *folklore* and *evermore*, and the song "us.," a single from her sophomore album *The Secret of Us* (2024) has Taylor featured. Their collaboration is a supreme endorsement, with Gracie's fan base overlapping Taylor's. Sabrina Carpenter has had a long career as a child television and music star and started, as many do, filming covers of songs and uploading them to her YouTube Channel. One video has Sabrina singing "White Horse" at nine years old. Fifteen years later, she sang the song with Taylor as a duet on the first night of the Sydney Eras Tour when her opening set was cancelled because of weather delays. Her new song, "Espresso," is a classic pop earworm, reminiscent of "Shake It Off" in all its viral glory. Her album *Short n' Sweet* will be released on August 23, 2024. Also known as mine and *Lover*'s birthday. As artists, these young women have Taylor as a significant influence. Taylor's legacy here is inescapable. The future is, indeed, female.

Taylor, the Political Influencer.
The 2020 *Miss Americana* documentary depicts Taylor as a 'voiceless good girl' when it comes to entering political conversation and this persona carried her through the first decade of her career. Just past the halfway mark of the film, there is a shift away from music, moving towards her changing views on politics and activism that emerges in the film's second half. She says,

part of the fabric of being a country artist is, don't force your politics on people, let people live their lives, that is grilled into us...throughout my whole career label executives and publishers would say, don't be like the Dixie Chicks, and I loved the Dixie Chicks...but a nice girl doesn't force their opinions on people, a nice girl smiles and waves and says thank you. A nice girl doesn't make people feel uncomfortable with her views.

This is a known part of American music history. On March 10, 2002, at a concert in Shepherd's Bush, London, Natalie Maines from The Dixie Chicks said in front of their English crowd, "We're ashamed the President of the United States is from Texas." Publicly voicing opposition to the invasion of Iraq meant receiving massive backlash in the US. They were blacklisted from country radio stations, and each band member received death threats. The polarising political landscape of the US is like none other in the world, bleeding into all industries, including music. We hear a journalist tell Taylor, "You've been very secretive about how you're voting, what you're voting for." She responds, "Well, you know, I just figure I'm a twenty-two-year-old singer, I don't know if people want to hear my political views, I think they just kinda want to hear me sing songs about break-ups and feelings." This was how the world's media knew her up until 2018. The midterm elections in 2018 were hugely impacted by the Senate votes in Tennessee. While being driven in a car, Taylor says to the camera, "I really care about my home state [Tennessee], and I know that at this point in time, my home state is a hugely important part of this midterm election...and I'm getting to the point where I can't listen to people telling me no, stay out of it."

In October, Taylor made the first political endorsement of her career. There is an intense (on Taylor's part, but not heated) argument between Taylor and her team in the documentary. Taylor says, "My team's really not happy with me right now. All I've talked about for the last couple of months is the election in Tennessee. It's not that I want to step into this, I can't not at this point, something is different in my life, completely and unchangeably different since the sexual assault trial last year and no man in my organisation and my family will ever understand what that was like." Taylor's political backing of Democratic candidates and, hence, taking a side brought about tension with her team. A section of *Miss Americana* focuses on her 2017 sexual assault case, and this, for Taylor, leads to a wider examination of systems that she believes are flawed and need changing. For her, it's a matter of social justice.

Taylor is very adamant when she says to the camera, "Next time there is any opportunity to change anything, you had better know what you stand for and what you want to say." A male team member can be heard saying, "For twelve years, we've not got involved with politics or religion…imagine if we can to you said we've got this idea that we could half the number of people that come to your next tour." That is what Taylor's team has learned to anticipate in regard to history because of The Dixie Chicks. But it did not happen to Taylor.

> I'm saying right now, that this is something that I know is right, and you guys, I need to be on the right side of history… I just really want you to know that this is important to me… it's right and wrong at this point I can't see another commercial and see her disguising these policies behind the words, Tennessee Christian values. Those aren't Tennessee Christian values, because I live in Tennessee and I'm a Christian and that's not what we stand for… Dad, I just need you to forgive me for doing it, 'cause I'm doing it.

The documentary records the moment when she posts her important endorsement and political comment on her social media, on October 8, sitting with her mum and her publicist, Tree Paine, who says, "I'm not gonna lie, I'm a little nervous." Taylor responds with "You should be." Taylor reflects further that she does not want to be hypocritical when it comes to her fans in the LGBTQ+ community. "I think that it is so frilly and spineless of me to stand on stage and go, 'Happy Pride Month, you guys' and then not say this when someone's literally coming for their necks." Her mother says, "Alright, cheers ladies, cheers, cheers to the Resistance." Then Taylor presses post to her social media. The lengthy statement in question was accompanied by a single black-and-white polaroid photo of Taylor staring down the camera's lens. I've included her post in full because she has not made a statement like this before, so it is significant.

> I'm writing this post about the upcoming midterm elections on November 6, in which I'll be voting in the state of Tennessee. In the past I've been reluctant to publicly voice my political opinions, but due to several events in my life and in the world in the past two years, I feel very differently about that now. I always have and always will cast my vote based on which candidate will protect and fight for the human rights I believe we all deserve in this country. I believe in the fight for LGBTQ rights, and that any form of discrimination based on sexual orientation or gender is WRONG. I believe that the systemic racism we still see in this country towards people of color is terrifying, sickening and prevalent.

> I cannot vote for someone who will not be willing to fight for dignity for ALL Americans, no matter their skin color, gender or who they love. Running for Senate in the state of Tennessee is a woman named Marsha Blackburn. As much as I have in the past and would like to continue voting for women in office, I cannot support Marsha Blackburn. Her voting record in Congress appals and terrifies me. She voted against equal pay for women. She voted against the Reauthorization of the Violence Against Women Act, which attempts to protect women from domestic violence,

stalking, and date rape. She believes businesses have a right to refuse service to gay couples. She also believes they should not have the right to marry. These are not MY Tennessee values. I will be voting for Phil Bredesen for Senate and Jim Cooper for House of Representatives. Please, please educate yourself on the candidates running in your state and vote based on who most closely represents your values. For a lot of us, we may never find a candidate or party with whom we agree 100% on every issue, but we have to vote anyway.

So many intelligent, thoughtful, self-possessed people have turned 18 in the past two years and now have the right and privilege to make their vote count. But first you need to register, which is quick and easy to do. October 9 is the LAST DAY to register to vote in the state of TN. Go to vote.org and you can find all the info. Happy Voting!

In the documentary, after Taylor heads into the stadium to rehearse for the day, a voiceover says, "Vote.org has reported there are more registrations in the last day, since Taylor's post than in all of August." Then Taylor reads a similar article, "Vote.org on Monday, nationwide there have been 51,308 new registrations in the past 24 hours." Those are the kind of numbers that she is capable of swaying. Andrea Hailey, CEO of Vote.org, called it a "highly encouraging sign of voter enthusiasm," Vote.org reported a 1,226% jump in participation in the hour after the post. "Our site was averaging 13,000 users every 30 minutes – a number that Taylor Swift would be proud of," Hailey said, referencing Swift's affinity for the number 13. Though Marsha Blackburn did win, the documentary shows a newsreel that says, "The Bredesen camp was very much hoping for 'the Swift Lift', as they called it, because young voter turnout spiked here by sevenfold from the previous midterm election." If there's a tool in her belt she's used successfully since the beginning of her career, it's her powers of persuasion.

The last ten minutes of *Miss Americana* were a treat for Swifties watching. It was the behind-the-scenes of a song that had never been heard before. Released on January 31, 2020, the single is called "Only The Young," and it was produced by Joel Little. The song references her failed hopes for the 2018 midterm, which led Marsha Blackburn to take office, where she still holds a senate position in 2024. There is another US election at the end of the year, so we will have to wait and see if Taylor will take the opportunity to speak up again. In a clip, Taylor tells her producer, Joel, "If you can shift the power in your direction by being bold enough, then it won't be like this forever." In typical Taylor style, the lyrics in "Only The Young" are both heart-breaking and triumphant. Where the first verse speaks about the anxiety and reality of emergency drills for school shooting scenarios (something unique to America) and has obvious references to Donald Trump, this song is a strong personal statement, much like many political speeches. In the documentary, she says, "I feel really good about not feeling muzzled anymore. And it was my own doing. I needed to learn a lot before turning 29, and it's time to take the masking tape off my mouth, like forever."

Taking a different political stance, released as *Lover's* second single on June 14, 2019, was Track 14 "You Need To Calm Down." The song is a deliberate choice to support the LQBTQI+ community in calling out discrimination and condemning hatred. She posted a letter to her senator on Instagram in conjunction with Pride Month. She started a Change.org petition for the United States Senate to pass the Equality Act, which would protect LGBTQ people from discrimination in their places of work, homes, schools, and other public spaces. At the fan-voted VMAs on August 26, she won Video of the Year, and said this in her acceptance speech.

> In this video, several points were made, you voting for this video means that you want a world where we're all treated equally under the law. At the end of this video, there was a

petition, and there still is a petition for the Equality Act, which basically just says we all deserve equal rights under the law...now it has half a million signatures, which is five times the amount that it would need to warrant a response from the White House...Thank you MTV, for lifting up this point in this video.

This isn't the first time Taylor has sung about human rights and marriage equality in her music. She encouraged people to be with who they want pairing girls and girls and boy and boys in "Welcome to New York" from 1989 in 2014, but six years later, this is a more pointed arrow aimed at homophobia. Jonathan Van Ness (who appeared in the music video alongside his *Queer Eye* presenters) said this about Taylor in the iHeart Music Awards presentation of her Innovator Award in 2023.

> It's not easy to be an ally, it's not easy to use your voice for something that you know people are going to be hateful about, and Taylor was fearless about using her voice, and using her platform to show up for queer and for trans people and I think that's beautiful, I think that's amazing and I think it's something she will continue to do.

Taylor said in the documentary, "I want to wear pink and tell you how I feel about politics, and I don't think that those things have to cancel each other out." Her statement was a pointed response to those who applauded her silence for not getting involved in politics and sticking to what she knows. That part of her life is well and truly over.

Taylor, the Educator.
Being nurtured into a fandom (fanatic kingdom, as I recently found out) is an incredible space to grow up; just ask any child who read or watched any franchise you can think of: *DC Comics, Star Trek, Star*

Wars, Harry Potter, The Hunger Games and many others. Spending time with like-minded people creates a foundational sense of belonging. Maybe you've watched a particular television show for decades or shared a love of pop culture through generations. But often, fan groups are discredited. At university I learned there is an intense intersection between fans and academia. Why? To simply put it, we know the most. Ask my dad about his favourite sports teams, ask my mum about ABBA and Kylie Minogue, ask my brother about Toyota Land Cruisers, and like anybody, you will find our passions. The same runs for every person you meet, and I love learning about the things people know lots about.

Four songs featured in *Fearless* were part of an academic study in 2011. "Fifteen," "White Horse," "You Belong With Me," and "Love Story" all were referenced in an academic paper titled "Songs as a Medium for Embedded Reproductive Messages" in *Evolutionary Psychology*. The authors, Dawn R. Hobbs and Gordon G. Gallup, Jr., from the University at Albany, found that "approximately 92% of the 174 songs that made it into the Top Ten in 2009 contained one or more reproductive messages, with an average of 10.49 reproductive phrases per song." "Love Story" was an example of one of the eighteen specific categories of reproductive messages dealing with commitment and fidelity, referencing "dedication, sincerity and long-term commitments to a relationship such as marriage." Analysis of songs is something that fans do the minute they hear them for the first time. We pull them to pieces, we find layers of meanings, we obsess over metaphors, and we memorise every word ready for recitation at any moment. Obsession is a word that, for a long time, has had negative connotations, but I never saw it as such. For me and everyone around the world who is "obsessed" with something: it as a speciality no one else has and not something you have to hide.

At this moment, there are approximately 25 universities across the world running courses focusing on aspects of Taylor's songwriting and cultural impact. Stanford University has two courses, 'All Too Well (Ten Week Version),' and 'The Last Great American Songwriter: Storytelling With Taylor Swift Through the Eras,' both looking at song analysis. St. Thomas University in Canada runs a course called 'Communications and Taylor Swift' that examines her marketing, strategies and social media usage. Three universities held academic conferences focused on Taylor's career; Indiana University's 'Taylor Swift: The Conference Era' was November 3-5, 2023, and the University of Melbourne held a 'Swiftposium' on February 11-13. The Institute of Popular Music at the University of Liverpool ran 'Tay Day: Liverpool's Version' on June 12, 2024. The full-day program included academic talks from subjects across the European continent including her impact on feminism, the LQBTQI+ community, and even the millipede that is named after her. The end of the day involved a "session of 'Critical Karaoke,' where researchers perform one-song essays to their chosen Taylor Swift track."

Melbourne and Liverpool's conference dates coincided with The Eras Tour stops in those cities. The keynote speakers of Melbourne's 'Swiftposium', have both focused their careers on Taylor Swift in different ways. Brittany Spanos, a writer for *Rolling Stone*, teaches the course 'Swiftology 101' at New York University's Clive Davis School of Recorded Music. Dr. Georgia Carroll is an academic whose focus is fan communities. She wrote her PhD in Sociology on Taylor Swift and the *Supernatural* (television series) fandom communities. Submitted in February 2023, it is titled, "'Oh My God, how did I spend all that money?': Lived experiences in two commodified fandom communities." In her work, she looks at social capital, "the benefits one can gain through group membership," fan consumption (in many cases the purchase of fan-related products, merchandise and concert tickets) and fan labour within communities, which she gives an example of as "participation on social media functions as a form of affective labour, both within the context of contributing to the value and creation of the site and in creating value-generating content for the object of fandom." The hundreds of dedicated Taylor Swift Facebook pages are evidence of this. People have interacted with strangers on the Internet because of Taylor and become close friends and have meet ups offline. This is also manifested in 2024, with the mass conceptualisation, creation, and distribution of friendship bracelets at her Eras concerts. Simple, beautiful, hand-made pieces have come to symbolise the fans' connection to each other and to Taylor because the messages on those bracelets are her lyrics. Georgia's PhD is an example of building knowledge and creating careers through fan communities.

In 2017, I attended a university class that taught digital and social media. The course examined trends and how influencers manipulated and used social platforms for commercial gain, widespread status and acknowledgement. It was the dawning of a new age of celebrity. The class was run by Dr. Jonathan Hutchinson, now the Chair of the Media and Communication Discipline at the University of Sydney. The same year, the university ran a series called Raising the Bar, which involved bringing academic talks into non-academic settings and encouraging deeper thought and conversation. With twenty talks happening simultaneously across different bars on one night (October 25), one of these presentations was called, "Look what you made me do: Taylor Swift and (un)social media." The speaker was my lecturer, Dr. Hutchinson. The title is clever but the content (and its impeccable timing) was better still – delivered less than a week before the release of her anticipated "comeback album" *reputation*. I didn't attend this talk, but with the transcript available online, I sorely wished I had.

In this talk, Jonathan acknowledged that, "She secretly, you know, reinvented that Instagram space and started posting material which was referencing her new album, and her new song, and her new shows. So, you know, it's really just marketing points in many ways." By "deleting all of her content, I think that's saying something about who we are within the social media space, and how we have lost control of our histories, or our right to be deleted in these spaces." The right to be deleted is interesting. By deleting it and starting it again with a shift towards album promotion and less sharing of personal stories, this was definitely a marked reaction to what burned her in the past; social media backlash. Jonathan said in his Raising the Bar talk,

> ...this is not just about social media where she's suddenly cutting off from her fans, she's really going back to what could be a traditional media type of response, where this is a one too many kind of thing. It's, 'This is my message; you will consume it,' [there will be no explanation, there will just be *reputation* was her rhyme] as opposed to this very sort of I guess two-way conversation which is prevalent to social media. So you might kind of ask yourself, you know, 'Why; why is she doing this to her social kind of media space? Why is she turning it into an unsocial media? You know, why is she making it broadcast only?' So it's an interesting moment for Taylor Swift.

Jonathan also speaks about, "the concept of performing our identities. We're consistently changing, we're always performing a new kind of person who we are. But often our social media platforms, they don't keep up with how we develop as people." And this is how I feel about Taylor Swift and her social media presence now in 2024. It was adjusted significantly in the post-*reputation* world. She posted a lot about her relationship with Calvin Harris for her fans to see (which was later deleted), and we didn't see that with Joe Alwyn; they both escaped the media constantly and did not post about each other but instead were photographed at events together. Right before the Taylor and Travis rumours began in July 2023, Taylor posted a photo for the Fourth of July, captioned "Happy belated Independence Day from your local neighbourhood independent girlies" with photos including Selena and the Haim sisters. Besides this, all of her other Instagram photos have been album announcements and tour updates. After almost a year of dating Travis Kelce, he finally made an appearance on her grid in a selfie with Prince William and his children at her London Eras shows in June 2024. A lot of celebrities do respond to fans using these spaces, and Taylor does sporadically now on TikTok and Tumblr, but there are sadly too many Internet trolls for her to make opening her comments possible.

Taylor, the Football Girlie.
If the only purpose for an examination of Taylor Swift's lyrics was to discover who the songs were written about, then it would be a shallow exploitation and a missed opportunity to analyse not only her songwriting skills but her impact on popular culture. Taylor herself has shed light on or shared their identities to help share more analysis on the songwriting because she is nothing if not cryptically specific. Upon the release of each album, journalists are always hungry for these answers, and they will never get them from Taylor herself; believe me, Ellen has tried. Her fans already know, and the rest of the world has seen the years of paparazzi photos; it's not a hard game to play. Dating Harry Styles and Jake Gyllenhaal shouldn't be the defining element of her career. The press is everyone's favourite aunt, asking the same questions about your relationship status over and over across the dinner table. It's humiliating and exhausting. When asked how she felt about the obsession with Taylor's relationships, my Swiftie friend Rebecca had a more measured view than me, showing how we perceive celebrity relationships.

"It's not something we should be fixating on as a society, but I think it's stupid to ignore the fact that her dating life has helped her; it is part of the brand and part of the business at the end of the day; all of her songs are about this. So it creates intrigue, that is part of the reason why people are so intrigued, and why they comb over lyrics, because she from the start let us into that part of her life."

Fans automatically love her, so we're obviously going to be interested in who she loves. Rebecca says,

"She's never hidden it; she's written about it too. It's kind of a double-edged sword because I feel bad sometimes; obviously, it's sometimes too much; it's fun to know who and then see them out and about, if she wants us to see them out, but people go way too far with it. It definitely interests me, when I hear a song, I want to know who that's about, and when I listen to the lyrics, I think I wonder if that's about that? And it's fun to piece it together, so as much as I could say I wish I didn't care, I definitely care, but it isn't the be-all and end-all, and it's not the only reason her music is interesting, because of who she's dating, but it's part of it."

At the time of writing, the pop culture world (particularly in the US) since the second half of 2023 has been spinning on the Taylor Swift and Travis Kelce axis. Oversaturation of boyfriend content means there is no escaping the news. Neither of them has posted about each other on their social media channels, but unlike Taylor and Joe's relationship, their affections are far from private. Travis Kelce has played for the Kansas City Chiefs since 2013, and euphemisms aside, I had to look up what his football position, 'tight end', was because I didn't know. He has had four Super Bowl appearances (2019, 2020, 2022 and 2023) in five seasons, winning the trophy three times. Behind the allure of sports fame, something highly prized in North American culture, there is an element of kindness and giving back to the community unexpected from such a sports star.

Travis started a charity called 'Eighty-Seven & Running' (his shirt number) in 2015. He watched as role models in his community left their hometown once becoming successful instead of staying and nurturing talent. He had support from friends and family. His charity "helps underserved youth strive to become productive citizens by mentoring and motivating them to explore and develop their abilities while learning critical life skills [and is] dedicated to providing resources and enrichment opportunities for youth and their communities through fundraising, athletic programs, mentoring, and outreach initiatives." After Travis attended the Kansas City stop of The Eras Tour in July 2023, the two made contact. This was before Taylor's first appearance at a Chiefs game in September, amidst a few months of dating rumours. She spoke about the relationship in her TIME Person of the Year interview with Sam Lansky in December,

> Travis very adorably put me on blast on his podcast, which I thought was metal as hell...We started hanging out right after that. So we actually had a significant amount of time that no one knew, which I'm grateful for, because we got to get to know each other. By the time I went to that first game, we were a couple. I think some people think that they saw our first date at that game? We would never be psychotic enough to hard launch a first date...When you say a relationship is public, that means I'm going to see him do what he loves, we're showing up for each other, other people are there and we don't care...The opposite of that is you have to go to an extreme amount of effort to make sure no one knows that you're seeing someone. And we're just proud of each other.

Travis spoke on *New Heights,* the podcast he shares with his football-famous brother Jason, the week after he attended the show. He said, "I was disappointed that she doesn't talk before or after her shows because she has to save her voice for the 44 songs that she sings, so I was a little butt-hurt I didn't get to hand her one of the bracelets I made for her. I received a bunch of them, being there, but I wanted to give Taylor Swift one with my number on it." Jason asks, "Your number as in 87? Or your phone number?" And you can tell Travis is grinning when he replies, "You know which one."

If Taylor and Travis' relationship seems familiar, it is because there are parallels with David and Victoria Beckham. When David and Victoria started dating, Victoria (of Posh Spice Girls fame) was more recognisable to international audiences than he was. When David Beckham came into the picture, the collision of their dual sports-meets-music celebrity made the tabloids explode. Taylor and Travis had their viral moment with the on-field embrace at the Chiefs' victorious Super Bowl in February 2024. Maybe it's because I am not from the US, where there is an understandable lack of American football tradition, but there is the specific acknowledgement and social phenomenon of Taylor as a football girlie, some labelling these fabulous women in sport as "WAGs" (Wives and Girlfriends) which in Victoria and Taylor's and case, they have both embraced and risen above.

On The Eras Tour in Buenos Aires, Argentina, on November 11, she included Travis in a lyric change on-stage in the song "Karma" from *Midnights*, she sang "Karma is the guy on the Chiefs, coming straight home to me." When Taylor shares her personal life with the public, the Internet goes into a tailspin. It could be said that Taylor feels "So High School" (a song on TTPD rife with football references) when she is with Travis, but she knew certain truths when she was "Fifteen" with lyrics about doing much greater things than dating boys on the football team. Almost 14 years later, those words she sung have come back full circle, much to the fans' delight. Swiftie Emma Coleman shed some light on this iconic merging of American cultural archetypes, country music and football.

"In terms of American football celebrity culture, it's very different from pop culture in terms of what Taylor experiences. Travis is really good at what he does at football, but it's not something where people are chasing him in the streets or anything like that. I know in Kansas City, people are really respectful of the players; they're not taking his picture in the supermarket and posting it online. Part of the euphoria in Kansas City is that there are so many Swifties here already, we packed Arrowhead Stadium two nights in a row. The more we've seen them together, I just think they're so cute, I hope they last, because just like I am with any of my friends, I never want it to be something where they're going to be heartbroken at the end, and I think Travis seems like a genuinely great, hilarious, goofy guy. The way he's been handling the press and the questions before the Super Bowl and how he talks about her, it's just refreshing to see in contrast to other situations and ways that guys have responded to being associated with her. It's a lot of fun, and I know people kind of joke that they're our American 'royal couple' because, obviously, we don't have royalty like everyone is excited to see them at the top of their games and killing it together."

Nate Jones wrote an article for *Business Insider* detailing a phenomenon that forges new relationships between fathers and daughters (talking about his own family experiences) because they are now watching football together, and Taylor has created a new demographic of football fans, just like she did with teenage girls and country music. Emma Coleman also reiterates this.

"I also think a big thing has been football dads and their little girls bonding because the girls are getting to see Taylor, their pop princess, having fun [at the Chiefs games] and the dads are having the opportunity to bond with their kids over that. The combining of worlds [between fangirls and universal (predominantly male) football fans] is for sure part of the attraction of the new-found pairing."

There is an element of "glory" in American sports that is only sometimes noticed outside of North America. One has to reach unbelievable levels of fame, emerging as invincible from endless hours of failure before success. The hard work and training it takes to have talent recognised exists long before the fame. Now, it seems, The Kelce Brothers (Travis' brother Jason Kelce played for the Philadelphia Eagles for 13 years) have both achieved major success in football, and now have been given a brighter spotlight, recognisable across the world, by Taylor fans and others alike as international celebrities.

With this intersection between two cultural worlds, there was a small amount of online backlash towards Taylor and her presence at the games. People said the focus on her was taking away from the broadcast time. That was simply untrue. During the Super Bowl broadcast, she had fifty-three 53 seconds of air time in CBS's four-hour television showing, with *Business Insider* reporting that less than a minute of broadcast focus on Taylor was worth about $12.4 million, based on the cost to run a 30-second commercial. Roger Goodell, NFL Commissioner, commented during a news conference before the Super Bowl, "Obviously, it creates a buzz," he said. "It creates another group of young fans, particularly young women, that are interested in seeing why is she going to this game, why is she interested in this game besides Travis. She is a football fan." An article in *Al Jazeera* on February 11, 2024, reported viewing statistics for the NFL before the Super Bowl,

> It has not only boosted Swift's brand value but has also helped bring new fans to the National Football League (NFL), especially women and girls...This has led to a 20 percent increase in sponsorships. The NFL's surge in female viewership cuts across different age demographics. Among teenage girls, NFL viewership has increased by 53 percent. Among the 18-24 age demographic, there has been an increase of 24 per cent. Even without the additional female fans, overall viewer numbers are up. According to NBC Sports, the game in which the Chiefs took on the New York Jets in October attracted 27 million people across all platforms, the highest number since the previous Super Bowl.

Apex Marketing Group conducted analysis on the Taylor Swift Effect on the NFL and the Super Bowl. The equivalent brand value ("EBV") derived from exposure received by Swift in association with the Kansas City Chiefs and the NFL for the period between September 24 and January 22 and from various media (TV, Radio, Newsprint, Digital News & Social Media) is $331.5,000,000 USD. Fanatics, an American manufacturer and online retailer of licensed sportswear, reported that Kelce-branded merchandise had a 400 per cent increase in sales after Taylor's first Chiefs game. Swiftonomics, a term used to describe her economic influence, is in full force here and has infiltrated a sector of society that has yet to be touched by Taylor Swift and her fans: football.

2023 brought Taylor and the NFL together in a beautiful union, but her connections to American sports go further back. At the beginning of her career, she starred in an ad campaign titled "It Stays With You" for the Nashville Predators NHL team in 2009. The video shows a mum and her daughter discussing a hockey game over breakfast, and the mum doesn't believe the daughter saw Taylor Swift at the game. The camera zooms out and Taylor appears sitting in the kitchen next to the daughter before she says, "I was there." As much as I don't understand American sports, I can understand the hype, and I appreciate the female viewership boost that she has given it. Taylor continues to nurture inclusion wherever she goes, and as far as the future of her and Travis is concerned, she knows all the fans want is for her to live her best life, and we will support her no matter who she spends her time with. I can see myself buying a Kelce 87 Chiefs jersey one day just for the fun of it.

Taylor, my Secret Best Friend.
I share this sentiment with a lot of Swifties: listening to every one of her albums feels like a best friend who reassures me, even on days when I don't believe her when she says everything is going to be okay. There lies the simplicity of the expert-level parasocial relationship she has nurtured with her fans. Kelsey Barnes pens

this perfectly in her essay for *Off Chance*, "Making The Case for Parasocial Relationships: Taylor's Version."

> Despite the phrase 'parasocial relationship' typically being thrown as something negative, it does create a ripple effect of fan creation. It's why people are handing out friendship bracelets at concerts and events for figures that aren't Taylor Swift, entire books are written because of one lyric or story she told in a song, and new songs are created after indulging in someone else's work, like for Swift after seeing [the 2019 film] "Someone Great." Like the rest of the world, I don't know Taylor Swift outside of the work she's given us. I tweeted a few years ago that I had the urge to wish her a happy birthday despite not knowing her and many agreed. It's a silly thing, but I see it as a respectful way to throw some love towards someone who has endlessly inspired me and countless others. And yes – I will be wishing her a happy birthday again this year, regardless of whether she will see it or not.

Taylor knows the extent of her fans' love, I am certain. Perhaps it's unrealistic, but my wish is to sit for a couple of hours with a bottle of wine and bring her up to speed on the moments when she's been lyrically and physically present in my life. In interviews, there's an impression of normality for someone who has led their life in the spotlight and under scrutiny. Her friends and celebrities who have shared their opinions of her often attest to this. I cannot count the number of times Taylor's music, and by extension, Taylor herself has assured me that heartbreaks hurt because I truly felt something magical. Her lyrics tell us not to lose that spark. Romantic love will come back around. I just have to be fearless, like the first time I heard her songs. She reassures us that it is okay to write letters that will never be read or see the light of day (something that my psychologist also supports) and that we should speak now and be courageous. We are allowed to long for a love that is gone because it will never change colours in our minds. It will always be the same memories that come back in burning red, black and white or golden because they were meaningful. I saw an uncredited quote on the Internet recently that said, "Don't ask me how I survived; ask me what song I played on repeat when I thought my whole world was over." When new music is released, regardless of the artist, the music ceases belonging to the artist and enters the sphere of collective experience. I've heard Maggie Rogers, Maisie Peters and Ed Sheeran say the same. We pick apart the lines, bridges, choruses and whole songs; they are ours now. Those are the lyrics that live in my phone, written down when I can't sleep and there's a song in my head.

In the *folklore: the long pond studio sessions* documentary, we see Jack Antonoff and Aaron Dessner sitting around a fire with Taylor, drinking wine and chatting about music. That image is what every fan feels: an intimate level of comfort. This is The Taylor Swift Effect. This is why we are supportive of everything she does. When the next album comes out, it will send us into a promotional spiral of conspiracy, drama and unhinged anticipation leading up to release day. My parents say I'm melodramatic. With everything that has happened in the last sixteen years of growing up listening to her, I know without her, my life would be radically different. Sometimes, I like to imagine myself (as I'm sure we all do) walking down the street with earphones in, like Meg Ryan in my own personal nineties romantic comedy. Life is good; things are looking up for the first time in a while, the words fit my exact mood, and the tempo of the song matches my footsteps. That song plays as the pivotal scene starts that will change the course of the film, and the main character (me) smiles. The song that plays for me will *always* be one of Taylor's.

At the end of the day, her legacy will forever and always be her songs and lyrics. I hope this is the story she would want me to write. I am glad to have lived happy, free, confused and lonely at the same mystical and magical time as Taylor Swift.

Taylor Swift (Caitlin's Version)

There exists a space in my record collection for my artist of the decades,
on my nan's old, dusty, almost-broken turntable I play songs
that can just as easily be heard without scratches in my headphones.

I collect vinyls like some collect typewriters, old relics of replaced technologies
their purpose the same, their lived nostalgia being tangible and satisfying,
to lift the needle and change the side that plays is the same as pushing a typewriter sideways.

I've memorised her words like the Bible, every commandment and prophecy,
wise psalms, prayers that cry out for help, and joyful choruses.

I've written them in my heart and on my school books and my phone notes to read
when I can't sleep at the witching hour.

She teaches you to love unconditionally even when it hurts, and cry with all of your heart,
because it meant you weren't afraid to feel something.

She teaches you to dance with joy even when the world is upside down, and to find
the people who stay with you in the middle of the dancefloor of life.

She teaches you to have day dreams, live fearlessly, take chances, be on your worst behaviour,
and most of all to not be silent.

We must use our voice, whispering at first, then screaming from cliff tops if no one listens.
Even if the cries of women are often discredited as hysterical or 'too much'. Keep going she says.

Somewhere far away from here there is a girl sitting in an English class,
in her first year of being a teenager, she believes in fairy tales, and in love at first sight,
and she probably has a crush on the boy that asks her questions in their lessons.

THE STORY OF US

She has one earphone in, and yet fully pays attention,
because these stories of everyone else's happily ever afters are all around her.

She wanders the corridors floating through flaky friend groups, and some days when
her mum picks her up from school, she will lean her head on the window and the tears will fall silently.

A song plays on the radio that she recognises and immediately her mood changes,
she lifts her head up, smiles and starts singing.

How could it be that I have sang the same words as that bright-eyed teenager? Are we the same?
The answer is yes, I am her, just a little bit older. But there are lots of us.

As the dawn of a new decade of life breaks, she understands now that all she has to do is write
about the feelings. All of them.

Joy doesn't come without pain; people like us are gone forever if you treat as we don't deserve.
Because at the end of the day, as midnight falls – the reminder comes; aren't we all just tortured poets?

album secret messages

"I wanted to do something that incentivised fans to read the lyrics because the lyrics are what I'm most proud of."
– Taylor on Jimmy Fallon, 2021.

These secret messages in Taylor's first five records, exist in the physical album booklets – the lyrics stylised in lowercase with random capitalised letters where there isn't normally (the 1989 booklet does the reverse). In most cases it summarises the song, in other times leaves more clues for the fans to decode and in some instances, she indicates and confirms who or where the song is about exactly. Instead of sharing this information when she is interviewed by journalists, she hides it in plain sight, and also a lot of the journalists were rude? Some of these secrets, like easter eggs on a hunt are easier to find out about than others and that is the thrill of the game.

In the cases of the first four albums the messages standalone but in the case of 1989 the messages retell a cohesive tale of the previous two years of music. *The Guardian* penned their take on 1989's messages, "The embedded story is an entertaining twist on the playful gimmick that has helped to make all of Swift's albums feel like slumber party secrets whispered in your ear, and it helps to shift the narrative around the pop star from her former perception as a boy-crazy serial dater to her current status as a thoughtful and self-assured adult." The *(Taylor's Version)* releases with new vault songs and some deluxe edition tracks (on debut, *Red* and 1989) sadly don't feature secret messages. But when they were released out of the vault, the letters were presented jumbled up in an internet video where fans were required to unscramble them, so she has never lost the cryptic touch.

Taylor Swift
1. Tim McGraw – Can't tell me nothin'.
2. Picture to Burn – Date nice boys.
3. Teardrops on My Guitar – He will never know.
4. A Place in This World – I found it.
5. Cold As You – Time to let go.
6. The Outside – You are not alone.
7. Tied Together With A Smile – You are loved.
8. Stay Beautiful – Shake n bake.
9. Should've Said No – Sam, Sam, Sam, Sam, Sam, Sam.
10. Mary's Song (Oh My My My) – Sometimes, love is forever.
11. Our Song – Live in love.

Fearless
1. Fearless – I loved you before I met you.
2. Fifteen – I cried while recording this.
3. Love Story – Someday I'll find this.
4. Hey Stephen – Love and theft.
5. White Horse – All I ever wanted was the truth.
6. You Belong With Me – Love is blind, so you couldn't see me.
7. Breathe – I'm sorry, I'm sorry, I'm sorry.
8. Tell Me Why – Guess I was fooled by your smile.
9. You're Not Sorry – She can have you.
10. The Way I Loved You – We can't go back.
11. Forever and Always – If you play these games, we're both going to lose.
12. The Best Day – God bless Andrea Swift.
13. Change – You made things change for me.

<u>Platinum Edition</u>
1. Jump Then Fall – Last summer was magical.
2. Untouchable – We always want what we can't reach.
3. Forever & Always (Piano) – Still miss who I thought he was.
4. Come in with the Rain – Won't admit that I wish you'd come back.
5. SuperStar – I'll never tell.
6. The Other Side of the Door – What I was really thinking when I slammed the door.

Speak Now
1. Mine – Toby.
2. Sparks Fly – Portland, Oregon.
3. Back To December – Tay.
4. Speak Now – You always regret what you don't say.
5. Dear John – Loved you from the very first day.
6. Mean – I thought you got me.
7. The Story of Us – CMT Music Awards.
8. Never Grow Up – I moved out in July.
9. Enchanted – Adam.
10. Better Than Revenge – You thought I would forget.
11. Innocent – Life is full of little interruptions.
12. Haunted – Still to this day.
13. Last Kiss – Forever and always.
14. Long Live – For you.

<u>Deluxe Edition</u>
15. Ours – Mayor.
16. If This Was a Movie – Let's press rewind.
17. Superman – Today I am saved.

Red
1. State of Grace – I love you doesn't count after goodbye.
2. Red – SAG.
3. Treacherous – Won't stop till it's over.
4. I Knew You Were Trouble – When you saw me dancing.

5. All Too Well – Maple Latte.
6. 22 – Ashley Dianna Claire Selena.
7. I Almost Do – Wrote this instead of calling.
8. We Are Never Ever Getting Back Together – When I stopped caring what you thought.
9. Stay Stay Stay – Daydreaming about real love.
10. The Last Time – LA on your break.
11. Holy Ground – When you came to the show in SD.
12. Sad Beautiful Tragic – While you were on a train.
13. The Lucky One – Wouldn't you like to know?
14. Everything Has Changed – Hyannis Port.
15. Starlight – For Ethel.
16. Begin Again – I wear heels now.

1989

1. Welcome to New York – We begin our story in New York.
2. Blank Space – There once was a girl known by everyone and no one.
3. Style – Her heart belonged to someone who couldn't stay.
4. Out of the Woods – They loved each other recklessly.
5. All You Had to Do Was Stay – They paid the price.
6. Shake It Off – She danced to forget him.
7. I Wish You Would – He drove past her street each night.
8. Bad Blood – She made friends and enemies.
9. Wildest Dreams – He only saw her in his dreams.
10. How You Get the Girl – Then one day he came back.
11. This Love – Timing is a funny thing.
12. I Know Places – And everyone was watching.
13. Clean – She lost him, but she found herself, and somehow, that was everything.

The Tortured Poets Department

Apple Music fans were treated to an extra treasure hunt in the lead up to the release of *The Tortured Poets Department*. From April 15, 2024, the bio of Apple Music's socials said "A word a day 'til the taylor swift album drops." These capitals were hidden in songs from different albums across Taylor's discography and once rearranged, each unscrambled word spells out, "We Hereby Conduct This Post Mortem", which are the opening lines of track 20, "How Did It End?" For me, this recalls *reputation*'s "Look What You Made Me Do" line, "the old Taylor can't come to the phone right now, why? "Cause she's dead."

1. "Glitch" – Hereby
2. "Peace" – Conduct
3. "Better Than Revenge" – This
4. "Clean" – Post
5. "We Were Happy" – We
6. "Begin Again" – Mortem

acknowledgements

i consider this my dissertation to a course that i've been enrolled in for sixteen years. i Wrote this book in blinding speed, in just over five months and as much as it felt like it was just me sitting alone Hammering furiously on my computer, biting my fingernails and nErvously pulling at my hair trying to make my own writing make sense; listening to taylor, and telling two histories at the same time, this was Not a solo effort.

siobhán; thank You for being an incredible and tolerant housemate, i apologise for the fact that, three mOnths to the day before i started writing this book, my headphones snapped and i left another pair in germany at christmas, so i appreciate you listening to taylor with me and spending your days in our hampstead home. **steph, lucas** and **ned;** my london swifties, this city woUldn't be the magical place that it is wiThout you by my side. **jo tuscano;** my trusty editor and the brilliant woman who has shown me you can have a career writing books. from our lockdown lunches in your House in glebe talking about my poetry, to you now editing thIs book from the other side of the world. thaNk you endlessly, i owe you a lot more than you know. thanK you to **serena yang** for the incredible cover photography and **matt broughton** for the cover design. **bec;** we celebrate Two *decades* of friendship this year. you live life in capital letters, filled with sunshine, pArties and most of all...music. i wouldn't be obsessed with taylor if it wasn't for You. it has been my joy to watch you chase adventures around the world and stilL come home to the central coast and have you there, forever and always you have a perfectly goOd heart. **my girlzsquad;** annalise, bridie and maRy. i am nothing without you three; i have said it once and i will say it again and again – you are bigger than the whole sky, the oneS i dreamed about when i was fourteen and reading alone in the school library with *fearless* in my headphones. you talk me doWn from my anxiety mountains with a phone call from across the other side of the world, I love you, see you soon. thank you to **the black spring press group** team for believing in the power of a Fandom and giving me the opportunity of a lifetime in publishing this book. **todd swifT, evie rowan, cate myddelton-evans,** and **jane collins,** your support for this book has been indescribable.

to my mum; there Is no me without you, there would be no book witHout you giving me the time, space and place to chase my dreams, and there would be no fangirl without you taking me to see her in 2010. **dad,** i know you don't love tay, but just focus on the fact your little girl wrote a whole damn book, okay? **lachie,** i love that you told me "lOve story" is your favourite taylor song, i love you so much and i can't wait to surf with you again soon. i love you three from the bottom of my heart, and words are supPosed to be my thing but, no words will ever be Enough.

and, to all the boys who broke my heart, you did your best work. but taYlor was the one who mended it.

i wrOte this book for two distinct groups; first and foremost, for the swifties; the people who have been on this journey with me growing Up with taylor in our lives for sixteen years, i acknowledge there will be pieces of the story that i haven't mentioned, i hope This book makes you love taylor all over again. the second is the neutral appreciators – you like Her music but wouldn't call yourselves obsessed, and that Is okay. you bought this book regardless, and my hope for you is that you read something that you didn't know about her, and if your appreciation for expaNds even a little, i've done my job right.

to everyone who contributed to interviews in this booK; bryce and sarah, olive and amelia, gabby, ed, rebecca, emma, alex, thank you a milliOn times for sharing your taylor stories. i meant what i said in the *Fearless* chapter about starting to write this book in 2008. it has been a journey. from being a fan and sharing in incredible memories with others around Me, concerts and albums, that that have materialised from my piles of merchandise on my bedroom floor to now being an author of this 'little golden book' that other people will have in their bookshelves (i hope) for a long timE.

why all the random capital letters in strange places, you ask?
some of you already know the answer, but go back and find them all for a surprise, I had to have my turn at a secret message.

pre-orders

An idea of my publisher, as an incentive to buy this book was to give a special mention inside to those kind enough to pre-order before the release date. On top of this, an idea of mine, to go with every pre-order was a friendship bracelet. Because that has become part of the currency of being a Swiftie, and I love how unique they are. I could have quite easily thrown the bracelets I received on top of any random book order but instead I tried really hard to pair the words on the bracelets with the people who bought them. At the Eras Tour, when swapping bracelets with strangers you would often ask people you traded with, "Do you have a favourite song or favourite album?" and then we would try to match preferences.

Every single bracelet has been handmade, either by myself or four women I found after posting online. I used Facebook groups to outsource Swifties who had made literally hundreds in preparation for them to be traded at the Eras Tour. So, to Lindsay who sold me the beads I used to make my own concert bracelets, and to the bracelet makers; Sam, Kirstie, Becky and Michelle, thank you. Thank you for the time and dedication you have donated, they are beautiful. To my pre-orders, I will forever and always be grateful to the people who cared first about reading the words I wrote.

Steph	Fiona	Sarina	Nicola
Emily	Hannah	Alex	Daniella
Will	Emma	Holly	Adam
Elliot	Kelli	Rebecca	William
Isobel	Annalise	Lily	Olivia
Alison	Bridie	Jacqueline	Ruby
Louise	Alex	Giana	Suneha
Sophie	Gemma	Nicole	Maizie
Megan	Hannah	Gabrielle	Mimi
Annaliese	dad	Guy	Jennie
Mary	Rachel G	Reuben	Amber
Sam	Rachel F	Callum	April
Tania	Caitlin	Amelia	Amanda
Jemma	Lucy	Ava	Angela
Helen	Antoine	Amelia	Lucinda
Skyler	Tyler	Abigail	Keavy
Bethany	Rachel	Laura	Mike
Narelle	Zariah	Natasha	Eva
Tracey	Lulu	Jill	Georgia
Hamish	Rebecca	Jayne	Nel
Joeley	Chels	Jennifer	Nikki
Alanah	Hannah	Catherine	Charlotte
Jodie	Sophie	Kerry	Stefanie
Vickie	Alice	Amber	Tori
mum	Claudia	Stacey	Rosie
Catherine	Nathan	Clare	Tina
Jess	Olive	Sarah	Caitlin
Sarah	Amelia	Adrienne	Isla
Jane	Greta	Ciara	
Gracie	Jenn	Shylena	
Danielle	Ffion	Vivienne	

CAITLIN ROBSON

Works Cited (Caitlin's Version)

@epiphany-in-exile. 2020. Tumblr. 25 May. https://epiphany-in-exile.tumblr.com/post/619086408567619584/its-an-undercover-band.

@HannahRae1327. 2023. X. 4 December. https://x.com/HannahRae1327/status/1731496446015250892.

2DayFMSydney. 2014. *Taylor Swift's 1989 secrets and response to SEXIST song speculation* [FULL INTERVIEW]. 20 October. https://www.youtube.com/watch?v=5xvlDW_jd8U.

Al Jazeera Staff. 2024. *How has the Taylor Swift effect boosted American football?* 11 February. https://www.aljazeera.com/news/2024/2/11/has-taylor-swift-helped-boost-nfl-popularity-in-the-us.

Apple Music. 2019. *Taylor Swift: 'Lover', Politics, & Friendship with Selena Gomez | Apple Music*. 30 October. https://www.youtube.com/watch?v=TC1UnBDfrQA-&t=9s.

Arnold, Bella. 2023. *The Taylor Swiftification of The Summer I Turned Pretty*. 24 August. https://www.vulture.com/2023/08/taylor-swift-summer-i-turned-pretty.html.

Austen, Jane. 1813. *Pride and Prejudice*. London: Thomas Egerton.

Barnes, Kelsey. n.d. *Making The Case For Parasocial Relationships: Taylor's Version*. https://off-chance.com/articles/parasocial-relationships-taylor-swift.

—. 2022. *On Taylor Swift's 'Midnights' and the beauty of staying the same*. 10 November. https://www.coupdemainmagazine.com/taylor-swift/18897.

Barrie, Josh. 2024. *Josh Barrie On the Sauce at the Black Dog, Vauxhall: the London pub made famous by Taylor Swift*. 24 April. https://www.standard.co.uk/going-out/foodanddrink/the-black-dog-vauxhall-taylor-swift-b1153327.html.

Battle, Myisha. 2023. "Situationships Are the Future of Dating. That's Not a Bad Thing." *TIME*, 18 March.

BBC Radio 1. 2019. *Taylor Swift talks music, politics and life with Radio 1's Clara Amfo*. 13 September. https://www.youtube.com/watch?v=2AUUnLixsFQ.

Beckner, Justin. 2024. "What guitar does Taylor Swift use? The varied and unique instruments of The Eras Tour." *Guitar.com*, 15 March.

Berckelman, Holly. 2024. *'The surprising detail in Taylor Swift's Eras tour that I can't stop thinking about'*. 27 February. https://www.bodyandsoul.com.au/wellness/

taylor-swift-the-eras-tour-cultivates-a-sense-of-belonging/news-story/o4ecceegdf239197ffde178a008b1ac9.

Bieber, Justin. 2016. *Instagram*. 2 August. https://www.instagram.com/p/BIm-WNPuBnXq/?utm_source=ig_embed&ig_rid=ff64985c6-50a9-4a5f-b95b-0a9cbe8d31ab.

—. 2019. *Instagram*. 30 June. https://www.instagram.com/p/BzWYdS9Hj5R/.

Billboard. 2019. *Taylor Swift Accepts Woman of the Decade Award | Women In Music*. 13 December. https://www.youtube.com/watch?v=ZVpkFb9-fts.

Borchetta, Scott. 2019. *So, It's Time For Some Truth....* 30 June. https://www.bigmachinelabelgroup.com/so-its-time-some-truth/.

Brocklehurst, Harrison. 2023. *All of the infamously devastating Taylor Swift track fives, ranked from worst to best*. 16 November. https://thetab.com/uk/2023/11/16/all-of-the-infamously-devastating-taylor-swift-track-fives-ranked-from-worst-to-best-337831.

Caramanica, Jon. 2008. "My Music, MySpace, My Life." *The New York Times*, 7 November.

Carroll, Georgia. 2018-2023. "'Oh My God, how did I spend all that money?': Lived experiences in two commodified fandom communities". PhD, Doctor of Philosophy, University of Sydney, Sydney: University of Sydney.

CBS Sunday Morning. 2019. *Taylor Swift on "Lover" and haters*. 25 August. https://www.youtube.com/watch?v=nDzhoofkRJI&t=1s.

Chapelle, Sarah. 2011. *TaylorSwiftStyle*. October. https://taylorswiftstyle.com.

2009. *Hannah Montana: The Movie*. Directed by Peter Chelsom. Produced by Walt Disney Pictures.

Clarkson, Kelly. 2019. *X*. 13 July. https://x.com/kellyclarkson/status/1150168164853882880?lang=en-GB.

Coleman, Emma. 2019. *Instagram*. 5 August. https://www.instagram.com/p/BozH-PHpuRY/?utm_source=ig_web_copy_link.

Conger, Bill. 2010. *Taylor Swift Talks About Her Album Speak Now, Her Hits "Mine" And "Speak Now," And Writing Her Songs*. 11 October. https://www.songwriteruniverse.com/taylorswift2010.htm.

Congreve, William. 1697 (pub. 1753). *The Mourning Bride: A Tragedy*. London: Dublin: J. and R. Tonson and S. Draper in the Strand.

Coscarelli, Joe. 2024. "How Big Is Taylor Swift?" *The New York Times*, 17 May.

Cox, Jamieson. 2016. *The Top 10 Best Songs*. 22 November. https://time.com/collection-post/4575319/top-10-best-songs-2016/.

Dailey, Hannah. 2024. *Taylor Swift's Fans Predict She'll Release 5 Versions of 'Tortured Poets' Representing the Stages of Grief.* 26 February. https://www.billboard.com/music/music-news/taylor-swift-tortured-poets-stages-of-grief-fan-theory-explained-1235615006/.

Davet, Stéphane. 2019. *Musique: opération séduction de Taylor Swift à l'Olympia.* 10 September. https://www.lemonde.fr/culture/article/2019/09/10/musique-operation-seduction-de-taylor-swift-a-l-olympia_5508568_3246.html.

Dixon-Smith, Matilda. 2017. "Taylor Swift Maybe Dragged Kim Kardashian Over Paris Robbery." *Junkee,* 28 August.

do, almost. 2021. *ellen making taylor swift uncomfortable for 5 minutes straight.* 30 June. https://www.youtube.com/watch?v=6n_STneD82I.

Dockterman, Eliana. 2017. "'I Was Angry.' Taylor Swift on What Powered Her Sexual Assault Testimony." *TIME,* 6 December.

Doyle, Patrick. 2020. "Musicians on Musicians: Taylor Swift & Paul McCartney." *Rolling Stone,* 13 November.

Elizabeth, De. 2022. "Taylor Swift "Karma" Fan Theory Explained." *Teen Vogue,* 6 October.

Elvis Duran Show. 2019. *Taylor Swift Tells the Stories Behind 'Lover' | Elvis Duran Show.* 23 August. https://www.youtube.com/watch?v=t7CUAaotCVw&t=827s.

Entertainment Tonight. 2015. *Taylor Swift Talks Going 'Home to Her Cats' After the Grammys: 'Men Get Me In Trouble!'.* 9 February. https://www.youtube.com/watch?v=Us1CudkeC4I.

Forde, Eamonn. 2024. *Taylor-made deals: how artists are following Swift's rights example.* 9 January. https://www.theguardian.com/music/2024/jan/09/taylor-swift-deals-how-artists-rights-example#:~:text=Olivia%20Rodrigo%20made%20ownership%20of,her%20own%20label%2C%20Sommer%20House.

Garcia, Joe. 2023. "Listening to Taylor Swift in Prison: Her music makes me feel that I'm still part of the world I left behind." *The New Yorker,* 2 September.

Gevinson, Tavi. 2015. *Taylor Swift Has No Regrets.* 7 May. https://www.elle.com/fashion/a28210/taylor-swift-elle-june-cover-2015/.

Global Citizen. 2020. *Taylor Swift performs "Soon You'll Get Better" | One World: Together At Home.* 19 April. https://www.youtube.com/watch?v=2P-uLAQ9FCI.

Global News. 2014. *Taylor Swift: Reacts to being named the voice of her generation.* 30

December. https://www.youtube.com/watch?v=eVSdF_Q_fLA.

Goldsborough, Susie. 2024. "This Swiftie is delighted, but 31 songs is too many." *The Times*, 22 April.

Good Morning America. 2019. *Taylor Swift says she'll re-record her old albums | Live on GMA*. 22 August. https://www.youtube.com/watch?v=ellK-CXh7B4.

2007. Great American Country: Ask The Artist. 28 February. https://archive.ph/20070708082423/http://blogs.gactv.com/gactv/asktheartist/taylor-swift/.

Griffiths, Charlotte. 2020. *Talk of the Town: Taylor Swift begs Phoebe Waller-Bridge to let her little brother Austin sing on the soundtrack of Killing Eve*. 9 February. https://www.dailymail.co.uk/tvshowbiz/article-7982493/Taylor-Swift-begs-Phoebe-Waller-Bridge-let-brother-sing-Killing-Eve-soundtrack.html.

Hiatt, Brian. 2019. "Taylor Swift: The Rolling Stone Interview." *Rolling Stone*, 18 September.

Hobbs, Dawn R., and Gordon G. Gallop Jnr. 2011. "Songs as a Medium for Embedded Reproductive Messages." *Evolutionary Psychology* 9 (3): 390-416.

Horton, Helena. 2016. "#TaylorSwiftIsOverParty: Katy Perry and social media users target Taylor Swift after Calvin Harris revelations." *The Telegraph*, 14 July.

Hudson, Anne. 2010. *Vintage Taylor Swift Interview (Sept. 2006)*. 29 September. https://www.youtube.com/watch?v=BG2hANOUU2Y.

Hutchinson, Jonathon. 2017. *Look what you made me do: Taylor Swift and (un)social media*. 25 October. https://www.sydney.edu.au/engage/events-sponsorships/raising-the-bar/podcast-transcripts.html.

Ingram, Kelseigh. 2016. *It's Time To Stop Pretending Taylor Swift Is A Feminist*. 24 October. https://www.huffpost.com/entry/its-time-to-stop-pretendi_b_12602028.

Jones, Nate. 2024. *It took Taylor Swift for my daughter to get into football. I'm watching the Super Bowl with her for the first time*. 11 February. https://www.businessinsider.com/taylor-swift-football-super-bowl-dad-daughter-relationship-2024-2.

Kelce, Travis, and Jason Kelce. 2023. *New Heights with Jason and Travis Kelce*.

Kermode, Mark. 2010. "Mark Kermode's DVD round-up: Green Zone; Life During Wartime; Leap Year; Valentine's Day; Lourdes." *The Guardian*, 11 July.

Klosterman, Chuck. 2015. "Taylor Swift on "Bad Blood," Kanye West, and How

People Interpret Her Lyrics." *GQ*, 15 October.

Kolirin, Lianne. 2024. *Olivia Colman says if she were a man, she'd be earning 'a f**k of a lot more'*. 25 March. https://edition.cnn.com/2024/03/25/entertainment/olivia-colman-pay-gap-gbr-scli-intl-gbr/index.html.

Kopstein, Jeannie. 2024. *TIME VIDEO: The Swifties Who Turned Their Fandom Into a Career*. 18 April. https://time.com/6968735/swifties-turned-fandom-into-career/.

Kornhaber, Spencer. 2019. "Taylor Swift's 'ME!' Is Everything Wrong With Pop." *The Atlantic*, 26 April.

Lampen, Claire, and Olivia Craighead. 2024. *Tortured Poets Department: All the Lyrics, Conspiracies, and Easter Eggs*. 22 April. https://www.thecut.com/article/taylor-swift-tortured-poets-department-explainer-lyrics-easter-eggs.html.

Lansky, Sam. 2023. *Person of the Year: Taylor Swift*. December 6. https://time.com/6342806/person-of-the-year-2023-taylor-swift/.

Lee, Benjamin. 2020. "Miss Americana review – Taylor Swift doc is too stage-managed to truly sing." *The Guardian*, 24 January.

Light, Alan. 2020. "Evermore Isn't About Taylor Swift. It's About Storytelling." *esquire*, 11 December.

Lipshutz, Jason. 2019. *Billboard Woman of the Decade Taylor Swift: 'I Do Want My Music to Live On'*. 12 December. https://www.billboard.com/music/pop/taylor-swift-cover-story-interview-billboard-women-in-music-2019-8545822/.

Low, Harry. 2024. *Taylor Swift fans 'overwhelming' London pub The Black Dog*. 22 April. https://www.bbc.co.uk/news/uk-england-london-68876725.

McCartney, Paul. 2021. *The Lyrics: 1956 To The Present*. London: Penguin Books.

McClellan, Laura. 2016. *Kelsea Ballerini and Taylor Swift are still besties*. 27 January. https://tasteofcountry.com/kelsea-ballerini-taylor-swift-girls-night/.

Mendez, Malia. 2023. *Jenny Han explains how Taylor Swift's songs and other pop music is central to 'Summer I Turned Pretty'*. 19 August. https://www.latimes.com/entertainment-arts/tv/story/2023-08-19/summer-i-turned-pretty-music-jenny-han-taylor-swift.

Meyers, Late Night with Seth. 2021. *Taylor Swift Full Interview on Late Night with Seth Meyers*. 14 November. https://www.youtube.com/watch?v=DYIOaifhjQU.

Moran, Robert. 2024. "I saw Taylor Swift on her first Australian tour. Here's what happened." *The Sydney Morning Herald*, 15 February.

MTV. 2019. *Taylor Swift Wins Video of the Year | 2019 Video Music Awards*. 27 August.

https://www.youtube.com/watch?v=8z4icNgFSPI.

News, Taylor Swift. 2020. "Jack Leopards & The Dolphin Club 🎵". 25 May. https://twitter.com/TSwiftNZ/status/1264819008387182592?s=20.

Nicks, Stevie. 2010. "The 2010 TIME 100: Taylor Swift." TIME, 29 April.

NPR Music. 2019. *Taylor Swift: NPR Music Tiny Desk Concert*. 28 October. https://www.youtube.com/watch?v=FvVnP8G6ITs.

Nugent, Annabel. 2023. *Taylor Swift review, Speak Now (Taylor's Version): A stunning rediscovery of a musician at a crossroads*. 7 July. https://www.independent.co.uk/arts-entertainment/music/reviews/taylor-swift-speak-now-lyrics-review-b2371332.html.

Orr, Gillian. 2009. "Taylor Swift, Shepherd's Bush Empire, London`." *The Independent*, 11 May.

Pullman, Laura. 2024. *Joe Alwyn: 'The end of a long relationship is a hard thing to navigate'*. 15 June. https://www.thetimes.com/culture/film/article/joe-alwyn-interview-end-relationship-taylor-swift-fzb3k5ffj.

Robinson, Jennifer Kaytin. 2019. *Instagram*. 23 August. https://www.instagram.com/p/B1fthzAJeQd/?hl=en.

Roche, Valheria. 2023. *Happy Lover-versary*. 23 August. https://substack.com/home/post/p-136344460.

Rodulfo, Kristina. 2016. "Kanye West Says Taylor Swift Actually Came Up With Those Taylor Swift Lyrics." *ELLE*, 12 February.

Rubin. 2021. *Andrew Lloyd Webber Says Writing a Song With Taylor Swift Was the Only Enjoyable Part of 'Cats' Movie*. 12 October. https://variety.com/2021/film/news/andrew-lloyd-webber-taylor-swift-cats-only-enjoyable-part-1235087324/.

Sales, Leigh. 2024. *Using your head to explain Taylor Swift's unparalleled success doesn't work. Her appeal comes from somewhere else*. 22 February. https://www.abc.net.au/news/2024-02-23/taylor-swift-success-from-the-heart-not-head/103497328.

Shepherd, Julianne Escobedo. 2016. *Kanye West's Surreal Album Launch: Fashion and Music Collide*. 12 February. https://www.rollingstone.com/music/music-news/kanye-wests-surreal-album-launch-fashion-and-music-collide-171160/.

SLN Staff Writer. 2010. *Taylor Swift Hosts 14.5 Hour Meet & Greet*. 16 June. https://www.soundslikenashville.com/news/taylor-swift-hosts-14-5-hour-meet-greet/.

Snapes, Laura. 2020. *Taylor Swift: Folklore review – bombastic pop makes way for emo-*

tional acuity. 24 July. https://www.theguardian.com/music/2020/jul/24/taylor-swift-folklore-review-bombastic-pop-makes-way-for-emotional-acuity.

Sodomsky, Sam. 2020. "Evermore (album review)." *Pitchfork*, 15 December.

—. 2020. "The National's Aaron Dessner Talks Taylor Swift's New Album folklore." *Pitchfork*, 24 July.

Spanos, Brittany. 2022. "Is 'Karma' Real? Inside The Mystery of Taylor Swift's 'Lost' Album." *Rolling Stone*, 26 September.

Steele, Anne. 2019. "Scooter Braun Makes $300 Million Deal for Big Machine Records." *The Wall Street Journal*, 30 June.

Sullivan, Becky. 2023. *A Taylor Swift Instagram post helped drive a surge in voter registration.* 22 September. https://www.npr.org/2023/09/22/1201183160/taylor-swift-instagram-voter-registration.

Suskind, Alex. 2019. "New Reputation: Taylor Swift shares intel on TS7, fan theories, and her next era." *Entertainment Weekly*, 9 May.

Swift, Taylor. 2006. *Taylor Swift*.

Swift, Taylor. 2017. *Reputation*.

Swift, Taylor. 2019. *Lover*.

Swift, Taylor. 2020. *folklore*.

Swift, Taylor. 2020. *evermore*.

Swift, Taylor. 2021. *Fearless (Taylor's Version)*.

Swift, Taylor. 2021. *Red (Taylor's Version)*.

Swift, Taylor. 2022. *Midnights*.

Swift, Taylor. 2023. *Speak Now (Taylor's Version)*.

Swift, Taylor. 2023. *1989 (Taylor's Version)*.

Swift, Taylor. 2024. *The Tortured Poets Department*.

—. 2018. "The Trick To Holding On." *British Vogue*, January.

—. 2019. *Don't know what else to do.* 14 November. https://www.tumblr.com/taylorswift/189068976205/dont-know-what-else-to-do.

—. 2019. "30 Things I Learned Before Turning 30." *Elle Magazine*, 6 March.

2020. *Folklore: The Long Pond Studio Sessions*. Directed by Taylor Swift. Produced by Taylor Swift, Robert Allen and Bart Peters. Disney+.

—. 2018. "Taylor Swift Interviews Rock 'n' Roll Icon Pattie Boyd on Songwriting, Beatlemania, & the Power of Being a Muse." *Harper's Bazaar*, 10 July.

—. 2015. "Just so you know…,". 9 April. http://taylorswift.tumblr.com/post/115942142045/just-so-you-know.

—. 2018. *Instagram*. 8 October. https://www.instagram.com/p/BopoXpYnCes/.
—. 2020. *Instagram*. 23 July. https://www.instagram.com/p/CC-9usjDzUw/?hl=en.
2020. *Miss Americana*. Directed by Lana Wilson. Produced by Morgan Neville, Caitrin Rogers and Christine O'Malley. Performed by Taylor Swift. Netflix.
—. 2014. *Taylor Swift's Gift Giving of 2014 | SWIFTMAS*. 31 December. https://www.youtube.com/watch?v=j3yyF31jbKo.
—. 2019. *Tumblr*. 30 June. https://www.tumblr.com/taylorswift/185958366550/for-years-i-asked-pleaded-for-a-chance-to-own-my.
—. 2020. *X*. 16 November. Accessed 2020. https://x.com/taylorswift13/status/1328471874318311425.
—. 2020. *X*. 2 December. https://twitter.com/taylorswift13/status/1334144808693223425.
—. 2020. *X*. 25 May. https://twitter.com/taylorswift13/status/1264740730771300359.
—. April. *X*. 17 2020. https://x.com/taylorswift13/status/1251193743912456192.
The Boot. 2015. *Taylor Swift, 'Our Song' — Story Behind the Song*. 30 January. https://theboot.com/story-behind-the-song-our-song-taylor-swift/.
TIFF Originals. 2022. *TAYLOR SWIFT | In Conversation With... | TIFF 2022*. 16 September. https://www.youtube.com/watch?v=1lbg54tnj_g.
Travers, Peter. 2010. "At the Movies With Peter Travers: "Valentine's Day" and "The Wolfman"." *Rolling Stone*, 11 February.
tswiftmyspace. n.d. *Tumblr*. https://tswiftmyspace.tumblr.com/bloglist.
VideoSwiftie. 2013. *Taylor Swift CMT Insider Special Edition Thanksgiving 2008 (part 1/2)*. 28 August. https://www.youtube.com/watch?v=WWxhIIdNQzI&t=427s.
Vogue. 2016. *73 Questions With Taylor Swift*. 19 April . https://www.youtube.com/watch?v=XnbCSboujF4.
Warner, Denise. 2019. *Taylor Swift Reveals Which 'Lover' Song She May Never Play Live During SiriusXM Town Hall*. 23 August. https://www.billboard.com/music/pop/taylor-swift-acoustic-versions-lover-siriusxm-8528223/.
Weaver, Caity. 2016. " Kim Kardashian West on Kanye and Taylor Swift, What's in O.J.'s Bag, and Understanding Caitlyn." *GQ*, 16 June.
Widdicombe, Lizzie. 2011. "You Belong With Me." *The New Yorker*, 3 October.
Willman, Chris. 2010. "Princess Crossover." *New York Magazine*, 7 October.
—. 2020. "Taylor Swift: No Longer 'Polite at All Costs'." *Variety*, 21 January.
WSMV4. 2023. *Taylor Swift throwback interview*. 11 July. https://www.wsmv.com/video/2023/07/11/taylor-swift-throwback-interview/.
Zacharek, Stephanie, Eliana Dockterman, and Haley Sweetland Edwards. 2017.

"Person of the Year 2017: The Silence Breakers." TIME, 6 December.

Zoladz, Lindsey. 2024. On 'The Tortured Poets Department,' Taylor Swift Could Use an Editor. 23 April. https://www.nytimes.com/2024/04/19/arts/music/taylor-swift-album-tortured-poets-department-review.html.